.NET Framework

PROGRAMMER'S REFERENCE

Dan Rahmel

McGraw-Hill/Osborne
New York Chicago San Francisco
Lisbon London Madrid Mexico City
Milan New Delhi San Juan
Seoul Singapore Sydney Toronto

About the Author

Dan Rahmel is a Windows programmer with over 14 years of experience designing and implementing information systems and deploying mid-sized client/server solutions using Visual Basic, ASP, C++, and SQL Server. He has authored numerous books including the *Visual Basic Programmer's Reference*, first and second editions; *Building Web Database Applications with Visual Studio*; *Teach Yourself Database Programming in 24 Hours*; and *Developing Client-Server Applications with Visual Basic*. He is a contributor to *DBMS*, *Internet Advisor*, and *American Programmer* magazines.

McGraw-Hill/Osborne
2600 Tenth Street
Berkeley, California 94710
U.S.A.

To arrange bulk purchase discounts for sales promotions, premiums, or fund-raisers, please contact **McGraw-Hill**/Osborne at the above address. For information on translations or book distributors outside the U.S.A., please see the International Contact Information page immediately following the index of this book.

.NET Framework Programmer's Reference

Publisher Brandon A. Nordin
Vice President & Associate Publisher Scott Rogers
Acquisitions Editor Jim Schachterle
Project Editor Mark Karmendy
Acquisitions Coordinator Tim Madrid
Technical Editor Steve Juntunen
Copy Editor Dennis Weaver
Proofreader John Gildersleeve
Indexer David Heiret
Computer Designers Lucie Ericksen and Lauren McCarthy
Illustrators Michael Mueller and Lyssa Wald
Series Design Peter F. Hancik

1234567890 DOC DOC 0198765432

ISBN 0-07-219466-9

This book was composed with Corel VENTURA ™ Publisher.

In the wake of the September 11th attacks, I would like to dedicate this book to all the people who use their passion and energy to create rather than to destroy—and to the survivors who must find the courage to build again.

CONTENTS

ACKNOWLEDGMENTS

It was a pleasure to work with the people at Osborne. Combining the creation of the book with the superior Osborne staff often made the difficult seem easy. I'd like to thank the people on the Osborne staff with whom I often interacted (Jim Schachterle, Tim Madrid, Steve Juntunen, and Mark Karmendy) and all the others who had to work tirelessly in production and editing to produce this book.

I'd like to thank my parents (Ron and Marie), siblings (David and Darlene), and friends (David Rahmel, Don Murphy, Greg Mickey, John Taylor, Juan Leonffu, Joel Harris, Ed Gildred, Lorinda Pate, Weld O'Connor) for their unconditional support. To David Rahmel, who made fantastic suggestions on how to improve the book, my many thanks.

Most of all, I'd like to thank the reader. By buying this book, you make it possible for all of us in the book industry to labor to produce good work. When pulling the long hours to complete a book, knowing that every little improvement will help the development community is what really makes the difference. Thanks.

INTRODUCTION

Welcome to the *.NET Framwork Programmer's Reference.* Microsoft has opened an exciting new world with the introduction of Visual Studio .NET. Along with the challenges presented by the new development environment, a VS programmer now has to master the vast and sometimes overwhelming framework that embodies all access to the Windows system for Visual Basic, C#, C++, and Visual FoxPro programmers. This book will serve as both a reference map and a handy guidebook to this new programming landscape.

With the somewhat overwhelming panorama that the .NET development system represents, I hope this book will help ease you into the system. I've also written a sister volume, the *Visual Basic® .NET Programmer's Reference* (ISBN 0-07-219534-7), that holds reference information, sample code, and object model diagrams for the Visual Basic .NET language. If you find this volume useful, you may find the companion book helpful as well.

What this Book Covers

The book you hold in your hands contains reference information for the .NET Framework that supplies the foundation of all applications developed in Visual Studio .NET. Reference material is included in this book to describe the most important classes found in the framework.

Chapter 1 provides a general overview of the entire .NET Framework. This includes a brief look at the Visual Studio system, a structural outline of the functional delineation of the .NET namespace, and the ways in which .NET can interact with other aspects of the system (such as COM objects, DLLs, and the SOAP interface). An explanation is provided to help you understand the new meta-code basis of .NET execution and the Microsoft Intermediate Language (MSIL) into which all source code is now compiled. Additionally, a list of keyboard shortcuts will help you use the Visual Studio programming environment more effectively.

The main body of this book includes descriptions of the classes of the framework that are divided into chapters based on various areas of functionality (security, GUI, XML, etc.). Each chapter begins with a brief description of the capabilities included in the enumerated classes. The chapter then provides one or more coding examples to demonstrate various aspects of the framework. The step-by-step examples show common operations of the classes as they are used in real code.

Following the examples is the alphabetical sequence of class entries. At a minimum, each entry includes the name of the class, a description of its function, and its namespace location. A majority of the entries also provide the hierarchical inheritance and a full list of available members. The members of a class may include constructors, properties, methods, and events. In the method entries, standard Microsoft formatting conventions are used such as enclosing optional parameters in a set of square brackets ([ ]) and using the bar symbol (|) to indicate an Or selection between different parameter data types (such as *myVar As Integer | Float*).

Most of the example code and general headers have been presented in Visual Basic format. I chose this format because of the clarity for reading and conversion and in an attempt to expand on the existing Visual Studio documentation. Even though I've been programming in C++ for more years than Visual Basic, I still generally find VB code to be easier to read. In my experience, it is far easier to convert most VB code to C, than vice versa. Secondly, much of the auxiliary Visual Studio documentation is written with examples in C#. This reference book, therefore, expands on the information that ships with the Visual Studio package. If the sample code is incomprehensible to a C++/C# programmer, there will often be an example of the class included in the Visual Studio documentation that is coded in these languages.

I hope you find this book as useful as the people at Coherent Data (www.coherentdata.com) already have. I also hope you'll provide feedback with any suggestions you have or mistakes you find. You'll find a page devoted to this book on the Coherent Data site. Please stop by.

Chapter 1
Getting Started: The New Visual Studio

For most Visual Studio programmers, mastering with the .NET technology will be a new challenge. Microsoft has reengineered Visual Studio from top to bottom to create a standardized, shared development environment that is common to all the primary programming languages (Visual Basic, C#, C++, and other third-party languages). This new environment approaches development and code compilation in a way far more like Sun's Java technology than previous Visual Studio incarnations.

The core of the entire .NET execution system is the metalanguage known as the Microsoft Intermediate Language (MSIL). Once program source code has been compiled from any of the VS languages into MSIL (see Figure 1-1), it must be loaded into the .NET environment to execute.

The MSIL code for the program is introduced into the .NET system and run through a Just-In-Time (JIT) compiler. The compiler converts the MSIL code into the native machine code that's actually executed

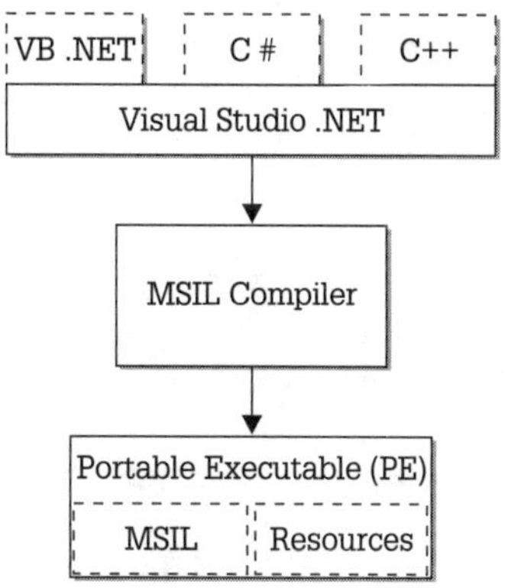

Figure 1-1. The compilation process converts source code (VB, C#, etc.) into MSIL code.

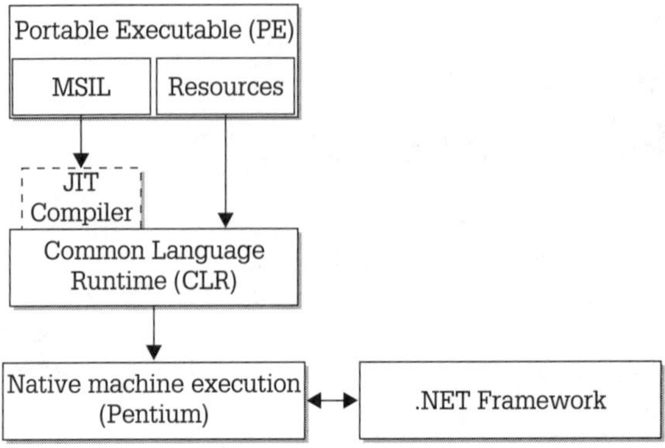

Figure 1-2. Running a .NET program converts the MSIL code to native machine code and executes it.

on the machine (see Figure 1-2). Program code executing under .NET may place calls or instantiate objects from the library of classes contained in the .NET framework. The .NET framework provides functionality for everything from opening windows to accessing data sources to parsing XML files.

For the C++ programmer with experience with the Microsoft Foundation Classes (MFC), using the .NET framework will be somewhat familiar. Visual Basic programmers may be familiar with the organized hierarchical nature of the framework from accessing various object models (such as ADO). With .NET, all of the programmer's interaction with the operating system will occur through objects found in the framework.

Structural Overview of the .NET Framework

An overview of the general outline of the framework can help you to understand how it's structured. The .NET framework is a set of extensible, reusable classes that provide access to events, graphics, I/O, Web services, networking, memory management, thread management, and all other system services.

At the root level of the framework hierarchy are two classes: System and Microsoft (see Figure 1-3). The hierarchy of classes and their organization is called a *namespace*.

The System namespace holds the classes that represent a majority of the .NET framework. Most of the standard operations a program might need (from opening windows to managing threads) are supplied in the System namespace and its subclasses. The System branch of the framework tree represents most of the functions earlier provided by the Win32 API.

The Microsoft namespace contains classes that manage events raised by the system itself (such as changes in power management), provide interoperability with unmanaged code, supply avenues to access and change registry settings, and manipulate compilation of code from source languages (such as C#, JScript, and Visual Basic) to MSIL. A majority of applications will have no need to access the Microsoft classes.

When creating a new Windows application, the Visual Studio development system adds, by default, namespace references for the following classes: Microsoft.Win32.Interop, System, System.Configuration, System.Data, System.Diagnostics, System.Drawing, System.WinForms, System.WinForms.Design, and System.XML.Serialization. Only a single Microsoft class is included in this default set: Microsoft.Win32.Interop. The Interop classes provide interoperability with unmanaged code (such as ActiveX/COM controls) as well as access to the legacy Win32 API.

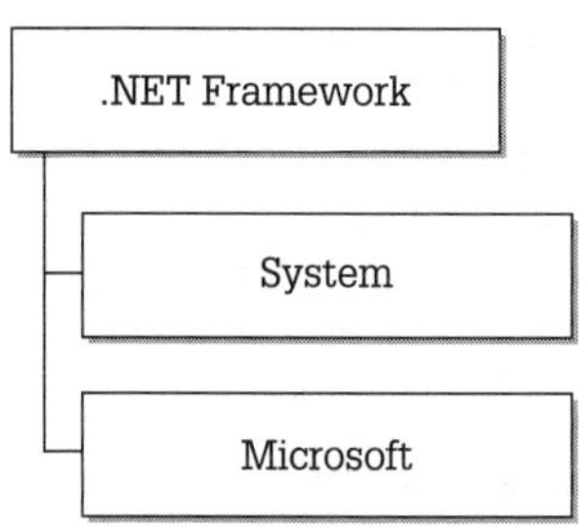

Figure 1-3. The root level of the .NET framework contains two primary classes.

NOTE: Although most classes in .NET provide class inheritance (which allows you to create a child class from an existing one), a class may be flagged to prohibit inheritance. In the documentation, you will see the prefix "Not Inheritable" before the name of such a class. Classes with this prefix forbid their use as a parent class for further extension.

Microsoft Intermediate Language (MSIL)

The Microsoft Intermediate Language (MSIL) is the "metalanguage" executed by the Just-In-Time (JIT) compiler. MSIL code is a set of CPU-independent instructions that are compiled by the JIT into native processor code. The environment in the .NET technology that actually executes the MSIL code is known as the Common Language Runtime (CLR).

One of the advantages of MSIL code is the ability to do strict data type testing. When data is addressed, the CLR can make certain that it is type compatible with the destination variable or memory allocation. Type testing prevents memory overwrites and faults that often occur in programs written in traditional languages such as C++. In addition to execution safety, it also provides greater protection for system security since overflow holes cannot be found to trip up the execution process.

Common Language Runtime (CLR)

At the core of the .NET system is the Common Language Runtime (CLR). The CLR is the code execution environment that processes the MSIL bytecode and converts it to executable machine code that is native to the processor that is executing the program. Code that executes in the CLR is called *managed code* because all object allocation, instancing, resource allocation, and garbage collection is managed by the runtime itself. That way, programs can avoid problems such as memory leaks and poor resource management.

Security in the CLR is robust because it can be controlled at the runtime level and enforced just before execution. Each application and execution environment can have a defined level of trust that allows the CLR to adjust its restrictions. For example, an Internet application executing within the runtime may not be given access to the local file system when it is executed on a remote machine.

For code to execute in the CLR, it must have a metadata header that describes the class and functions to be executed. This header is automatically generated by the Visual Studio compilers, and it complies with the Common Language Specification (CLS).

The CLR provides the following services:

- Access to the .NET Framework of classes
- Compilation of MSIL into native machine code through a JIT compiler
- Processing of managed data including automatic garbage collection
- Security restrictions to limit access for various application types
- Access to class metadata
- Isolation of executing applications in separate memory spaces
- Error exception handling
- Interfacing between managed applications, managed components, and external unmanaged applications and DLLs
- Development debugging

Since the CLR executes all the code in MSIL regardless of the source language (VB, C#, and so on) used to create it, objects written in any language can be integrated and freely interact with each other at the class level. While the class for one object may be written in VB and another in C#, they can call each other and seamlessly exchange information.

Common Type System (CTS)

The typing of data variables (such as Integer, Double, and so on) is standardized in the CLR through the Common Language Specification (CLS). CLS is a standards specification submitted by Microsoft to an open standards committee for industry approval. The design of the CLS provides for creating languages compatible with the CLR. The CLS defines language syntax interpretation and specific data types. The CLS standard supports the following primitive data types: Byte, Int16, Int32, Int64, Single, Double, Boolean, Char, Decimal, IntPtr, and String.

By adopting the CLS standard, when a VB program passes an Integer to a component written in C#, it can be assured that the variable type is exactly the same. Previously, most languages had varying definitions for everything from integers to the lowest index number available in an array. The CLS creates a uniform definition for all of the most common variable types.

Additionally, the definition of new data types has been standardized. New types used by a class or assembly are stored in an XML metadata file. This metadata can be accessed by the CLR in order to understand how to manage and interpret the custom type. The standard means that component compatibility, versioning, and replication are more efficient.

NOTE: In this section ["Common Type System (CTS)"], the industry standard meaning of the term "type" is used. It denotes specifically a data type or a variable or other variable memory allocation. In much of Microsoft's documentation, classes are referred to as *types*. Microsoft is seeking to redefine every data, code, and programming structure under the common term of "type." To avoid confusion and until Microsoft succeeds in changing the industry lexicon, I have chosen to use the current meaning of industry terms throughout the book. Therefore, *class* is used wherever possible to specify a class, while *type* is used to denote a data variable type.

The metadata for the custom data types is written in tokenized form and is not accessible with a standard text editor. Only with tools such as the MSIL Disassembler or the Runtime Debugger can you view this data. The metadata description of classes contained in a Portable Executable (PE) or an assembly fill much of the same role that Interface Definition Language (IDL) and type library files have served for other object interface methods such as COM, CORBA, and Java RMI.

Assemblies

An assembly is a collection or library of related classes and resources. This collection can be treated as a unit for deployment, security, and scope. For example, all of the routines related to XML processing are stored in an assembly named System.XML.dll. Any assembly can also bind one or more Portable Executable (PE) files together for versioning.

NOTE: If you are already familiar with Java programming, you might recognize the resemblance of *assemblies* to Java *packages*. Microsoft has extended the concept of packages to include additional features such as more robust versioning, multigranular security, and XML-based reflection.

A single file assembly includes four primary pieces:

- **Assembly metadata/manifest** A structure similar to a Java package manifest.
- **Type metadata** The header of the single class held in the assembly.
- **MSIL code** The MSIL code for the class
- **Resources** The resources (such as text or bitmaps) that will be used by the class.

A multifile assembly can be much more complex and might even include such items as graphics (GIF files, JPEG files, and other graphics), modules of compiled code, or data files required by the assembly. A multifile assembly is also a common method of assembling a number of class files that are written in different languages.

The *assembly manifest* (assembly metadata) file describes the format of the file or files that make up an assembly and how the various elements of that assembly relate to each other. The manifest may contain the following descriptive information: name, version number, culture or language specifications, strong name information, list of files in the assembly, list of class metadata files, and a list of static assemblies that are addressed by class files in the assembly.

For versioning, an assembly is the smallest granularity unit that may be specified within the CLR. The CLR versioning is stored in the manifest of each assembly. A unique assembly version number is assigned as part of the version identity. This number (such as 1.2.82.0) is formatted with the following structure: [MajorVersion].[MinorVersion].[BuildNumber].[Revision].

There are two different types of assemblies: private assemblies and shared assemblies.

Private Assemblies

A private assembly is used by only a single application and is stored in the installation directory of that application. Private assemblies are commonly used by individual programmers for building a single monolithic application. If an assembly is to be used by two or more applications, it must be placed in a common system directory and registered as a shared assembly.

Shared Assemblies

A shared assembly is not merely a private assembly placed in a public directory location for common access. Shared assemblies use a combined cache called the *global assembly cache*. Much like making a variable global within a class, a global assembly should be used only when necessary. Code references to an assembly not held in the application's directory can be confusing. Additionally, deployment and maintenance of a global assembly solution is far more complicated than simple private assembly applications. To ease global assembly deployment, you can specify the global attribute in the application installer script, and the infrastructure registration will be handled by the installer.

To make sure each assembly is unique, a shared assembly must be compiled with a cryptographic strong name (known as a *shared name*). Because of the unique name, you can implement security versioning so that only the author of the assembly has the key to produce a new edition of that assembly. The assembly is signed with a utility called Strong Name (SN.exe) that is included with the .NET SDK. The syntax for the command-line activation of the Strong Name application appears like this:

```
SN [-q(uiet)] <option> [<parameters>]
```

The following utility parameters may be passed from the console:

Parameter	Description
`-?` or `-h`	Displays help file of all of the parameters.
`-c [<csp>]`	Sets or resets the name of the Cryptographic Service Provider (CSP).
`-d <container>`	Deletes the named key container.

Parameter	Description
-D <assembly1> <assembly2>	Compares differences between assembly1 and assembly2 and makes sure they only differ in signature.
-e <assembly> <outputfile>	Extracts the public key from the assembly and writes it into the specified output file.
-i <inputfile> <container>	Reads key from input file and installs in specified key container.
-k <outputfile>	Creates new key pair and writes it into specified output file.
-m [y|n]	Enables machine-specific key containers (y), disable (n), or (left blank) check.
-o <inputfile> [<outputfile>]	Converts inputfile public key to comma delimited list of decimal byte values. If outputfile is specified, write into file otherwise store to clipboard.
-p <inputfile> <outputfile>	Reads public key from inputfile and write it to outputfile.
-pc <container> <outputfile>	Writes public key from container into outputfile.
-q	Quiet mode suppresses any output other than error messages. Must be first command sent to SN.exe.
-R <assembly> <inputfile>	Re-signs assembly with key pair supplied in inputfile.
-Rc <assembly> <container>	Re-signs assembly with key pair in containers.
-t <inputfile>	Displays token of public key from inputfile.
-tp <inputfile>	Displays token of public key and public key from inputfile.
-T <assembly>	Displays token of public key from assembly.
-Tp <assembly>	Displays token of public key and public key from assembly.

Parameter	Description
`-v[f] <assembly>`	Verifies strong name signature in assembly. If -vf switch is used, force verification even if verification is disabled.
`-Vl`	Displays verify list setting for this machine.
`-Vr <assembly> [<userlist>]`	Sets verification skipping on specified assembly. Wildcard (*) specifies all assemblies and wildcard with token `(*,<public key token>)` will specify all assemblies with matching token (string of hex digits). Optional comma-separated list of usernames to which skipping will be applied.
`-Vu <assembly>`	Removes verification skipping using same rules for `<assembly>` specification as `-Vr`.
`-Vx`	Removes verification skipping on all entries.

You can examine all the assemblies currently stored in the global assemblies cache by opening the \Assembly folder stored in your Windows directory. A special viewer automatically activates (similar to the one used when the Internet cache folder is displayed), and each assembly is listed with a Global Assembly Name, assembly type, current version, culture, and public key token.

Framework Assemblies

Visual Studio stores the foundation assemblies of the .NET Framework in approximately 30 separate DLL files. These files can be found in the .NET directory of the System directory. On a Windows 2000 machine, for example, the path may be

```
c:\WinNT\Microsoft.NET\Framework\v1.0.3617
```

The final directory name will be the current version of the .NET framework stored on your machine. In that directory, you will find the following .NET assembly files:

Microsoft.JScript.dll
Microsoft.Jscript.resources.dll
Microsoft.VisualBasic.dll
Microsoft.VisualBasic.Vsa.dll
Microsoft.VisualBasic.Compatibility.dll
Microsoft.VisualBasic.Compatibility.Data.dll
Microsoft.VisualC.dll
Microsoft.VisualStudio.VSHelp.dll
Microsoft.Vsa.dll
System.dll
System.Configuration.Install.dll
System.Data.dll
System.Design.dll
System.DirectoryServices.dll
System.Drawing.dll
System.Drawing.Design.dll
System.EnterpriseServices.dll
System.EnterpriseServices.Thunk.dll
System.Management.dll
System.Runtime.Remoting.Serialization.Formatters.Soap.dll
System.Security.dll
System.ServiceProcess.dll
System.Web.dll
System.Web.RegularExpressions.dll
System.Web.Services.dll
System.Windows.Forms.dll
System.XML.dll

Each of these files contains a number of classes for the framework. You can examine the namespaces of these files using the MSIL Disassembler. The Disassembler will convert the namespace of a designation file into a hierarchical outline similar to the Explorer interface. For example, to examine the class System.Windows.Forms, you would use the following instruction at the MS-DOS command line or command prompt to execute the Disassembler:

```
ildasm
```

Once the Disassembler has been activated, you can open any of the assembly files. In Figure 1-4 you can see the hierarchy tree of one of the assembly files. You can double-click on the entry for the Manifest of the assembly, and it will be displayed in the Notepad application.

The core assembly library used by the .NET framework has the filename of *mscorlib.dll* and can be found in the \Framework folder:

```
C:\WinNT\Microsoft.NET\Framework\v1.0.3617\mscorlib.dll
```

Custom class libraries that will be used by multiple applications are located in the \Assembly directory:

```
C:\WinNT\Assembly
```

Private assemblies for use with ASP.NET should be located in the \bin directory of the application directory that will use it. For example:

```
C:\inetpub\wwwroot\HelloNetWorld\bin
```

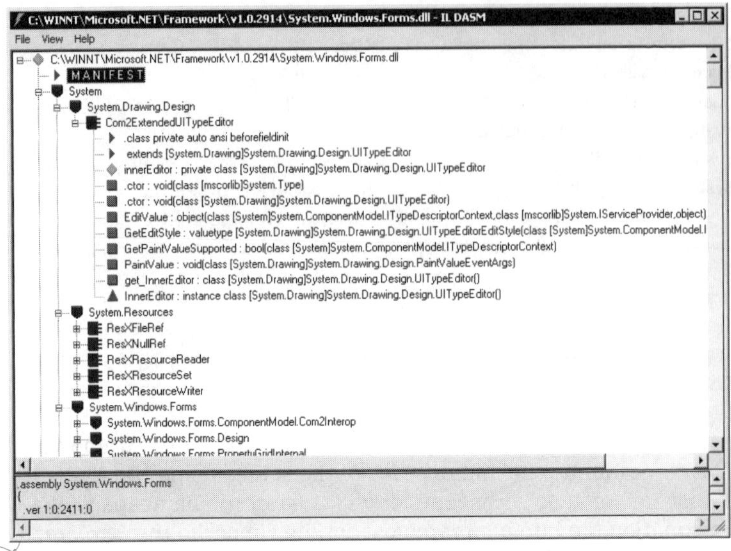

Figure 1-4. Opening an assembly file in the Disassembler allows you to examine the hierarchy stored in the file.

ASP.NET

One of the key aspects of .NET initiative is the ASP.NET technology. ASP.NET is the infrastructure that allows you to execute .NET routines and applications using the framework for Web-based solutions. ASP.NET, like ASP, is an ISAPI DLL that executes under the Internet Information Server (IIS).

ASP.NET files are recognizable by their extensions that end with the letter "X", such as .aspx and .asax. These files can be nearly identical to the traditional .asp and .asa files, or they can use the features of the .NET system. Changing an .asp or .asa extension to .aspx or .asax, respectively, will allow existing files to execute almost seamlessly on the new ASP.NET engine. However, changing the extension back if .NET functionality has been added will generate errors.

Visual Studio Environment

Since the Visual Studio environment is common to all languages, you can see most of the common portions of the environment in Figure 1-5. In the figure, the Solution Explorer and class view appear in the top-right pane of the window. The class view lets you examine all of the classes that are constructed within the project, including methods, properties, and subclasses.

Server Explorer and the Toolbox

The Server Explorer and the Toolbox are both pop-out windows that appear to run down the left side of the window. The Server

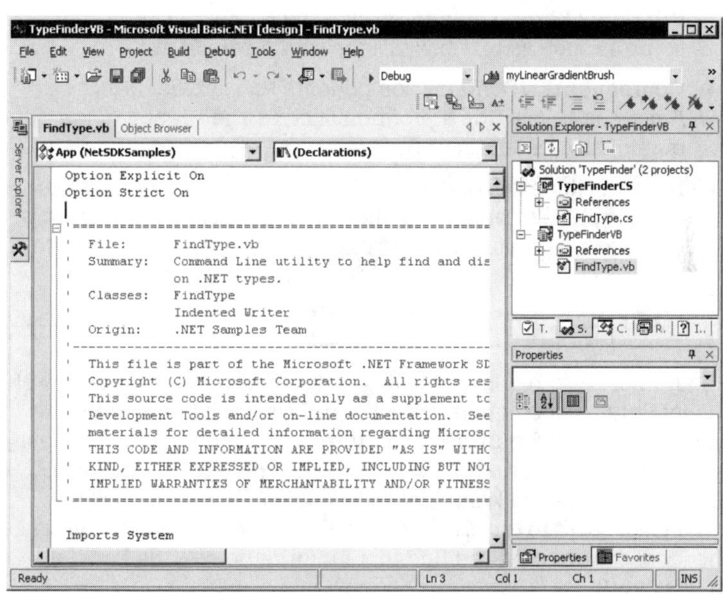

Figure 1-5. The Visual Studio environment is shown displaying an example Visual Basic project.

Explorer contains data connections and servers that can be addressed from the current system. The Server Explorer can be used to

- Investigate existing data connections
- Add new connections (through the right-click menu)
- Create new databases on an SQL Server platform
- Examine the available servers in the Network Neighborhood
- Add additional server connections to the current machine
- Provide access to event logs, message queues, performance counters, services, and Crystal services to which permission has been granted

The Toolbox will be familiar to seasoned users of any of the Visual Studio languages. It contains different categories of items that can be placed on forms. The four tabs are

- **General** Contains the general form pointer.
- **Windows Forms** Features all of the familiar user interface controls such as text boxes, labels, and scroll bars.
- **Components** Contains components that provide access to functionality outside a program such as the event log, message queue, or performance counter.
- **Data** Includes all of the controls needed to bind data to a form. These controls can be used in conjunction with the Windows Forms controls such as the TextBox, CheckBox, and DataGrid.

Properties, Dynamic Help

The Properties tab will be familiar to users of previous versions of Visual Studio. One new feature is the class listing shown for the selected item. In Figure 1-6, the Properties window in the bottom-right corner shows that the control named labelID is followed by the notation *System.Windows.Forms.Label.* This describes the hierarchical path to the class in the .NET Framework that instantiates the label control. You can find more information on the Label class in Chapter 9.

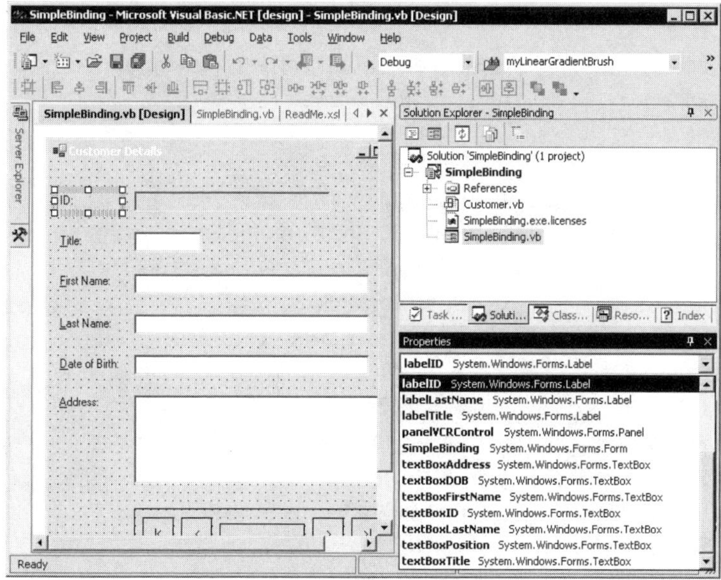

Figure 1-6. The Properties window shows the class that is used to instantiate the selected control.

Menu Options

While some of the menu options will change depending on the language that you will be developing in, most of the commands will remain the same. Here is a list of shortcut keys for the most common menu commands:

Shortcut	Description
ALT-F12	Find symbol
ALT-SHIFT-A	Add existing item
CTRL-A	Select all
CTRL-ALT-P	Examine debug processes
CTRL-B	Add new breakpoint
CTRL-F	Find

Shortcut	Description
CTRL-F1	Dynamic help
CTRL-F5	Start execution without debugging
CTRL-G	Go to (line number)
CTRL-H	Replace
CTRL-N	New file
CTRL-O	Open file
CTRL-P	Print
CTRL-S	Save item
CTRL-SHIFT-A	Add new item
CTRL-SHIFT-B	Build current project
CTRL-SHIFT-F	Find in files
CTRL-SHIFT-F9	Clear all breakpoints
CTRL-SHIFT-H	Replace in files
CTRL-SHIFT-N	New project
CTRL-SHIFT-O	Open project
CTRL-SHIFT-S	Save all
CTRL-SHIFT-U	Make uppercase
CTRL-U	Make lowercase
CTRL-Y	Redo
CTRL-Z	Undo
F1	Help
F3	Find again
F4	Properties window
F5	Start execution
F7	View code
F9	Set breakpoint
F10	Step over
F11	Step into
SHIFT-ALT-ENTER	Display in full screen mode

Object Browser

The Object Browser is an integrated help system that allows you to examine any object in the available framework. For each object, all of the methods and properties are displayed. Selecting a method will show the argument requirements for passing and receiving values. Selecting a property will display the variable type that is represented by the property name.

NOTE: In the past, components have been called VBXs, OCXs, OLE controls, COM controls, and finally ActiveX controls. With .NET, these components have now been recast as managed Windows Forms controls. ActiveX controls will now be subclassed off the Windows.Forms.UserControl class. The UserControl has a complete graphical user interface and can be compiled into a separate DLL or included in your main project.

The Object Browser can also be used to display enumerated values types. For example, the MsgBox function can return a cancel value of 2 to indicate the user clicked the Cancel button. These enumerated types as well as others such as Abort, Ignore, Yes, No, etc., can be examined and their numeric values determined.

Accessing Classes

To simplify access to external classes by a program, the name of the external class may be included at the beginning of the program. In VB, C#, and C++, the command for doing this is different. To use the classes in the System namespace, for example, the following commands would be used:

Language	Command
Visual Basic	Imports System
C#	using System;
C++	using namespace System;

Once the namespace has been included, the object hierarchy can be navigated in the way that is traditional for each language. VB and C# use the dot(.) separator while C++ uses the double colon (::) as an object reference operator. Without these references, external classes may still be used, although a fully qualified namespace string is required in each code instance (such as variable definition or method activation).

External Access

Although the capabilities of the .NET languages and the .NET Framework are robust, there will often be the need to take advantage of other systems. For example, although C++ does not support the higher-level features of .NET (that are supported in C#), traditional C++ can be used to program the .NET Framework. Additionally, programs within .NET can be used to call outside to unmanaged code created using more traditional languages.

Managed Extensions for C++

C++ can access most of the functionality of the .NET system through technology called *Managed Extensions for C++*. The Managed Extensions allows a C++ program to use everything from the classes in the .NET framework to the garbage collection and object management capabilities.

The Managed Extensions are required for C++ to access the .NET system. Therefore, whenever C++ is mentioned in this book, it is implicit that the Managed Extensions are being used. To make C++ compile into managed code, you need to specify the command-line switch (/CLR) because it is not managed by default. Even with this switch set, data created in C++ is not automatically managed data. You must use the __gc keyword when the C++ objects are instantiated to mark them as managed data.

NOTE: While any programming language that provides access to the COM/ActiveX interface can address the .NET Framework, much of the functionality is sacrificed by using this method. The inheritance, overloading, garbage collection, and many other features are not available when driving .NET through its COM interface.

Using DLLs and COM Objects from .NET

Calls to existing Win32 or external DLL routines can be made from within .NET. DLL functions can be invoked using the System.Runtime.InteropServices class. You can use a Declare statement in Visual Basic, or you can use the new DLLImport function (available in both VB and C#). The following VB code makes a shell function to the message box call in the Win32 library:

```
Imports System
Imports System.Runtime.InteropServices
   <DllImport("user32.dll", EntryPoint:=" MessageBox")> _
Public Shared Function MessageBox(ByVal hWnd As Integer,
  ByVal strMessage As String, ByVal strCaption As String,
  ByVal uiType As UInt32) As Integer
    ' No code is required, this function is just a shell.
    ' The DLLImport supplies the code.
End Function
```

COM components (or ActiveX controls) are much easier to address. They may be selected through the traditional References dialog box. The Visual Studio system will automatically generate a Runtime Callable Wrapper (RCW). This allows access to any registered standard ActiveX DLLs or components. It is also possible to write a custom RCW for non-ActiveX interfaces.

A .NET component may be accessed from outside the .NET system (such as from a Visual Studio 6 application) through a COM Callable Wrapper (CCW). A CCW can be automatically generated for a .NET class by selecting that option in the Project Options dialog box, or one may be manually defined.

Simple Object Access Protocol (SOAP)

Previously in Windows, the dominant method of object interaction across a network (or the Internet) was through the Distributed COM (DCOM) protocol. The .NET system has adopted the open standard know as SOAP (Simple Object Access Protocol) to allow objects to communicate. SOAP is a standard that communicates through HTTP and conducts most of its data interaction through XML-based transmissions.

NOTE: The utility SoapSuds.exe can be used to generate a metadata proxy file to allow communication.

Chapter 2
Graphical User Interface

2

The graphical user interface (GUI) of a program or component is the presentation that the user sees and manipulates. A GUI includes forms, scroll bars, buttons, tree views, combo boxes, and all other display items of the standard user experience. These familiar GUI elements of the Windows OS can be addressed through the System.Windows.Forms class.

This chapter provides a reference to each of the classes contained in the System.Windows.Forms class. A short description of each class is included. For the most important classes, the headers of all available constructors, methods, and properties are shown. The inheritance of each important class is described since many of the classes inherit methods and properties from their parent or foundation classes.

NOTE: Many of the functions in the Microsoft.Win32 class parallel older function calls in the Win32 DLLs and the Microsoft Foundation Classes (MFCs) used by C++ programmers. For Visual Basic 6 compatibility, you will find the user interface elements that mirror VB6 components in the class library of Microsoft.VisualBasic.Compatibility.VB6.

Before the general class reference begins, there are some simple windowing examples included. These provide a framework to observe how the classes are actually used in code. The code has been presented in Visual Basic, although each program is easily adaptable to any of the other Visual Studio languages.

Creating a Window

The .NET framework makes it easy to create new windows. Populating a window with controls is also a fairly simple process. When you use the Visual Studio environment, code is automatically generated to create and manage the window forms and the controls on them. However, there are times when you will want to modify this code for specific uses or create your own. In the new Visual

Studio, all of the user interface elements are generated as code that can be manually modified.

The following code is generated automatically for you by the Windows Form Designer. It can provide an instructive sample of how the Visual Studio system creates and manages forms. The InitializeComponent() routine that is included in the New() constructor is necessary to initialize the resources used by user interface elements created by the Windows Form Designer. Likewise, the code found in the Dispose() routine eliminates these resources.

```
Imports System.ComponentModel
Imports System.Drawing
Imports System.Windows.Forms

#Region " Windows Form Designer generated code "

  Public Sub New()
    MyBase.New()
    InitializeComponent()

    'Add custom initialization code here
  End Sub

  Protected Overloads Overrides Sub Dispose(ByVal _
    disposing As Boolean)
    If disposing Then
      If Not (components Is Nothing) Then
        componentsDispose()
      End If
    End If
    MyBase.Dispose(disposing)
  End Sub

  'Required by the Windows Form Designer
  Private components As System.ComponentModel.Container

  'NOTE: Only modify this code using the
  '      Windows Form Designer.
  <System.Diagnostics.DebuggerStepThrough()>
Private Sub InitializeComponent()
  Me.AutoScaleBaseSize = New System.Drawing.Size(5, 13)
  Me.ClientSize = New System.Drawing.Size(292, 273)
  Me.Name = "Form1"
```

```
  Me.Text = "Form1"
End Sub
#End Region
```

This code, while generated by macros in the Form Designer, could be written by hand in the code window. From a programming standpoint, forms in .NET are treated in much the same manner as in previous versions of the Visual Studio languages. Unfortunately, the system has not been augmented to allow code to be compiled at runtime (although late binding is still available), but adding a form from an existing template can easily provide much of this functionality.

NOTE: The New() subroutine of Visual Basic.NET that is shown in the code above replaces both the Form_Load and the Form_Initialize events available in previous versions of Visual Basic. When the code in the New() routine is called, the form has already been loaded and all of the controls on it have been initialized.

There is no definitional difference between modal (dialog boxes) and modal-less windows—the difference occurs in activation. For modal windows, the ShowDialog() routine is used. The following code demonstrates calling this method from Visual Basic and C#:

```
myForm.ShowDialog(Me)         ' Visual Basic
myForm.ShowDialog( this );  // C#
```

To create a simple form to be used as a dialog box, you could generate it entirely from within a program. The following Visual Basic code, when activated through the Click event of a command button, creates such a form and populates it with a button and a list box. If the form's AcceptButton property was set to reference myButton and the ShowDialog method was used, you could have a completely coded dialog box.

```
Sub cmdNewForm_Click()
  Dim myForm As New Form()
  Dim myButton As New Button()
  Dim myListBox As New ListBox()

  ' Set form caption
  myForm.Text = "Hello World Form"
  ' Set location to the center of the screen
  myForm.StartPosition = FormStartPosition.CenterScreen

  ' Setup button location
```

```
  myButton.Location = New Point(150, 10)
  ' Set button text
  myButton.Text = "&OK"

  ' Set listbox location
  myListBox.Location = New Point(10, 10)
  ' Add one item to listbox
  myListBox.Items.Add("Hello World!")

  ' Add both controls to myForm
  myForm.Controls.Add(myButton)
  myForm.Controls.Add(myListBox)
  ' Display myForm
  myForm.Show()
End Sub
```

Adding User Interface Elements

More common than creating a form from code is the need to add controls to the various collections of an existing form. After creating a window within Visual Studio, you quickly can add controls such as radio buttons and text fields from code that is executing within the form itself.

The following code demonstrates adding a number of buttons to an existing form. The placement and naming of the buttons are determined by the number of controls that already exist on the form. If you place this code within a button on a form, when you execute the application and click the button, it will generate a dynamically created button and display it on the form.

```
Sub cmdAddButton_Click()
  Dim myButton As New Button()
  ' Setup button location & use the Me keyword to get
  ' an object reference to the current form
  myButton.Location = New Point(10, Me.Controls.Count * 30)
  ' Set button text to the control number
  myButton.Text = "Control #" & Me.Controls.Count
  Me.Controls.Add(myButton)
End Sub
```

Displaying a Save Dialog Box

Not all forms must be created from scratch. There are a number of common dialog boxes that are included as part of the standard Windows OS. These dialog boxes are derived from a foundation class called CommonDialog and are accessible through their individual classes. There are five types of dialog boxes included in the .NET framework: ColorDialog, FileDialog, FontDialog, PageSetupDialog, and PrintDialog.

Below is simple Visual Basic code to configure and display the Save dialog box and retrieve the entry of the user. The code shown here executes when a button named cmdSaveDialog is clicked.

```
Sub cmdSaveDialog_Click()
  Dim saveDialog As New SaveFileDialog()
  Dim myResult As DialogResult

  ' Setup file filter for Save dialog
  saveDialog.Filter = _
    "Data files (*.dat)|*.dat|All files (*.*)|*.*"

  ' Display Save dialog and place result in variable
  myResult = saveDialog.ShowDialog()
  ' Check result value
  If myResult = DialogResult.OK Then
    MsgBox("Thanks for saving: " + saveDialog.FileName)
  End If
End Sub
```

AccessibleObject Class

Provides the settings of an accessibility application for examination.

Inheritance—Object.MarshalByRefObject.AccessibleObject

```
public class System.Windows.Forms.AccessibleObject
  ' Constructors
  AccessibleObject()
```

```
' Properties
Bounds As System.Drawing.Rectangle (read only)
DefaultAction As System.String (read only)
Description As System.String (read only)
Help As System.String (read only)
KeyboardShortcut As System.String (read only)
Name As System.String
Parent As
  System.Windows.Forms.AccessibleObject (read only)
Role As System.Windows.Forms.AccessibleRole (read only)
State As
  System.Windows.Forms.AccessibleStates (read only)
Value As System.String
' Methods
DoDefaultAction()
GetChild(index As Int32) As AccessibleObject
GetChildCount() As Int32
GetFocused() As AccessibleObject
GetHelpTopic(fileName As String&) As Int32
GetSelected() As AccessibleObject
HitTest(x As Int32, y As Int32) As AccessibleObject
Navigate(navdir As AccessibleNavigation)
  As AccessibleObject
Select(flags As AccessibleSelection)
```

AmbientProperties Class

Holds properties that, if not set on the current instance, retrieve their data from the same property on the parent control. If the object has no parent and the property is not set, the value is determined through the Site property.

Inheritance—Object.AmbientProperties

```
public class System.Windows.Forms.AmbientProperties
  ' Constructors
  AmbientProperties()
  ' Properties
  BackColor As System.Drawing.Color
  Cursor As System.Windows.Forms.Cursor
  Font As System.Drawing.Font
  ForeColor As System.Drawing.Color
```

Application Class

Static class that provides methods and properties for the manipulation of facets of an application such as execution, termination, startup and data access paths, etc.

Inheritance—Object.Application

```
public class System.Windows.Forms.Application
  ' Properties
  AllowQuit As System.Boolean (read only)
  CommonAppDataPath As System.String (read only)
  CommonAppDataRegistry As
    Microsoft.Win32.RegistryKey (read only)
  CompanyName As System.String (read only)
  CurrentCulture As System.Globalization.CultureInfo
  CurrentInputLanguage As
    System.Windows.Forms.InputLanguage
  ExecutablePath As System.String (read only)
  LocalUserAppDataPath As System.String (read only)
  MessageLoop As System.Boolean (read only)
  ProductName As System.String (read only)
  ProductVersion As System.String (read only)
  SafeTopLevelCaptionFormat As System.String
  StartupPath As System.String (read only)
  UserAppDataPath As System.String (read only)
  UserAppDataRegistry As
    Microsoft.Win32.RegistryKey (read only)
  ' Methods
  AddMessageFilter(value As IMessageFilter)
  DoEvents()
  Exit()
  ExitThread()
  OleRequired() As ApartmentState
  OnThreadException(t As Exception)
  RemoveMessageFilter(value As IMessageFilter)
  Run(mainForm As Form)
  Run()
  Run(context As ApplicationContext)
  ' Events
  ApplicationExit As System.EventHandler
  Idle As System.EventHandler
```

```
  ThreadException As
    System.Threading.ThreadExceptionEventHandler
  ThreadExit As System.EventHandler
```

ApplicationContext Class

Allows configuration of the context of the execution threads of an application, such as redefining the conditions that cause a thread to exit.

Inheritance—Object.ApplicationContext

```
public class System.Windows.Forms.ApplicationContext
  ' Constructors
  ApplicationContext(mainForm As Form)
  ApplicationContext()
  ' Properties
  MainForm As System.Windows.Forms.Form
  ' Methods
  Dispose()
  ExitThread()
  ' Events
  ThreadExit As System.EventHandler
```

AxHost Class

Provides a wrapper class for ActiveX controls and exposes them as Windows.Forms controls. This class is not meant to be instantiated as a stand-alone class, but rather provides a base class that is used as the parent of other classes. Most of the properties of this class are only valid if the wrapped ActiveX control supports them.

Inheritance—Object.MarshalByRefObject.Component.Control.AxHost

```
public class System.Windows.Forms.AxHost
  ' Properties
  BackColor As System.Drawing.Color
  BackgroundImage As System.Drawing.Image
  ContainingControl As
    System.Windows.Forms.ContainerControl
```

```
ContextMenu As System.Windows.Forms.ContextMenu
Cursor As System.Windows.Forms.Cursor
EditMode As System.Boolean (read only)
Enabled As System.Boolean
Font As System.Drawing.Font
ForeColor As System.Drawing.Color
HasAboutBox As System.Boolean (read only)
OcxState As System.Windows.Forms.AxHost+State
RightToLeft As System.Boolean
Site As System.ComponentModel.ISite (write only)
Text As System.String
' Methods
BeginInit()
DoVerb(verb As Int32)
EndInit()
GetOcx() As Object
HasPropertyPages() As Boolean
InvokeEditMode()
MakeDirty()
PreProcessMessage(msg As Message&) As Boolean
ShowAboutBox()
ShowPropertyPages()
ShowPropertyPages(control As Control)
' Events
BackColorChanged As System.EventHandler
BackgroundImageChanged As System.EventHandler
BindingContextChanged As System.EventHandler
ChangeUICues As System.Windows.Forms.UICuesEventHandler
Click As System.EventHandler
ContextMenuChanged As System.EventHandler
CursorChanged As System.EventHandler
DoubleClick As System.EventHandler
DragDrop As System.Windows.Forms.DragEventHandler
DragEnter As System.Windows.Forms.DragEventHandler
DragLeave As System.EventHandler
DragOver As System.Windows.Forms.DragEventHandler
EnabledChanged As System.EventHandler
FontChanged As System.EventHandler
ForeColorChanged As System.EventHandler
GiveFeedback As
  System.Windows.Forms.GiveFeedbackEventHandler
HelpRequested As System.Windows.Forms.HelpEventHandler
ImeModeChanged As System.EventHandler
KeyDown As System.Windows.Forms.KeyEventHandler
KeyPress As System.Windows.Forms.KeyPressEventHandler
KeyUp As System.Windows.Forms.KeyEventHandler
Layout As System.Windows.Forms.LayoutEventHandler
MouseDown As System.Windows.Forms.MouseEventHandler
MouseEnter As System.EventHandler
```

2

```
MouseHover As System.EventHandler
MouseLeave As System.EventHandler
MouseMove As System.Windows.Forms.MouseEventHandler
MouseUp As System.Windows.Forms.MouseEventHandler
MouseWheel As System.Windows.Forms.MouseEventHandler
Paint As System.Windows.Forms.PaintEventHandler
QueryAccessibilityHelp As System.Win-
  dows.Forms.QueryAccessibilityHelpEventHandler
QueryContinueDrag As
  System.Windows.Forms.QueryContinueDragEventHandler
RightToLeftChanged As System.EventHandler
StyleChanged As System.EventHandler
TabIndexChanged As System.EventHandler
TabStopChanged As System.EventHandler
TextChanged As System.EventHandler
```

BaseCollection Class

The foundation class used to create collections. This class is not meant to be instantiated as a stand-alone class, but rather provides a base class that is used as the parent of other classes. The following classes use this class as a parent: BindingsCollection, GridColumnStylesCollection, and GridTableStylesCollection.

Inheritance—Object.MarshalByRefObject. BaseCollection

```
public class System.Windows.Forms.BaseCollection
  ' Constructors
  BaseCollection()
  ' Properties
  Count As System.Int32 (read only)
  IsReadOnly As System.Boolean (read only)
  IsSynchronized As System.Boolean (read only)
  SyncRoot As System.Object (read only)
  ' Methods
  CopyTo(ar As Array, index As Int32)
  GetEnumerator() As IEnumerator
```

Binding Class

Provides simple binding between the property of an object and the property of a control.

Inheritance—Object.Binding

```
public class System.Windows.Forms.Binding
  ' Constructors
  Binding(propertyName As String, dataSource As Object,
    dataMember As String)
  ' Properties
  BindingManagerBase As
    System.Windows.Forms.BindingManagerBase (read only)
  BindingMemberInfo As
    System.Windows.Forms.BindingMemberInfo (read only)
  Control As System.Windows.Forms.Control (read only)
  DataSource As System.Object (read only)
  IsBinding As System.Boolean (read only)
  PropertyName As System.String (read only)
  ' Events
  Format As System.Windows.Forms.ConvertEventHandler
  Parse As System.Windows.Forms.ConvertEventHandler
```


BindingContext Class

Manages a collection of objects created from the BindingManagerBase class.

Inheritance—Object.BindingContext

```
public class System.Windows.Forms.BindingContext
  ' Constructors
  BindingContext()
  ' Properties
  IsReadOnly As System.Boolean (read only)
  Item As
    System.Windows.Forms.BindingManagerBase (read only)
  Item As
    System.Windows.Forms.BindingManagerBase (read only)
  ' Methods
  Contains(dataSource As Object [,dataMember As String])
    As Boolean
  ' Events
  CollectionChanged As
    System.ComponentModel.CollectionChangeEventHandler
```

BindingManagerBase Class

Provides management of Binding objects that connect the source to a control for a particular data source and data member.

Inheritance—Object.BindingManagerBase

```
public class System.Windows.Forms.BindingManagerBase
  ' Constructors
  BindingManagerBase()
  ' Properties
  Bindings As
    System.Windows.Forms.BindingsCollection (read only)
  Count As System.Int32 (read only)
  Current As System.Object (read only)
  Position As System.Int32
  ' Methods
  AddNew()
  CancelCurrentEdit()
  EndCurrentEdit()
  GetItemProperties() As PropertyDescriptorCollection
  RemoveAt(index As Int32)
  ResumeBinding()
  SuspendBinding()
  ' Events
  CurrentChanged As System.EventHandler
  PositionChanged As System.EventHandler
```

BindingsCollection Class

Used by the system to hold a collection of Binding objects for a control. Found as System.Windows.Forms.**BindingsCollection**.

Button Class

Provides the class used to create an instance of a Windows command button control.

Inheritance—Object.MarshalByRefObject.Component.Control.ButtonBase.Button

```
public class System.Windows.Forms.Button
  ' Constructors
  Button()
  ' Properties
  DialogResult As System.Windows.Forms.DialogResult
  ' Methods
  NotifyDefault(value As Boolean)
  PerformClick()
  ToString() As String
  ' Events
  DoubleClick As System.EventHandler
```

ButtonBase Class

Provides the foundation class functionality used for Windows button types, such as the Button, CheckBox, and RadioButton controls.

Inheritance—Object.MarshalByRefObject.Component.Control.ButtonBase

```
public class System.Windows.Forms.ButtonBase
  ' Properties
  FlatStyle As System.Windows.Forms.FlatStyle
  Image As System.Drawing.Image
  ImageAlign As System.Drawing.ContentAlignment
  ImageIndex As System.Int32
  ImageList As System.Windows.Forms.ImageList
  ImeMode As System.Windows.Forms.ImeMode
  TextAlign As System.Drawing.ContentAlignment
```

CheckBox Class

Provides the class used to create an instance of a Windows CheckBox control.

Inheritance—Object.MarshalByRefObject. Component.Control.ButtonBase.CheckBox

```
public class System.Windows.Forms.CheckBox
  ' Constructors
  CheckBox()
  ' Properties
  Appearance As System.Windows.Forms.Appearance
  AutoCheck As System.Boolean
  CheckAlign As System.Drawing.ContentAlignment
  Checked As System.Boolean
  CheckState As System.Windows.Forms.CheckState
  TextAlign As System.Drawing.ContentAlignment
  ThreeState As System.Boolean
  ' Methods
  ToString() As String
  ' Events
  AppearanceChanged As System.EventHandler
  CheckedChanged As System.EventHandler
  CheckStateChanged As System.EventHandler
```

CheckedListBox Class

Provides the class used to create an instance of a Windows ListBox control that displays a checkbox to the left of each list item.

Inheritance—Object.MarshalByRefObject. Component.Control.ListControl.ListBox. CheckedListBox

```
public class System.Windows.Forms.CheckedListBox
  ' Constructors
  CheckedListBox()
  ' Properties
  CheckedIndices As System.Windows.Forms.CheckedListBox+
    CheckedIndexCollection (read only)
  CheckedItems As System.Windows.Forms.CheckedListBox+
    CheckedItemCollection (read only)
  CheckOnClick As System.Boolean
  DrawMode As System.Windows.Forms.DrawMode
  ItemHeight As System.Int32
```

```
Items As System.Windows.Forms.CheckedListBox+
  ObjectCollection (read only)
SelectionMode As System.Windows.Forms.SelectionMode
ThreeDCheckBoxes As System.Boolean
' Methods
GetItemChecked(index As Int32) As Boolean
GetItemCheckState(index As Int32) As CheckState
SetItemChecked(index As Int32, value As Boolean)
SetItemCheckState(index As Int32, value As CheckState)
' Events
Click As System.EventHandler
DrawItem As System.Windows.Forms.DrawItemEventHandler
ItemCheck As System.Windows.Forms.ItemCheckEventHandler
MeasureItem As
  System.Windows.Forms.MeasureItemEventHandler
```


Clipboard Class

Static class that provides access to the system Clipboard. The DataFormats objects hold the information on the type or types of data held in the clipboard.

Inheritance—Object.Clipboard

```
public class System.Windows.Forms.Clipboard
  ' Methods
  GetDataObject() As IDataObject
  SetDataObject(data As Object, copy As Boolean)
  SetDataObject(data As Object)
```

ColorDialog Class

Used to display a color picker dialog box for user selection of colors and definition of custom colors. This class represents one of the common dialog boxes provided by the system. *See also* the FileDialog, FontDialog, PageSetupDialog, and PrintDialog classes.

Inheritance—Object.MarshalByRefObject.Component.CommonDialog.ColorDialog

```
public class System.Windows.Forms.ColorDialog
  ' Constructors
  ColorDialog()
  ' Properties
  AllowFullOpen As System.Boolean
  AnyColor As System.Boolean
  Color As System.Drawing.Color
  CustomColors As System.Int32()
  FullOpen As System.Boolean
  ShowHelp As System.Boolean
  SolidColorOnly As System.Boolean
  ' Methods
  Reset()
  ToString() As String
```

ColumnHeader Class

Holds the column header of a single column for a ListView control. Found as System.Windows.Forms.**ColumnHeader**.

ComboBox Class

Provides the class used to create an instance of a Windows ComboBox control. Use the Add() method to insert individual new elements to the ComboBox object and the AddRange() method to add all object references held in an array.

Inheritance—Object.MarshalByRefObject.Component.Control.ListControl.ComboBox

```
public class System.Windows.Forms.ComboBox
  ' Constructors
  ComboBox()
  ' Properties
```

```
BackColor As System.Drawing.Color
BackgroundImage As System.Drawing.Image
DrawMode As System.Windows.Forms.DrawMode
DropDownStyle As System.Windows.Forms.ComboBoxStyle
DropDownWidth As System.Int32
DroppedDown As System.Boolean
Focused As System.Boolean (read only)
ForeColor As System.Drawing.Color
IntegralHeight As System.Boolean
ItemHeight As System.Int32
Items As System.Windows.Forms.ComboBox+
  ObjectCollection (read only)
MaxDropDownItems As System.Int32
MaxLength As System.Int32
PreferredHeight As System.Int32 (read only)
SelectedIndex As System.Int32
SelectedItem As System.Object
SelectedText As System.String
SelectionLength As System.Int32
SelectionStart As System.Int32
Sorted As System.Boolean
Text As System.String
' Methods
BeginUpdate()
EndUpdate()
FindString(s As String [,startIndex As Int32]) As Int32
FindStringExact(s As String [,startIndex As Int32])
  As Int32
GetItemHeight(index As Int32) As Int32
Select(start As Int32, length As Int32)
SelectAll()
ToString() As String
' Events
DrawItem As System.Windows.Forms.DrawItemEventHandler
DropDown As System.EventHandler
DropDownStyleChanged As System.EventHandler
MeasureItem As
  System.Windows.Forms.MeasureItemEventHandler
SelectedIndexChanged As System.EventHandler
SelectionChangeCommitted As System.EventHandler
```

2

CommonDialog Class

Provides the foundation class used to create all of the common dialog boxes for user selection of color, file, font, page setup, and printing options. *See also* the ColorDialog, FileDialog, FontDialog, PageSetupDialog, and PrintDialog classes.

Inheritance—Object.MarshalByRefObject.Component.CommonDialog

```
public class System.Windows.Forms.CommonDialog
  ' Constructors
  CommonDialog()
  ' Methods
  Reset()
  ShowDialog() As DialogResult
  ' Events
  HelpRequest As System.EventHandler
```

ContainerControl Class

Provides a foundation class for containers (such as forms, property grids, and user controls) of other controls.

Inheritance—Object.MarshalByRefObject.Component.Control.ScrollableControl.ContainerControl

```
public class System.Windows.Forms.ContainerControl
  ' Constructors
  ContainerControl()
  ' Properties
  ActiveControl As System.Windows.Forms.Control
  BindingContext As System.Windows.Forms.BindingContext
  ParentForm As System.Windows.Forms.Form (read only)
  ' Methods
  Validate() As Boolean
```

ContextMenu Class

Provides a class to create object instances of a context, shortcut, or right-click menu. *See also* the Menu class.

Inheritance—Object.MarshalByRefObject.Component.Menu.ContextMenu

```
public class System.Windows.Forms.ContextMenu
  ' Constructors
  ContextMenu()
  ContextMenu(menuItems As MenuItem())
  ' Properties
  RightToLeft As System.Windows.Forms.RightToLeft
  SourceControl As System.Windows.Forms.Control (read only)
  ' Methods
  Show(control As Control, pos As Point)
  ' Events
  Popup As System.EventHandler
```

Control Class

Provides a foundation class for all controls or components with a visual implementation. This class provides functionality to handle keyboard and input device entry as well as message routing and security. New controls are generally not created as children of this class, but rather inherit from the UserControl class.

Inheritance—Object.MarshalByRefObject.Component.Control

```
public class System.Windows.Forms.Control
  ' Constructors
  Control(parent As Control, text As String, left As Int32,
    top As Int32, width As Int32, height As Int32)
  Control(text As String, left As Int32, top As Int32,
    width As Int32, height As Int32)
```

```
Control(parent As Control, text As String)
Control(text As String)
Control()
' Properties
AccessibilityObject As
  System.Windows.Forms.AccessibleObject (read only)
AccessibleDefaultActionDescription As System.String
AccessibleDescription As System.String
AccessibleName As System.String
AccessibleRole As System.Windows.Forms.AccessibleRole
AllowDrop As System.Boolean
Anchor As System.Windows.Forms.AnchorStyles
BackColor As System.Drawing.Color
BackgroundImage As System.Drawing.Image
BindingContext As System.Windows.Forms.BindingContext
Bottom As System.Int32 (read only)
Bounds As System.Drawing.Rectangle
CanFocus As System.Boolean (read only)
CanSelect As System.Boolean (read only)
Capture As System.Boolean
CausesValidation As System.Boolean
ClientRectangle As System.Drawing.Rectangle (read only)
ClientSize As System.Drawing.Size
CompanyName As System.String (read only)
ContainsFocus As System.Boolean (read only)
ContextMenu As System.Windows.Forms.ContextMenu
Controls As System.Windows.Forms.Control+
  ControlCollection (read only)
Created As System.Boolean (read only)
Cursor As System.Windows.Forms.Cursor
DataBindings As
  System.Windows.Forms.ControlBindingsCollection
  (read only)
DefaultBackColor As System.Drawing.Color (read only)
DefaultFont As System.Drawing.Font (read only)
DefaultForeColor As System.Drawing.Color (read only)
DisplayRectangle As System.Drawing.Rectangle (read only)
Disposing As System.Boolean (read only)
Dock As System.Windows.Forms.DockStyle
Enabled As System.Boolean
Focused As System.Boolean (read only)
Font As System.Drawing.Font
ForeColor As System.Drawing.Color
Handle As System.IntPtr (read only)
HasChildren As System.Boolean (read only)
Height As System.Int32
ImeMode As System.Windows.Forms.ImeMode
InvokeRequired As System.Boolean (read only)
IsAccessible As System.Boolean
IsDisposed As System.Boolean (read only)
IsHandleCreated As System.Boolean (read only)
Left As System.Int32
```

```
Location As System.Drawing.Point
ModifierKeys As System.Windows.Forms.Keys (read only)
MouseButtons As
  System.Windows.Forms.MouseButtons (read only)
MousePosition As System.Drawing.Point (read only)
Name As System.String
Parent As System.Windows.Forms.Control
ProductName As System.String (read only)
ProductVersion As System.String (read only)
RecreatingHandle As System.Boolean (read only)
Region As System.Drawing.Region
Right As System.Int32 (read only)
RightToLeft As System.Windows.Forms.RightToLeft
Site As System.ComponentModel.ISite
Size As System.Drawing.Size
TabIndex As System.Int32
TabStop As System.Boolean
Tag As System.Object
Text As System.String
Top As System.Int32
TopLevelControl As
  System.Windows.Forms.Control (read only)
Visible As System.Boolean
Width As System.Int32
WindowTarget As System.Windows.Forms.IWindowTarget
' Methods
BeginInvoke(method As Delegate [,args As Object()])
  As IAsyncResult
BringToFront()
CallWndProc(msg As Int32, wparam As IntPtr,
  lparam As IntPtr) As IntPtr
Contains(ctl As Control) As Boolean
CreateControl()
CreateGraphics(dc As IntPtr) As Graphics
CreateGraphics() As Graphics
DoDragDrop(data As Object, allowedEffects As
  DragDropEffects) As DragDropEffects
EndInvoke(asyncResult As IAsyncResult) As Object
FindForm() As Form
Focus() As Boolean
FromChildHandle(handle As IntPtr) As Control
FromHandle(handle As IntPtr) As Control
GetChildAtPoint(pt As Point) As Control
GetContainerControl() As IContainerControl
GetNextControl(ctl As Control, forward As Boolean)
  As Control
Hide()
Invalidate()
Invalidate(invalidateChildren As Boolean)
Invalidate(rc As Rectangle
  [,invalidateChildren As Boolean])
Invalidate(region As Region
  [,invalidateChildren As Boolean])
```

```
Invoke(method As Delegate [,args As Object()]) As Object
IsMnemonic(charCode As Char, text As String) As Boolean
PerformLayout()
PerformLayout(affectedControl As Control,
  affectedProperty As String)
PointToClient(p As Point) As Point
PointToScreen(p As Point) As Point
PreProcessMessage(msg As Message&) As Boolean
RectangleToClient(r As Rectangle) As Rectangle
RectangleToScreen(r As Rectangle) As Rectangle
Refresh()
ResetBackColor()
ResetBindings()
ResetCursor()
ResetFont()
ResetForeColor()
ResetImeMode()
ResetRightToLeft()
ResetText()
ResumeLayout()
ResumeLayout(performLayout As Boolean)
Scale(ratio As Single)
Scale(dx As Single, dy As Single)
Select()
SelectNextControl(ctl As Control, forward As Boolean,
  tabStopOnly As Boolean, nested As Boolean,
  wrap As Boolean) As Boolean
SendToBack()
SetBounds(x As Int32, y As Int32, width As Int32,
  height As Int32, specified As BoundsSpecified)
SetBounds(x As Int32, y As Int32, width As Int32,
  height As Int32)
Show()
SuspendLayout()
Update()
' Events
BackColorChanged As System.EventHandler
BackgroundImageChanged As System.EventHandler
BindingContextChanged As System.EventHandler
CausesValidationChanged As System.EventHandler
ChangeUICues As System.Windows.Forms.UICuesEventHandler
Click As System.EventHandler
ContextMenuChanged As System.EventHandler
ControlAdded As System.Windows.Forms.ControlEventHandler
ControlRemoved As
  System.Windows.Forms.ControlEventHandler
CursorChanged As System.EventHandler
DockChanged As System.EventHandler
DoubleClick As System.EventHandler
```

```
DragDrop As System.Windows.Forms.DragEventHandler
DragEnter As System.Windows.Forms.DragEventHandler
DragLeave As System.EventHandler
DragOver As System.Windows.Forms.DragEventHandler
EnabledChanged As System.EventHandler
Enter As System.EventHandler
FontChanged As System.EventHandler
ForeColorChanged As System.EventHandler
GiveFeedback As
  System.Windows.Forms.GiveFeedbackEventHandler
GotFocus As System.EventHandler
HandleCreated As System.EventHandler
HandleDestroyed As System.EventHandler
HelpRequested As System.Windows.Forms.HelpEventHandler
ImeModeChanged As System.EventHandler
Invalidated As
  System.Windows.Forms.InvalidateEventHandler
KeyDown As System.Windows.Forms.KeyEventHandler
KeyPress As System.Windows.Forms.KeyPressEventHandler
KeyUp As System.Windows.Forms.KeyEventHandler
Layout As System.Windows.Forms.LayoutEventHandler
Leave As System.EventHandler
LocationChanged As System.EventHandler
LostFocus As System.EventHandler
MouseDown As System.Windows.Forms.MouseEventHandler
MouseEnter As System.EventHandler
MouseHover As System.EventHandler
MouseLeave As System.EventHandler
MouseMove As System.Windows.Forms.MouseEventHandler
MouseUp As System.Windows.Forms.MouseEventHandler
MouseWheel As System.Windows.Forms.MouseEventHandler
Move As System.EventHandler
Paint As System.Windows.Forms.PaintEventHandler
ParentChanged As System.EventHandler
QueryAccessibilityHelp As System.
  Windows.Forms.QueryAccessibilityHelpEventHandler
QueryContinueDrag As
  System.Windows.Forms.QueryContinueDragEventHandler
Resize As System.EventHandler
RightToLeftChanged As System.EventHandler
SizeChanged As System.EventHandler
StyleChanged As System.EventHandler
SystemColorsChanged As System.EventHandler
TabIndexChanged As System.EventHandler
TabStopChanged As System.EventHandler
TextChanged As System.EventHandler
Validated As System.EventHandler
Validating As System.ComponentModel.CancelEventHandler
VisibleChanged As System.EventHandler
```

ControlBindingsCollection Class

Provides the objects that bind a control to a data source and data member. Found as System.Windows.Forms.**ControlBindings Collection**.

ControlPaint Class

Provides the functionality to paint common Windows controls. The UserPaint bit of the control (accessed with the GetStyle() and SetStyle() methods) must be set to True to allow manipulation of the control painting process.

Inheritance—Object.ControlPaint

```
public class System.Windows.Forms.ControlPaint
  ' Properties
  ContrastControlDark As System.Drawing.Color (read only)
  ' Methods
  CreateHBitmap16Bit(bitmap As Bitmap,
    background As Color) As IntPtr
  CreateHBitmapColorMask(bitmap As Bitmap,
    monochromeMask As IntPtr) As IntPtr
  CreateHBitmapTransparencyMask(bitmap As Bitmap) As IntPtr
  Dark(baseColor As Color) As Color
  Dark(baseColor As Color, percOfDarkDark As Single)
    As Color
  DarkDark(baseColor As Color) As Color
  DrawBorder(graphics As Graphics, bounds As Rectangle,
    leftColor As Color, leftWidth As Int32, leftStyle As
    ButtonBorderStyle, topColor As Color, topWidth As
    Int32, topStyle As ButtonBorderStyle, rightColor As
    Color, rightWidth As Int32, rightStyle As
    ButtonBorderStyle, bottomColor As Color, bottomWidth
    As Int32, bottomStyle As ButtonBorderStyle)
  DrawBorder(graphics As Graphics, bounds As Rectangle,
    color As Color, style As ButtonBorderStyle)
  DrawBorder3D(graphics As Graphics, x As Int32,
    y As Int32, width As Int32, height As Int32)
  DrawBorder3D(graphics As Graphics, x As Int32,
    y As Int32, width As Int32, height As Int32,
    style As Border3DStyle)
```

DrawBorder3D(graphics As Graphics, x As Int32, y As Int32, width As Int32, height As Int32, style As Border3DStyle, sides As Border3DSide)

DrawBorder3D(graphics As Graphics, rectangle As Rectangle)

DrawBorder3D(graphics As Graphics, rectangle As Rectangle, style As Border3DStyle)

DrawBorder3D(graphics As Graphics, rectangle As Rectangle, style As Border3DStyle, sides As Border3DSide)

DrawButton(graphics As Graphics, x As Int32, y As Int32, width As Int32, height As Int32, state As ButtonState)

DrawButton(graphics As Graphics, rectangle As Rectangle, state As ButtonState)

DrawCaptionButton(graphics As Graphics, x As Int32, y As Int32, width As Int32, height As Int32, button As CaptionButton, state As ButtonState)

DrawCaptionButton(graphics As Graphics, rectangle As Rectangle, button As CaptionButton, state As ButtonState)

DrawCheckBox(graphics As Graphics, x As Int32, y As Int32, width As Int32, height As Int32, state As ButtonState)

DrawCheckBox(graphics As Graphics, rectangle As Rectangle, state As ButtonState)

DrawComboButton(graphics As Graphics, x As Int32, y As Int32, width As Int32, height As Int32, state As ButtonState)

DrawComboButton(graphics As Graphics, rectangle As Rectangle, state As ButtonState)

DrawContainerGrabHandle(graphics As Graphics, bounds As Rectangle)

DrawFocusRectangle(graphics As Graphics, rectangle As Rectangle, foreColor As Color, backColor As Color)

DrawFocusRectangle(graphics As Graphics, rectangle As Rectangle)

DrawGrabHandle(graphics As Graphics, rectangle As Rectangle, primary As Boolean, enabled As Boolean)

DrawGrid(graphics As Graphics, area As Rectangle, pixelsBetweenDots As Size, backColor As Color)

DrawImageDisabled(graphics As Graphics, image As Image, x As Int32, y As Int32, background As Color)

DrawLockedFrame(graphics As Graphics, rectangle As Rectangle, primary As Boolean)

DrawMenuGlyph(graphics As Graphics, x As Int32, y As Int32, width As Int32, height As Int32, glyph As MenuGlyph)

DrawMenuGlyph(graphics As Graphics, rectangle As Rectangle, glyph As MenuGlyph)

DrawMixedCheckBox(graphics As Graphics, x As Int32, y As Int32, width As Int32, height As Int32, state As ButtonState)

```
DrawMixedCheckBox(graphics As Graphics, rectangle As
  Rectangle, state As ButtonState)
DrawRadioButton(graphics As Graphics, x As Int32,
  y As Int32, width As Int32, height As Int32,
  state As ButtonState)
DrawRadioButton(graphics As Graphics, rectangle As
  Rectangle, state As ButtonState)
DrawReversibleFrame(rectangle As Rectangle,
  backColor As Color, style As FrameStyle)
DrawReversibleLine(start As Point, end As Point,
  backColor As Color)
DrawScrollButton(graphics As Graphics, x As Int32,
  y As Int32, width As Int32, height As Int32,
  button As ScrollButton, state As ButtonState)
DrawScrollButton(graphics As Graphics,
  rectangle As Rectangle, button As ScrollButton,
  state As ButtonState)
DrawSelectionFrame(graphics As Graphics,
  active As Boolean, outsideRect As Rectangle,
  insideRect As Rectangle, backColor As Color)
DrawSizeGrip(graphics As Graphics, backColor As Color,
  x As Int32, y As Int32, width As Int32,
  height As Int32)
DrawSizeGrip(graphics As Graphics, backColor As Color,
  bounds As Rectangle)
DrawStringDisabled(graphics As Graphics, s As String,
  font As Font, color As Color, layoutRectangle As
  RectangleF, format As StringFormat)
FillReversibleRectangle(rectangle As Rectangle,
  backColor As Color)
Light(baseColor As Color) As Color
Light(baseColor As Color, percOfLightLight As Single)
  As Color
LightLight(baseColor As Color) As Color
```

CreateParams Class

Holds the parameters used to initially create an instance of a control. These parameters define the control's state and appearance. Most controls that are children of the Control class override the CreateParams propery that stores this object to pass values received from their constructors.

Inheritance—Object.CreateParams

```
public class System.Windows.Forms.CreateParams
  ' Constructors
```

```
CreateParams()
' Properties
Caption As System.String
ClassName As System.String
ClassStyle As System.Int32
ExStyle As System.Int32
Height As System.Int32
Param As System.Object
Parent As System.IntPtr
Style As System.Int32
Width As System.Int32
X As System.Int32
Y As System.Int32
' Methods
ToString() As String
```


CurrencyManager Class

Manages the list of current bound controls through a collection of Binding objects.

Inheritance—Object.BindingManagerBase. CurrencyManager

```
public class System.Windows.Forms.CurrencyManager
  ' Properties
  Count As System.Int32 (read only)
  Current As System.Object (read only)
  List As System.Collections.IList (read only)
  Position As System.Int32
  ' Methods
  AddNew()
  CancelCurrentEdit()
  EndCurrentEdit()
  GetItemProperties() As PropertyDescriptorCollection
  Refresh()
  RemoveAt(index As Int32)
  ResumeBinding()
  SuspendBinding()
  ' Events
  ItemChanged As
    System.Windows.Forms.ItemChangedEventHandler
```

Cursor Class

Contains the information used to paint the current mouse cursor on the screen.

Inheritance—Object.Cursor

```
public class System.Windows.Forms.Cursor
  ' Constructors
  Cursor(type As Type, resource As String)
  Cursor(fileName As String)
  Cursor(handle As IntPtr)
  Cursor(stream As Stream)
  ' Properties
  Clip As System.Drawing.Rectangle
  Current As System.Windows.Forms.Cursor
  Handle As System.IntPtr (read only)
  Position As System.Drawing.Point
  Size As System.Drawing.Size (read only)
  ' Methods
  CopyHandle() As IntPtr
  Dispose()
  Draw(g As Graphics, targetRect As Rectangle)
  DrawStretched(g As Graphics, targetRect As Rectangle)
  Equals(obj As Object) As Boolean
  GetHashCode() As Int32
  Hide()
  Show()
  ToString() As String
```

Cursors Class

A static class that holds a set of default cursors available for use by a Windows application.

Inheritance—Object.Cursors

```
public class System.Windows.Forms.Cursors
  ' Properties
```

```
AppStarting As System.Windows.Forms.Cursor (read only)
Arrow As System.Windows.Forms.Cursor (read only)
Cross As System.Windows.Forms.Cursor (read only)
Default As System.Windows.Forms.Cursor (read only)
Hand As System.Windows.Forms.Cursor (read only)
Help As System.Windows.Forms.Cursor (read only)
HSplit As System.Windows.Forms.Cursor (read only)
IBeam As System.Windows.Forms.Cursor (read only)
No As System.Windows.Forms.Cursor (read only)
NoMove2D As System.Windows.Forms.Cursor (read only)
NoMoveHoriz As System.Windows.Forms.Cursor (read only)
NoMoveVert As System.Windows.Forms.Cursor (read only)
PanEast As System.Windows.Forms.Cursor (read only)
PanNE As System.Windows.Forms.Cursor (read only)
PanNorth As System.Windows.Forms.Cursor (read only)
PanNW As System.Windows.Forms.Cursor (read only)
PanSE As System.Windows.Forms.Cursor (read only)
PanSouth As System.Windows.Forms.Cursor (read only)
PanSW As System.Windows.Forms.Cursor (read only)
PanWest As System.Windows.Forms.Cursor (read only)
SizeAll As System.Windows.Forms.Cursor (read only)
SizeNESW As System.Windows.Forms.Cursor (read only)
SizeNS As System.Windows.Forms.Cursor (read only)
SizeNWSE As System.Windows.Forms.Cursor (read only)
SizeWE As System.Windows.Forms.Cursor (read only)
UpArrow As System.Windows.Forms.Cursor (read only)
VSplit As System.Windows.Forms.Cursor (read only)
WaitCursor As System.Windows.Forms.Cursor (read only)
```

DataFormats Class

A static class that provides the predefined Clipboard data format names. *See also* the DataObject class.

Inheritance—Object.DataFormats

```
public class System.Windows.Forms.DataFormats
  ' Methods
  GetFormat(id As Int32) As Format
  GetFormat(format As String) As Format
```

DataGrid Class

Provides the class used to create an instance of a Windows DataGrid control. The DataGrid control may be bound to one of the following data source types: DataSet object, DataTable object, DataView object, DataViewManager object, single dimension array, or components implementing the IList or IListSource interfaces.

Inheritance—Object.MarshalByRefObject.Component.Control.DataGrid

```
public class System.Windows.Forms.DataGrid
  ' Constructors
  DataGrid()
  ' Properties
  AllowNavigation As System.Boolean
  AllowSorting As System.Boolean
  AlternatingBackColor As System.Drawing.Color
  BackColor As System.Drawing.Color
  BackgroundColor As System.Drawing.Color
  BackgroundImage As System.Drawing.Image
  BorderStyle As System.Windows.Forms.BorderStyle
  CaptionBackColor As System.Drawing.Color
  CaptionFont As System.Drawing.Font
  CaptionForeColor As System.Drawing.Color
  CaptionText As System.String
  CaptionVisible As System.Boolean
  ColumnHeadersVisible As System.Boolean
  CurrentCell As System.Windows.Forms.DataGridCell
  CurrentRowIndex As System.Int32
  Cursor As System.Windows.Forms.Cursor
  DataMember As System.String
  DataSource As System.Object
  FirstVisibleColumn As System.Int32 (read only)
  FlatMode As System.Boolean
  ForeColor As System.Drawing.Color
  GridLineColor As System.Drawing.Color
  GridLineStyle As System.Windows.Forms.DataGridLineStyle
  HeaderBackColor As System.Drawing.Color
  HeaderFont As System.Drawing.Font
  HeaderForeColor As System.Drawing.Color
  Item As System.Object
  Item As System.Object
  LinkColor As System.Drawing.Color
  LinkHoverColor As System.Drawing.Color
  ParentRowsBackColor As System.Drawing.Color
```

```
ParentRowsForeColor As System.Drawing.Color
ParentRowsLabelStyle As
  System.Windows.Forms.DataGridParentRowsLabelStyle
ParentRowsVisible As System.Boolean
PreferredColumnWidth As System.Int32
PreferredRowHeight As System.Int32
ReadOnly As System.Boolean
RowHeadersVisible As System.Boolean
RowHeaderWidth As System.Int32
SelectionBackColor As System.Drawing.Color
SelectionForeColor As System.Drawing.Color
TableStyles As
  System.Windows.Forms.GridTableStylesCollection
  (read only)
Text As System.String
VisibleColumnCount As System.Int32 (read only)
VisibleRowCount As System.Int32 (read only)
' Methods
BeginEdit(gridColumn As DataGridColumnStyle,
  rowNumber As Int32) As Boolean
BeginInit()
Collapse(row As Int32)
EndEdit(gridColumn As DataGridColumnStyle,
  rowNumber As Int32, shouldAbort As Boolean) As Boolean
EndInit()
Expand(row As Int32)
GetCellBounds(dgc As DataGridCell) As Rectangle
GetCellBounds(row As Int32, col As Int32) As Rectangle
GetCurrentCellBounds() As Rectangle
HitTest(position As Point) As HitTestInfo
HitTest(x As Int32, y As Int32) As HitTestInfo
IsExpanded(rowNumber As Int32) As Boolean
IsSelected(row As Int32) As Boolean
NavigateBack()
NavigateTo(rowNumber As Int32, relationName As String)
ResetAlternatingBackColor()
ResetBackColor()
ResetForeColor()
ResetGridLineColor()
ResetHeaderBackColor()
ResetHeaderFont()
ResetHeaderForeColor()
ResetLinkColor()
ResetLinkHoverColor()
ResetSelectionBackColor()
ResetSelectionForeColor()
Select(row As Int32)
SetDataBinding(dataSource As Object,
  dataMember As String)
SubObjectsSiteChange(site As Boolean)
```

```
UnSelect(row As Int32)
' Events
AllowNavigationChanged As System.EventHandler
BackButtonClick As System.EventHandler
BackgroundColorChanged As System.EventHandler
BorderStyleChanged As System.EventHandler
CaptionVisibleChanged As System.EventHandler
CurrentCellChanged As System.EventHandler
DataSourceChanged As System.EventHandler
FlatModeChanged As System.EventHandler
Navigate As System.Windows.Forms.NavigateEventHandler
ParentRowsLabelStyleChanged As System.EventHandler
ParentRowsVisibleChanged As System.EventHandler
ReadOnlyChanged As System.EventHandler
Scroll As System.EventHandler
ShowParentDetailsButtonClick As System.EventHandler
```

DataGridBoolColumn Class

Provides the class used by the DataGrid to specify a column containing CheckBox controls that represent Boolean values.

Inheritance—Object.MarshalByRefObject. Component.DataGridColumnStyle. DataGridBoolColumn

```
public class System.Windows.Forms.DataGridBoolColumn
  ' Constructors
  DataGridBoolColumn(prop As PropertyDescriptor,
    isDefault As Boolean)
  DataGridBoolColumn(prop As PropertyDescriptor)
  DataGridBoolColumn()
  ' Properties
  AllowNull As System.Boolean
  FalseValue As System.Object
  NullValue As System.Object
  TrueValue As System.Object
  ' Events
  AllowNullChanged As System.EventHandler
  FalseValueChanged As System.EventHandler
  TrueValueChanged As System.EventHandler
```

DataGridColumnStyle Class

Provides the style used for a DataGrid column, including appearance, text formatting, and behavior.

Inheritance—Object.MarshalByRefObject.Component.DataGridColumnStyle

```
public class System.Windows.Forms.DataGridColumnStyle
  ' Constructors
  DataGridColumnStyle()
  DataGridColumnStyle(prop As PropertyDescriptor)
  ' Properties
  Alignment As System.Windows.Forms.HorizontalAlignment
  DataGridTableStyle As
    System.Windows.Forms.DataGridTableStyle (read only)
  HeaderAccessibleObject As
    System.Windows.Forms.AccessibleObject (read only)
  HeaderText As System.String
  MappingName As System.String
  NullText As System.String
  PropertyDescriptor As
    System.ComponentModel.PropertyDescriptor
  ReadOnly As System.Boolean
  Width As System.Int32
  ' Methods
  ResetHeaderText()
  ' Events
  AlignmentChanged As System.EventHandler
  FontChanged As System.EventHandler
  HeaderTextChanged As System.EventHandler
  MappingNameChanged As System.EventHandler
  NullTextChanged As System.EventHandler
  PropertyDescriptorChanged As System.EventHandler
  ReadOnlyChanged As System.EventHandler
  WidthChanged As System.EventHandler
```

DataGridPreferredColumnWidthType ConverterClass

Converts the data value in a data grid column to a different type. Found as System.Windows.Forms.**DataGridPreferredColumnWidth TypeConverter**.

DataGridTableStyle Class

Defines the presentation style of the table referenced by the data grid object.

Inheritance—Object.MarshalByRefObject. Component.DataGridTableStyle

```
public class System.Windows.Forms.DataGridTableStyle
  ' Constructors
  DataGridTableStyle()
  DataGridTableStyle(listManager As CurrencyManager)
  DataGridTableStyle(isDefaultTableStyle As Boolean)
  ' Properties
  AllowSorting As System.Boolean
  AlternatingBackColor As System.Drawing.Color
  BackColor As System.Drawing.Color
  ColumnHeadersVisible As System.Boolean
  DataGrid As System.Windows.Forms.DataGrid
  ForeColor As System.Drawing.Color
  GridColumnStyles As
    System.Windows.Forms.GridColumnStylesCollection
    (read only)
  GridLineColor As System.Drawing.Color
  GridLineStyle As System.Windows.Forms.DataGridLineStyle
  HeaderBackColor As System.Drawing.Color
  HeaderFont As System.Drawing.Font
  HeaderForeColor As System.Drawing.Color
  LinkColor As System.Drawing.Color
  LinkHoverColor As System.Drawing.Color
  MappingName As System.String
  PreferredColumnWidth As System.Int32
  PreferredRowHeight As System.Int32
  ReadOnly As System.Boolean
  RowHeadersVisible As System.Boolean
  RowHeaderWidth As System.Int32
```

```
SelectionBackColor As System.Drawing.Color
SelectionForeColor As System.Drawing.Color
' Methods
BeginEdit(gridColumn As DataGridColumnStyle,
  rowNumber As Int32) As Boolean
EndEdit(gridColumn As DataGridColumnStyle,
  rowNumber As Int32, shouldAbort As Boolean) As Boolean
ResetAlternatingBackColor()
ResetBackColor()
ResetForeColor()
ResetGridLineColor()
ResetHeaderBackColor()
ResetHeaderFont()
ResetHeaderForeColor()
ResetLinkColor()
ResetLinkHoverColor()
ResetSelectionBackColor()
ResetSelectionForeColor()
' Events
AllowSortingChanged As System.EventHandler
AlternatingBackColorChanged As System.EventHandler
BackColorChanged As System.EventHandler
ColumnHeadersVisibleChanged As System.EventHandler
ForeColorChanged As System.EventHandler
GridLineColorChanged As System.EventHandler
GridLineStyleChanged As System.EventHandler
HeaderBackColorChanged As System.EventHandler
HeaderFontChanged As System.EventHandler
HeaderForeColorChanged As System.EventHandler
LinkColorChanged As System.EventHandler
LinkHoverColorChanged As System.EventHandler
MappingNameChanged As System.EventHandler
PreferredColumnWidthChanged As System.EventHandler
PreferredRowHeightChanged As System.EventHandler
ReadOnlyChanged As System.EventHandler
RowHeadersVisibleChanged As System.EventHandler
RowHeaderWidthChanged As System.EventHandler
SelectionBackColorChanged As System.EventHandler
SelectionForeColorChanged As System.EventHandler
```

DataGridTextBox Class

Defines the text box control used for a text cell within a data grid control. The DataGridTextBoxColumn class is used to host a DataGridTextBox object to allow direct value editing in a DataGrid control.

Inheritance—Object.MarshalByRefObject. Component.Control.TextBoxBase.TextBox. DataGridTextBox

```
public class System.Windows.Forms.DataGridTextBox
  ' Constructors
  DataGridTextBox()
  ' Properties
  IsInEditOrNavigateMode As System.Boolean
  ' Methods
  SetDataGrid(parentGrid As DataGrid)
```

DataGridTextBoxColumn Class

Holds the definition of a DataGridTextBox control for string editing in a DataGrid control.

Inheritance—Object.MarshalByRefObject. Component.DataGridColumnStyle. DataGridTextBoxColumn

```
public class System.Windows.Forms.DataGridTextBoxColumn
  ' Constructors
  DataGridTextBoxColumn(prop As PropertyDescriptor)
  DataGridTextBoxColumn()
  DataGridTextBoxColumn(prop As PropertyDescriptor,
    format As String)
  DataGridTextBoxColumn(prop As PropertyDescriptor,
    isDefault As Boolean)
  DataGridTextBoxColumn(prop As PropertyDescriptor,
    format As String, isDefault As Boolean)
  ' Properties
  Format As System.String
  FormatInfo As System.IFormatProvider
  PropertyDescriptor As
    System.ComponentModel.PropertyDescriptor (write only)
  ReadOnly As System.Boolean
  TextBox As System.Windows.Forms.TextBox (read only)
```

DataObject Class

Hosts a bridge object for transfer of single or multiple pieces of data for operations such as transferring a variable array to the system Clipboard. The GetFormats() method will provide information indicating the format or formats of the data stored in this object.

Inheritance—Object.DataObject

```
public class System.Windows.Forms.DataObject
  ' Constructors
  DataObject(format As String, data As Object)
  DataObject(data As Object)
  DataObject()
  ' Methods
  GetData(format As Type) As Object
  GetData(format As String [,autoConvert As Boolean])
    As Object
  GetDataPresent(format As String) As Boolean
  GetDataPresent(format As String, autoConvert As Boolean)
    As Boolean
  GetDataPresent(format As Type) As Boolean
  GetFormats(autoConvert As Boolean) As String()
  GetFormats() As String()
  SetData(format As Type, data As Object)
  SetData(data As Object)
  SetData(format As String, autoConvert As Boolean,
    data As Object)
  SetData(format As String, data As Object)
```

DateTimePicker Class

Provides the class used to create an instance of a Windows DateTimePicker control.

Inheritance—Object.MarshalByRefObject.Component.Control.DateTimePicker

```
public class System.Windows.Forms.DateTimePicker
  ' Constructors
  DateTimePicker()
  ' Properties
  BackColor As System.Drawing.Color
  BackgroundImage As System.Drawing.Image
  CalendarFont As System.Drawing.Font
  CalendarForeColor As System.Drawing.Color
  CalendarMonthBackground As System.Drawing.Color
```

```
CalendarTitleBackColor As System.Drawing.Color
CalendarTitleForeColor As System.Drawing.Color
CalendarTrailingForeColor As System.Drawing.Color
Checked As System.Boolean
CustomFormat As System.String
DropDownAlign As System.Windows.Forms.LeftRightAlignment
ForeColor As System.Drawing.Color
Format As System.Windows.Forms.DateTimePickerFormat
MaxDate As System.DateTime
MinDate As System.DateTime
PreferredHeight As System.Int32 (read only)
ShowCheckBox As System.Boolean
ShowUpDown As System.Boolean
Text As System.String
Value As System.DateTime
' Methods
ToString() As String
' Events
CloseUp As System.EventHandler
DropDown As System.EventHandler
FormatChanged As System.EventHandler
ValueChanged As System.EventHandler
```

DomainUpDown Class

The class used to create an instance of a Windows UpDown control for string values. *See also* the NumericUpDown class.

Inheritance—Object.MarshalByRefObject. Component.Control.ScrollableControl. ContainerControl.UpDownBase.DomainUpDown

```
public class System.Windows.Forms.DomainUpDown
  ' Constructors
  DomainUpDown()
  ' Properties
  Items As System.Windows.Forms.DomainUpDown+
    DomainUpDownItemCollection (read only)
  SelectedIndex As System.Int32
  SelectedItem As System.Object
  Sorted As System.Boolean
  Wrap As System.Boolean
  ' Methods
```

```
DownButton()
ToString() As String
UpButton()
' Events
SelectedItemChanged As System.EventHandler
```


ErrorProvider Class

Provides the user interface display of an error that has occurred in an editable user control (such as a TextBox control). The error for the control is indicated by displaying an icon next to the control (such as a small colored exclamation point) and a tool tip describing the error.

Inheritance—Object.MarshalByRefObject.Component.ErrorProvider

```
public class System.Windows.Forms.ErrorProvider
  ' Constructors
  ErrorProvider()
  ErrorProvider(parentControl As ContainerControl)
  ' Properties
  BlinkRate As System.Int32
  BlinkStyle As System.Windows.Forms.ErrorBlinkStyle
  ContainerControl As System.Windows.Forms.ContainerControl
  DataMember As System.String
  DataSource As System.Object
  Icon As System.Drawing.Icon
  Site As System.ComponentModel.ISite (write only)
  ' Methods
  BindToDataAndErrors(newDataSource As Object,
    newDataMember As String)
  CanExtend(extendee As Object) As Boolean
  GetError(control As Control) As String
  GetIconAlignment(control As Control)
    As ErrorIconAlignment
  GetIconPadding(control As Control) As Int32
  SetError(control As Control, value As String)
  SetIconAlignment(control As Control,
    value As ErrorIconAlignment)
  SetIconPadding(control As Control, padding As Int32)
  UpdateBinding()
```

FeatureSupport Class

A static class available for reading feature and version information related to the current system. *See also* the OSFeature class.

Inheritance—Object.FeatureSupport

```
public class System.Windows.Forms.FeatureSupport
  ' Methods
  GetVersionPresent(featureClassName As String,
    featureConstName As String) As Version
  GetVersionPresent(feature As Object) As Version
  IsPresent(featureClassName As String,
    featureConstName As String, minimumVersion As Version)
    As Boolean
  IsPresent(featureClassName As String, featureConstName
    As String) As Boolean
  IsPresent(feature As Object, minimumVersion As Version)
    As Boolean
  IsPresent(feature As Object) As Boolean
```

FileDialog Class

Provides a foundation class used by OpenFileDialog and SaveFileDialog to display a dialog box for user file selection.This class represents one of the common dialog boxes provided by the system. *See also* the ColorDialog, OpenFileDialog, SaveFileDialog, PageSetupDialog, and PrintDialog classes.

Inheritance—Object.MarshalByRefObject. Component.CommonDialog.FileDialog

```
public class System.Windows.Forms.FileDialog
  ' Properties
  AddExtension As System.Boolean
  CheckFileExists As System.Boolean
  CheckPathExists As System.Boolean
  DefaultExt As System.String
  DereferenceLinks As System.Boolean
  FileName As System.String
  FileNames As System.String() (read only)
```

```
Filter As System.String
FilterIndex As System.Int32
InitialDirectory As System.String
RestoreDirectory As System.Boolean
ShowHelp As System.Boolean
Title As System.String
ValidateNames As System.Boolean
' Methods
Reset()
ToString() As String
' Events
FileOk As System.ComponentModel.CancelEventHandler
```


FontDialog Class

Provides the display of a font dialog box for user selection of font type, style, and size. This class represents one of the common dialog boxes provided by the system. *See also* the ColorDialog, FileDialog, PageSetupDialog, and PrintDialog classes.

Inheritance—Object.MarshalByRefObject. Component.CommonDialog.FontDialog

```
public class System.Windows.Forms.FontDialog
  ' Constructors
  FontDialog()
  ' Properties
  AllowScriptChange As System.Boolean
  AllowSimulations As System.Boolean
  AllowVectorFonts As System.Boolean
  AllowVerticalFonts As System.Boolean
  Color As System.Drawing.Color
  FixedPitchOnly As System.Boolean
  Font As System.Drawing.Font
  FontMustExist As System.Boolean
  MaxSize As System.Int32
  MinSize As System.Int32
  ScriptsOnly As System.Boolean
  ShowApply As System.Boolean
  ShowColor As System.Boolean
  ShowEffects As System.Boolean
  ShowHelp As System.Boolean
  ' Methods
```

```
Reset()
ToString() As String
' Events
Apply As System.EventHandler
```

Form Class

Provides an object that appears to the user as either a window or a dialog box. This class can be used for borderless, floating, modal, MDI, standard, and tool windows. This class is the parent of the following classes: CollectionEditor, CollectionForm, CalendarAutoFormatDialog, RegexEditorDialog, ComponentEditorForm, and PrintPreviewDialog.

Inheritance—Object.MarshalByRefObject. Component.Control.ScrollableControl. ContainerControl.Form

```
public class System.Windows.Forms.Form
  ' Constructors
  Form()
  ' Properties
  AcceptButton As System.Windows.Forms.IButtonControl
  ActiveForm As System.Windows.Forms.Form (read only)
  ActiveMdiChild As System.Windows.Forms.Form (read only)
  AllowTransparency As System.Boolean
  AutoScale As System.Boolean
  AutoScaleBaseSize As System.Drawing.Size
  AutoScroll As System.Boolean
  BackColor As System.Drawing.Color
  BorderStyle As System.Windows.Forms.FormBorderStyle
  CancelButton As System.Windows.Forms.IButtonControl
  ClientSize As System.Drawing.Size
  ControlBox As System.Boolean
  DesktopBounds As System.Drawing.Rectangle
  DesktopLocation As System.Drawing.Point
  DialogResult As System.Windows.Forms.DialogResult
  FormBorderStyle As System.Windows.Forms.FormBorderStyle
  HelpButton As System.Boolean
  Icon As System.Drawing.Icon
  IsMdiChild As System.Boolean (read only)
```

```
IsMdiContainer As System.Boolean
IsRestrictedWindow As System.Boolean (read only)
KeyPreview As System.Boolean
MaximizeBox As System.Boolean
MaximumSize As System.Drawing.Size
MdiChildren As System.Windows.Forms.Form() (read only)
MdiParent As System.Windows.Forms.Form
Menu As System.Windows.Forms.MainMenu
MergedMenu As System.Windows.Forms.MainMenu (read only)
MinimizeBox As System.Boolean
MinimumSize As System.Drawing.Size
Modal As System.Boolean (read only)
Opacity As System.Double
OwnedForms As System.Windows.Forms.Form() (read only)
Owner As System.Windows.Forms.Form
ShowInTaskbar As System.Boolean
Size As System.Drawing.Size
SizeGripStyle As System.Windows.Forms.SizeGripStyle
StartPosition As System.Windows.Forms.FormStartPosition
TabIndex As System.Int32
TopLevel As System.Boolean
TopMost As System.Boolean
TransparencyKey As System.Drawing.Color
WindowState As System.Windows.Forms.FormWindowState
' Methods
Activate()
AddOwnedForm(ownedForm As Form)
Close()
GetAutoScaleSize(font As Font) As SizeF
LayoutMdi(value As MdiLayout)
RemoveOwnedForm(ownedForm As Form)
SetDesktopBounds(x As Int32, y As Int32,
  width As Int32, height As Int32)
SetDesktopLocation(x As Int32, y As Int32)
ShowDialog(owner As IWin32Window) As DialogResult
ShowDialog() As DialogResult
ToString() As String
' Events
Activated As System.EventHandler
Closed As System.EventHandler
Closing As System.ComponentModel.CancelEventHandler
Deactivate As System.EventHandler
InputLanguageChanged As
  System.Windows.Forms.InputLanguageChangedEventHandler
```

```
InputLanguageChanging As
  System.Windows.Forms.InputLanguageChangingEventHandler
Load As System.EventHandler
MaximizedBoundsChanged As System.EventHandler
MaximumSizeChanged As System.EventHandler
MdiChildActivate As System.EventHandler
MenuComplete As System.EventHandler
MenuStart As System.EventHandler
MinimumSizeChanged As System.EventHandler
```

GridColumnStylesCollection Class

Holds the collection of DataGridColumnStyle objects for a DataGrid control. Found as System.Windows.Forms.**GridColumnStyles Collection**.

GridItem Class

Provides a GridItem object for use as one row of a PropertyGrid control user interface.

Inheritance—Object.GridItem

```
public class System.Windows.Forms.GridItem
  ' Properties
  Expandable As System.Boolean (read only)
  Expanded As System.Boolean
  GridItems As
    System.Windows.Forms.GridItemCollection (read only)
  GridItemType As
    System.Windows.Forms.GridItemType (read only)
  Label As System.String (read only)
  Parent As System.Windows.Forms.GridItem (read only)
  PropertyDescriptor As
    System.ComponentModel.PropertyDescriptor (read only)
  Value As System.Object (read only)
  ' Methods
  Select() As Boolean
```

GridItemCollection Class

Holds a collection of GridItem objects for a PropertyGrid object. Found as System.Windows.Forms.**GridItemCollection**.

GridTableStylesCollection Class

Holds a collection of DataGridTableStyle objects for a DataGrid control. Found as System.Windows.Forms.**GridTableStyles Collection**.

GroupBox Class

Provides the class used to create an instance of the Windows GroupBox control that appears as a frame around other controls. Typically this class is used to group RadioButton controls. *See also* the Panel class.

Inheritance—Object.MarshalByRefObject.Component.Control.GroupBox

```
public class System.Windows.Forms.GroupBox
  ' Constructors
  GroupBox()
  ' Properties
  AllowDrop As System.Boolean
  Cursor As System.Windows.Forms.Cursor
  DisplayRectangle As System.Drawing.Rectangle (read only)
  FlatStyle As System.Windows.Forms.FlatStyle
  TabStop As System.Boolean
  Text As System.String
  ' Methods
  ToString() As String
  ' Events
  Click As System.EventHandler
  DoubleClick As System.EventHandler
```

```
KeyDown As System.Windows.Forms.KeyEventHandler
KeyPress As System.Windows.Forms.KeyPressEventHandler
KeyUp As System.Windows.Forms.KeyEventHandler
MouseDown As System.Windows.Forms.MouseEventHandler
MouseEnter As System.EventHandler
MouseLeave As System.EventHandler
MouseMove As System.Windows.Forms.MouseEventHandler
MouseUp As System.Windows.Forms.MouseEventHandler
```

Help Class

Static class that provides access to the Windows HTML Help engine. *See also* the HelpProvider class.

Inheritance—Object.Help

```
public class System.Windows.Forms.Help
  ' Methods
  ShowHelp(parent As Control, url As String,
    keyword As String)
  ShowHelp(parent As Control, url As String,
    command As HelpNavigator, param As Object)
  ShowHelp(parent As Control, url As String)
  ShowHelp(parent As Control, url As String,
    navigator As HelpNavigator)
  ShowHelpIndex(parent As Control, url As String)
  ShowPopup(parent As Control, caption As String,
    location As Point)
```

HelpProvider Class

Provides the help user interface of a pop-up text box or online help for a control. If the HelpNameSpace property is not set to point to the name of the proper help file (i.e. "C:\myPath\myHelp.chm"), use the SetHelpString() method to specify the actual help text.

Inheritance—Object.MarshalByRefObject. Component.HelpProvider

```
public class System.Windows.Forms.HelpProvider
  ' Constructors
```

```
HelpProvider()
' Properties
HelpNamespace As System.String
' Methods
CanExtend(target As Object) As Boolean
GetHelpKeyword(ctl As Control) As String
GetHelpNavigator(ctl As Control) As HelpNavigator
GetHelpString(ctl As Control) As String
GetShowHelp(ctl As Control) As Boolean
ResetShowHelp(ctl As Control)
SetHelpKeyword(ctl As Control, keyword As String)
SetHelpNavigator(ctl As Control,
  navigator As HelpNavigator)
SetHelpString(ctl As Control, helpString As String)
SetShowHelp(ctl As Control, value As Boolean)
ToString() As String
```


HScrollBar Class

The class used to create an instance of a Windows horizontal scroll bar control. All methods, properties, and events for this control are inherited from the ScrollBar class. Found as System.Windows.Forms.**HScrollBar**.

ImageIndexConverter Class

Converts image data within an image index to and from a string. Retrieve an instance of this class using the GetConverter() method of the TypeDescriptor object. *See also* the TreeViewImageIndex Converter class.

Inheritance—Object.TypeConverter.BaseNumber Converter.Int32Converter.ImageIndexConverter

```
public class System.Windows.Forms.ImageIndexConverter
  ' Constructors
  ImageIndexConverter()
  ' Methods
```

```
ConvertFrom(context As ITypeDescriptorContext,
  culture As CultureInfo, value As Object) As Object
ConvertTo(context As ITypeDescriptorContext,
  culture As CultureInfo, value As Object,
  destinationType As Type) As Object
GetStandardValues(context As ITypeDescriptorContext)
  As StandardValuesCollection
GetStandardValuesExclusive(context As
  ITypeDescriptorContext) As Boolean
GetStandardValuesSupported(context As
  ITypeDescriptorContext) As Boolean
```

ImageList Class

Provides a class that contains methods and properties that can be used to manage a list of Image objects. The ImageList object is used by controls such as ListView, Toolbar, and Treeview to manage display icons.

Inheritance—Object.MarshalByRefObject. Component.ImageList

```
public class System.Windows.Forms.ImageList
  ' Constructors
  ImageList(container As IContainer)
  ImageList()
  ' Properties
  ColorDepth As System.Windows.Forms.ColorDepth
  Handle As System.IntPtr (read only)
  HandleCreated As System.Boolean (read only)
  Images As System.Windows.Forms.ImageList+
    ImageCollection (read only)
  ImageSize As System.Drawing.Size
  ImageStream As System.Windows.Forms.ImageListStreamer
  TransparentColor As System.Drawing.Color
  ' Methods
  Draw(g As Graphics, pt As Point, index As Int32)
  Draw(g As Graphics, x As Int32, y As Int32,
    index As Int32)
  Draw(g As Graphics, x As Int32, y As Int32,
    width As Int32, height As Int32, index As Int32)
  ToString() As String
  ' Events
  RecreateHandle As System.EventHandler
```

InputLanguage Class

Static class that provides the functionality to manage the input language objects used for character screen display and keyboard layout. For more specific information on the input language selected on the current machine, access the culture and globalization settings available through the System.Globalization classes.

Inheritance—Object.InputLanguage

```
public class System.Windows.Forms.InputLanguage
  ' Properties
  Culture As System.Globalization.CultureInfo (read only)
  CurrentInputLanguage As
    System.Windows.Forms.InputLanguage
  DefaultInputLanguage As
    System.Windows.Forms.InputLanguage (read only)
  Handle As System.IntPtr (read only)
  InstalledInputLanguages As
    System.Windows.Forms.InputLanguageCollection
    (read only)
  LayoutName As System.String (read only)
  ' Methods
  Equals(value As Object) As Boolean
  FromCulture(culture As CultureInfo) As InputLanguage
  GetHashCode() As Int32
```

InputLanguageCollection Class

Holds a collection of InputLanguage objects. Found as System.Windows.Forms.**InputLanguageCollection**.

KeysConverter Class

Provides a converter to change the types of all Key objects.

Inheritance—Object.TypeConverter.KeysConverter

```
public class System.Windows.Forms.KeysConverter
  ' Constructors
  KeysConverter()
  ' Methods
  CanConvertFrom(context As ITypeDescriptorContext,
    sourceType As Type) As Boolean
  Compare(a As Object, b As Object) As Int32
  ConvertFrom(context As ITypeDescriptorContext,
    culture As CultureInfo, value As Object) As Object
  ConvertTo(context As ITypeDescriptorContext,
    culture As CultureInfo, value As Object,
    destinationType As Type) As Object
  GetStandardValues(context As ITypeDescriptorContext)
    As StandardValuesCollection
  GetStandardValuesExclusive(context As
    ITypeDescriptorContext) As Boolean
  GetStandardValuesSupported(context As
    ITypeDescriptorContext) As Boolean
```

Label Class

Provides the class used to create an instance of a Windows Label control. *See also* the LinkLabel class.

Inheritance—Object.MarshalByRefObject. Component.Control.Label

```
public class System.Windows.Forms.Label
  ' Constructors
  Label()
  ' Properties
  AutoSize As System.Boolean
  BackgroundImage As System.Drawing.Image
  BorderStyle As System.Windows.Forms.BorderStyle
  FlatStyle As System.Windows.Forms.FlatStyle
  Image As System.Drawing.Image
  ImageAlign As System.Drawing.ContentAlignment
  ImageIndex As System.Int32
  ImageList As System.Windows.Forms.ImageList
  ImeMode As System.Windows.Forms.ImeMode
  PreferredHeight As System.Int32 (read only)
  PreferredWidth As System.Int32 (read only)
  TabStop As System.Boolean
```

```
  TextAlign As System.Drawing.ContentAlignment
  UseMnemonic As System.Boolean
  ' Methods
  ToString() As String
  ' Events
  AutoSizeChanged As System.EventHandler
  KeyDown As System.Windows.Forms.KeyEventHandler
  KeyPress As System.Windows.Forms.KeyPressEventHandler
  KeyUp As System.Windows.Forms.KeyEventHandler
  TextAlignChanged As System.EventHandler
```


LinkLabel Class

The class used to create an instance of a Windows Label control that can display Web hyperlinks. *See also* the Label class.

Inheritance—Object.MarshalByRefObject.Component.Control.Label.LinkLabel

```
public class System.Windows.Forms.LinkLabel
  ' Constructors
  LinkLabel()
  ' Properties
  ActiveLinkColor As System.Drawing.Color
  DisabledLinkColor As System.Drawing.Color
  LinkArea As System.Windows.Forms.LinkArea
  LinkBehavior As System.Windows.Forms.LinkBehavior
  LinkColor As System.Drawing.Color
  Links As System.Windows.Forms.LinkLabel+LinkCollection
    (read only)
  LinkVisited As System.Boolean
  Text As System.String
  VisitedLinkColor As System.Drawing.Color
  ' Events
  LinkClicked As
    System.Windows.Forms.LinkLabelLinkClickedEventHandler
```

ListBindingConverter Class

Provides conversion of data types for Binding objects. Retrieve an instance of this class using the GetConverter() method of the TypeDescriptor object. Found as System.Windows.Forms.**ListBindingConverter**.

ListBox Class

Provides the class used to create an instance of a Windows ListBox control. All of the ListBox control items are represented in a collection held in the ObjectCollection property.

Inheritance—Object.MarshalByRefObject. Component.Control.ListControl.ListBox

```
public class System.Windows.Forms.ListBox
  ' Constructors
  ListBox()
  ' Properties
  BackColor As System.Drawing.Color
  BackgroundImage As System.Drawing.Image
  BorderStyle As System.Windows.Forms.BorderStyle
  ColumnWidth As System.Int32
  DrawMode As System.Windows.Forms.DrawMode
  ForeColor As System.Drawing.Color
  HorizontalExtent As System.Int32
  HorizontalScrollbar As System.Boolean
  IntegralHeight As System.Boolean
  ItemHeight As System.Int32
  Items As System.Windows.Forms.ListBox+ObjectCollection
    (read only)
  MultiColumn As System.Boolean
  PreferredHeight As System.Int32 (read only)
  RightToLeft As System.Windows.Forms.RightToLeft
  ScrollAlwaysVisible As System.Boolean
  SelectedIndex As System.Int32
  SelectedIndices As System.Windows.Forms.ListBox+
    SelectedIndexCollection (read only)
  SelectedItem As System.Object
  SelectedItems As System.Windows.Forms.ListBox+
    SelectedObjectCollection (read only)
  SelectionMode As System.Windows.Forms.SelectionMode
  Sorted As System.Boolean
  Text As System.String
  TopIndex As System.Int32
  UseTabStops As System.Boolean
  ' Methods
  BeginUpdate()
  ClearSelected()
```

```
  EndUpdate()
  FindString(s As String, startIndex As Int32) As Int32
  FindString(s As String) As Int32
  FindStringExact(s As String) As Int32
  FindStringExact(s As String, startIndex As Int32)
    As Int32
  GetItemHeight(index As Int32) As Int32
  GetItemRectangle(index As Int32) As Rectangle
  GetSelected(index As Int32) As Boolean
  IndexFromPoint(x As Int32, y As Int32) As Int32
  IndexFromPoint(p As Point) As Int32
  SetSelected(index As Int32, value As Boolean)
  ToString() As String
  ' Events
  Click As System.EventHandler
  DrawItem As System.Windows.Forms.DrawItemEventHandler
  MeasureItem As
    System.Windows.Forms.MeasureItemEventHandler
  SelectedIndexChanged As System.EventHandler
```

ListControl Class

Provides the foundation class used to create the ComboBox and ListBox controls.

Inheritance—Object.MarshalByRefObject.Component.Control.ListControl

```
public class System.Windows.Forms.ListControl
  ' Properties
  DataSource As System.Object
  DisplayMember As System.String
  SelectedIndex As System.Int32
  SelectedValue As System.Object
  ValueMember As System.String
  ' Methods
  GetItemText(item As Object) As String
  ' Events
  DataSourceChanged As System.EventHandler
  DisplayMemberChanged As System.EventHandler
  SelectedValueChanged As System.EventHandler
  ValueMemberChanged As System.EventHandler
```

ListView Class

Provides the class used to create an instance of a Windows ListView control that displays list items in one of four views (large icons, small icons, list, and details). Each item in the ListView control may be displayed with a caption and an optional image or icon.

Inheritance—Object.MarshalByRefObject.Component.Control.ListView

```
public class System.Windows.Forms.ListView
  ' Constructors
  ListView()
  ' Properties
  Activation As System.Windows.Forms.ItemActivation
  Alignment As System.Windows.Forms.ListViewAlignment
  AllowColumnReorder As System.Boolean
  AutoArrange As System.Boolean
  BackColor As System.Drawing.Color
  BackgroundImage As System.Drawing.Image
  BorderStyle As System.Windows.Forms.BorderStyle
  CheckBoxes As System.Boolean
  CheckedIndices As System.Windows.Forms.ListView+
    CheckedIndexCollection (read only)
  CheckedItems As System.Windows.Forms.ListView+
    CheckedListViewItemCollection (read only)
  Columns As System.Windows.Forms.ListView+
    ColumnHeaderCollection (read only)
  FocusedItem As
    System.Windows.Forms.ListViewItem (read only)
  ForeColor As System.Drawing.Color
  FullRowSelect As System.Boolean
  GridLines As System.Boolean
  HeaderStyle As System.Windows.Forms.ColumnHeaderStyle
  HideSelection As System.Boolean
  HoverSelection As System.Boolean
  Items As System.Windows.Forms.ListView+
    ListViewItemCollection (read only)
  LabelEdit As System.Boolean
```

```
LabelWrap As System.Boolean
LargeImageList As System.Windows.Forms.ImageList
ListViewItemSorter As System.Collections.IComparer
MultiSelect As System.Boolean
Scrollable As System.Boolean
SelectedIndices As System.Windows.Forms.ListView+
  SelectedIndexCollection (read only)
SelectedItems As System.Windows.Forms.ListView+
  SelectedListViewItemCollection (read only)
SmallImageList As System.Windows.Forms.ImageList
Sorting As System.Windows.Forms.SortOrder
StateImageList As System.Windows.Forms.ImageList
Text As System.String
TopItem As System.Windows.Forms.ListViewItem (read only)
View As System.Windows.Forms.View
' Methods
ArrangeIcons()
ArrangeIcons(value As ListViewAlignment)
BeginUpdate()
Clear()
EndUpdate()
EnsureVisible(index As Int32)
GetItemAt(x As Int32, y As Int32) As ListViewItem
GetItemRect(index As Int32) As Rectangle
GetItemRect(index As Int32, portion As
  ItemBoundsPortion) As Rectangle
Sort()
ToString() As String
' Events
AfterLabelEdit As
  System.Windows.Forms.LabelEditEventHandler
BeforeLabelEdit As
  System.Windows.Forms.LabelEditEventHandler
ColumnClick As
  System.Windows.Forms.ColumnClickEventHandler
ItemActivate As System.EventHandler
ItemCheck As System.Windows.Forms.ItemCheckEventHandler
ItemDrag As System.Windows.Forms.ItemDragEventHandler
SelectedIndexChanged As System.EventHandler
```

ListViewItem Class

Represents an item displayed in the ListView control.

Inheritance—Object.ListViewItem

```
public class System.Windows.Forms.ListViewItem
  ' Constructors
  ListViewItem()
  ListViewItem(items As String(), imageIndex As Int32,
    foreColor As Color, backColor As Color, font As Font)
  ListViewItem(subItems As ListViewSubItem(),
    imageIndex As Int32)
  ListViewItem(text As String)
  ListViewItem(items As String(), imageIndex As Int32)
  ListViewItem(items As String())
  ListViewItem(text As String, imageIndex As Int32)
  ' Properties
  BackColor As System.Drawing.Color
  Bounds As System.Drawing.Rectangle (read only)
  Checked As System.Boolean
  Focused As System.Boolean
  Font As System.Drawing.Font
  ForeColor As System.Drawing.Color
  ImageIndex As System.Int32
  ImageList As System.Windows.Forms.ImageList (read only)
  Index As System.Int32 (read only)
  ListView As System.Windows.Forms.ListView (read only)
  Selected As System.Boolean
  StateImageIndex As System.Int32
  SubItems As System.Windows.Forms.ListViewItem+
    ListViewSubItemCollection (read only)
  Tag As System.Object
  Text As System.String
  UseItemStyleForSubItems As System.Boolean
  ' Methods
  BeginEdit()
  Clone() As Object
  EnsureVisible()
  GetBounds(portion As ItemBoundsPortion) As Rectangle
  Remove()
  ToString() As String
```

ListViewItemConverter Class

Converts ListViewItem objects from one data type to another. Found as System.Windows.Forms.**ListViewItemConverter**.

MainMenu Class

Holds the designated menu functionality for a specified form or window. This class holds an array of MenuItem objects that represent the individual elements of the menu. *See also* the Menu class.

Inheritance—Object.MarshalByRefObject. Component.Menu.MainMenu

```
public class System.Windows.Forms.MainMenu
  ' Constructors
  MainMenu()
  MainMenu(items As MenuItem())
  ' Properties
  RightToLeft As System.Windows.Forms.RightToLeft
  ' Methods
  CloneMenu() As MainMenu
  GetForm() As Form
  ToString() As String
```

Menu Class

Provides a foundation class for all menus available through the Windows system. *See also* the ContextMenu, MainMenu, and MenuItem classes.

Inheritance—Object.MarshalByRefObject. Component.Menu

```
public class System.Windows.Forms.Menu
  ' Properties
  Handle As System.IntPtr (read only)
```

```
IsParent As System.Boolean (read only)
MdiListItem As System.Windows.Forms.MenuItem (read only)
MenuItems As System.Windows.Forms.Menu+
  MenuItemCollection (read only)
' Methods
FindMenuItem(type As Int32, value As IntPtr) As MenuItem
GetContextMenu() As ContextMenu
GetMainMenu() As MainMenu
MergeMenu(menuSrc As Menu)
ToString() As String
```

MenuItem Class

Represents an item that appears in a MainMenu or ContextMenu control.

Inheritance—Object.MarshalByRefObject. Component.Menu.MenuItem

```
public class System.Windows.Forms.MenuItem
  ' Constructors
  MenuItem(text As String, onClick As EventHandler,
    shortcut As Shortcut)
  MenuItem()
  MenuItem(text As String, items As MenuItem())
  MenuItem(mergeType As MenuMerge, mergeOrder As Int32,
    shortcut As Shortcut, text As String, onClick As
    EventHandler, onPopup As EventHandler, onSelect As
    EventHandler, items As MenuItem())
  MenuItem(text As String)
  MenuItem(text As String, onClick As EventHandler)
  ' Properties
  BarBreak As System.Boolean
  Break As System.Boolean
  Checked As System.Boolean
  DefaultItem As System.Boolean
  Enabled As System.Boolean
  Index As System.Int32
  IsParent As System.Boolean (read only)
  MdiList As System.Boolean
  MergeOrder As System.Int32
  MergeType As System.Windows.Forms.MenuMerge
```

```
Mnemonic As System.Char (read only)
OwnerDraw As System.Boolean
Parent As System.Windows.Forms.Menu (read only)
RadioCheck As System.Boolean
Shortcut As System.Windows.Forms.Shortcut
ShowShortcut As System.Boolean
Text As System.String
Visible As System.Boolean
' Methods
CloneMenu() As MenuItem
MergeMenu() As MenuItem
MergeMenu(itemSrc As MenuItem)
PerformClick()
PerformSelect()
ToString() As String
' Events
Click As System.EventHandler
DrawItem As System.Windows.Forms.DrawItemEventHandler
MeasureItem As
  System.Windows.Forms.MeasureItemEventHandler
Popup As System.EventHandler
Select As System.EventHandler
```

MessageBox Class

Used to create an instance of the Windows MessageBox that can display text and icons as well as receive simple user input (Yes, No, Cancel, OK, etc.). Input is returned in the form of a System.Windows. Forms.**DialogResult** object.

Inheritance—Object.MessageBox

```
public class System.Windows.Forms.MessageBox
  ' Methods
  Show(owner As IWin32Window, text As String,
    caption As String, buttons As MessageBoxButtons,
    icon As MessageBoxIcon) As DialogResult
  Show(owner As IWin32Window, text As String,
    caption As String, buttons As MessageBoxButtons,
    icon As MessageBoxIcon, defaultButton As
    MessageBoxDefaultButton) As DialogResult
  Show(owner As IWin32Window, text As String,
    caption As String, buttons As MessageBoxButtons,
    icon As MessageBoxIcon, defaultButton As
```

```
    MessageBoxDefaultButton, options As MessageBoxOptions)
    As DialogResult
  Show(owner As IWin32Window, text As String)
    As DialogResult
  Show(owner As IWin32Window, text As String,
    caption As String) As DialogResult
  Show(owner As IWin32Window, text As String,
    caption As String, buttons As MessageBoxButtons)
    As DialogResult
  Show(text As String, caption As String, buttons As
    MessageBoxButtons, icon As MessageBoxIcon)
    As DialogResult
  Show(text As String, caption As String, buttons As
    MessageBoxButtons, icon As MessageBoxIcon,
    defaultButton As MessageBoxDefaultButton)
    As DialogResult
  Show(text As String, caption As String, buttons As
    MessageBoxButtons, icon As MessageBoxIcon,
    defaultButton As MessageBoxDefaultButton,
    options As MessageBoxOptions) As DialogResult
  Show(text As String) As DialogResult
  Show(text As String, caption As String) As DialogResult
  Show(text As String, caption As String,
    buttons As MessageBoxButtons) As DialogResult
```

MonthCalendar Class

Provides the class used to create an instance of a Windows MonthCalendar control. *See also* the SelectionRange class.

Inheritance—Object.MarshalByRefObject. Component.Control.MonthCalendar

```
public class System.Windows.Forms.MonthCalendar
  ' Constructors
  MonthCalendar()
  ' Properties
  AnnuallyBoldedDates As System.DateTime()
  BackColor As System.Drawing.Color
  BackgroundImage As System.Drawing.Image
  BoldedDates As System.DateTime()
  CalendarDimensions As System.Drawing.Size
  FirstDayOfWeek As System.Windows.Forms.Day
  ForeColor As System.Drawing.Color
  ImeMode As System.Windows.Forms.ImeMode
  MaxDate As System.DateTime
```

```
MaxSelectionCount As System.Int32
MinDate As System.DateTime
MonthlyBoldedDates As System.DateTime()
ScrollChange As System.Int32
SelectionEnd As System.DateTime
SelectionRange As System.Windows.Forms.SelectionRange
SelectionStart As System.DateTime
ShowToday As System.Boolean
ShowTodayCircle As System.Boolean
ShowWeekNumbers As System.Boolean
SingleMonthSize As System.Drawing.Size (read only)
Text As System.String
TitleBackColor As System.Drawing.Color
TitleForeColor As System.Drawing.Color
TodayDate As System.DateTime
TodayDateSet As System.Boolean (read only)
TrailingForeColor As System.Drawing.Color
' Methods
AddAnnuallyBoldedDate(date As DateTime)
AddBoldedDate(date As DateTime)
AddMonthlyBoldedDate(date As DateTime)
GetDisplayRange(visible As Boolean) As SelectionRange
HitTest(x As Int32, y As Int32) As HitTestInfo
HitTest(point As Point) As HitTestInfo
RemoveAllAnnuallyBoldedDates()
RemoveAllBoldedDates()
RemoveAllMonthlyBoldedDates()
RemoveAnnuallyBoldedDate(date As DateTime)
RemoveBoldedDate(date As DateTime)
RemoveMonthlyBoldedDate(date As DateTime)
SetCalendarDimensions(x As Int32, y As Int32)
SetDate(date As DateTime)
SetSelectionRange(date1 As DateTime, date2 As DateTime)
ToString() As String
UpdateBoldedDates()
' Events
Click As System.EventHandler
DateChanged As System.Windows.Forms.DateRangeEventHandler
DateSelected As
  System.Windows.Forms.DateRangeEventHandler
DoubleClick As System.EventHandler
```

NativeWindow Class

Provides a low-level class for access to a window handle or procedure. When a handle is assigned to the window (through the AssignHandle() method), it is no longer available for garbage collection until it is explicitly released (through the DestroyHandle() or ReleaseHandle() methods).

Inheritance—Object.MarshalByRefObject.NativeWindow

```
public class System.Windows.Forms.NativeWindow
  ' Constructors
  NativeWindow()
  ' Properties
  Handle As System.IntPtr (read only)
  ' Methods
  AssignHandle(handle As IntPtr)
  CreateHandle(cp As CreateParams)
  DefWndProc(m As Message&)
  DestroyHandle()
  FromHandle(handle As IntPtr) As NativeWindow
  ReleaseHandle()
```

NotifyIcon Class

Provides the class used to create an instance of a Windows icon that appears in the system tray.

Inheritance—Object.MarshalByRefObject.Component.NotifyIcon

```
public class System.Windows.Forms.NotifyIcon
  ' Constructors
  NotifyIcon()
  NotifyIcon(container As IContainer)
  ' Properties
  ContextMenu As System.Windows.Forms.ContextMenu
  Icon As System.Drawing.Icon
  Text As System.String
  Visible As System.Boolean
  ' Events
  Click As System.EventHandler
  DoubleClick As System.EventHandler
  MouseDown As System.Windows.Forms.MouseEventHandler
  MouseMove As System.Windows.Forms.MouseEventHandler
  MouseUp As System.Windows.Forms.MouseEventHandler
```

NumericUpDown Class

Provides the class used to create an instance of a Windows UpDown control for display of numeric values. *See also* the DomainUpDown class.

Inheritance—Object.MarshalByRefObject.Component.Control.ScrollableControl.ContainerControl.UpDownBase.NumericUpDown

```
public class System.Windows.Forms.NumericUpDown
  ' Constructors
  NumericUpDown()
  ' Properties
  DecimalPlaces As System.Int32
  Hexadecimal As System.Boolean
  Increment As System.Decimal
  Maximum As System.Decimal
  Minimum As System.Decimal
  Text As System.String
  ThousandsSeparator As System.Boolean
  Value As System.Decimal
  ' Methods
  BeginInit()
  DownButton()
  EndInit()
  ToString() As String
  UpButton()
  ' Events
  ValueChanged As System.EventHandler
```

OpacityConverter Class

Provides functionality to convert opacity values to and from a string. Retrieve an instance of this class using the GetConverter() method of the TypeDescriptor object.

Inheritance—Object.TypeConverter.OpacityConverter

```
public class System.Windows.Forms.OpacityConverter
  ' Constructors
  OpacityConverter()
  ' Methods
  CanConvertFrom(context As ITypeDescriptorContext,
    sourceType As Type) As Boolean
  ConvertFrom(context As ITypeDescriptorContext,
    culture As CultureInfo, value As Object) As Object
  ConvertTo(context As ITypeDescriptorContext,
    culture As CultureInfo, value As Object,
    destinationType As Type) As Object
```

OpenFileDialog Class

Used to display an open file dialog box for user selection of file. Most of the functionality of this class is inherited from the FileDialog parent class. This class represents one of the common dialog boxes provided by the system. *See also* the ColorDialog, FileDialog, FontDialog, PageSetupDialog, and PrintDialog classes.

Inheritance—Object.MarshalByRefObject.Component.CommonDialog.FileDialog.OpenFileDialog

```
public class System.Windows.Forms.OpenFileDialog
  ' Constructors
  OpenFileDialog()
  ' Properties
  CheckFileExists As System.Boolean
  Multiselect As System.Boolean
  ReadOnlyChecked As System.Boolean
  ShowReadOnly As System.Boolean
  ' Methods
  OpenFile() As Stream
  Reset()
```

OSFeature Class

Static class that provides information on the version and available features of the operating system.

Inheritance—Object.FeatureSupport.OSFeature

```
public class System.Windows.Forms.OSFeature
  ' Properties
  Feature As System.Windows.Forms.OSFeature (read only)
  ' Methods
  GetVersionPresent(feature As Object) As Version
```

PageSetupDialog Class

Provides the functionality of the page setup dialog box for user selection of page settings, such as paper size, orientation, number of copies, collation factors, etc. This class represents one of the common dialog boxes provided by the system. *See also* the ColorDialog, FileDialog, FontDialog, and PrintDialog classes.

Inheritance—Object.MarshalByRefObject. Component.CommonDialog.PageSetupDialog

```
public class System.Windows.Forms.PageSetupDialog
  ' Constructors
  PageSetupDialog()
  ' Properties
  AllowMargins As System.Boolean
  AllowOrientation As System.Boolean
  AllowPaper As System.Boolean
  AllowPrinter As System.Boolean
  Document As System.Drawing.Printing.PrintDocument
  MinMargins As System.Drawing.Printing.Margins
  PageSettings As System.Drawing.Printing.PageSettings
  PrinterSettings As
```

```
    System.Drawing.Printing.PrinterSettings
  ShowHelp As System.Boolean
  ShowNetwork As System.Boolean
  ' Methods
  Reset()
```

Panel Class

The class used to create an instance of a Windows Panel control. By default, a Panel control is displayed without any borders.

Inheritance—Object.MarshalByRefObject.Component.Control.ScrollableControl.Panel

```
public class System.Windows.Forms.Panel
  ' Constructors
  Panel()
  ' Properties
  BorderStyle As System.Windows.Forms.BorderStyle
  TabStop As System.Boolean
  Text As System.String
  ' Methods
  ToString() As String
  ' Events
  KeyDown As System.Windows.Forms.KeyEventHandler
  KeyPress As System.Windows.Forms.KeyPressEventHandler
  KeyUp As System.Windows.Forms.KeyEventHandler
```

PictureBox Class

The class used to create an instance of a Windows PictureBox control. This control can display various image types including icon, BMP, GIF, WMF, and JPEG.

Inheritance—Object.MarshalByRefObject.Component.Control.PictureBox

```
public class System.Windows.Forms.PictureBox
  ' Constructors
  PictureBox()
```

```
' Properties
AllowDrop As System.Boolean
BorderStyle As System.Windows.Forms.BorderStyle
CausesValidation As System.Boolean
Font As System.Drawing.Font
ForeColor As System.Drawing.Color
Image As System.Drawing.Image
ImeMode As System.Windows.Forms.ImeMode
RightToLeft As System.Windows.Forms.RightToLeft
SizeMode As System.Windows.Forms.PictureBoxSizeMode
TabIndex As System.Int32
TabStop As System.Boolean
Text As System.String
' Methods
ToString() As String
' Events
Enter As System.EventHandler
KeyDown As System.Windows.Forms.KeyEventHandler
KeyPress As System.Windows.Forms.KeyPressEventHandler
KeyUp As System.Windows.Forms.KeyEventHandler
Leave As System.EventHandler
SizeModeChanged As System.EventHandler
```


PrintControllerWithStatusDialogClass

Provides a PrintController object that manages the operation of printing and can display a dialog box to relay the status of the current print job to the user. This class augments the PrintController class by adding the status dialog box.

Inheritance—Object.PrintController. PrintControllerWithStatusDialog

```
public class
  System.Windows.Forms.PrintControllerWithStatusDialog
  ' Constructors
  PrintControllerWithStatusDialog(underlyingController
    As PrintController [,dialogTitle As String])
  ' Methods
  OnEndPage(document As PrintDocument,
    e As PrintPageEventArgs)
  OnEndPrint(document As PrintDocument,
    e As PrintEventArgs)
  OnStartPage(document As PrintDocument,
    e As PrintPageEventArgs) As Graphics
  OnStartPrint(document As PrintDocument,
    e As PrintEventArgs)
```

PrintDialog Class

Provides the functionality of the Print dialog box for user selection of printer name, number of copies, page print ranges, etc. This class represents one of the common dialog boxes provided by the system. *See also* the ColorDialog, FileDialog, FontDialog, and PageSetupDialog classes.

Inheritance—Object.MarshalByRefObject. Component.CommonDialog.PrintDialog

```
public class System.Windows.Forms.PrintDialog
  ' Constructors
  PrintDialog()
  ' Properties
  AllowPrintToFile As System.Boolean
  AllowSelection As System.Boolean
  AllowSomePages As System.Boolean
  Document As System.Drawing.Printing.PrintDocument
  PrinterSettings As
    System.Drawing.Printing.PrinterSettings
  PrintToFile As System.Boolean
  ShowHelp As System.Boolean
  ShowNetwork As System.Boolean
  ' Methods
  Reset()
```

PrintPreviewControl Class

The class used to create an instance of a Windows PrintPreview control that displays the actual preview of the print area. This control is used by the Print Preview dialog box, but can be used separately for a custom printing preview window.

Inheritance—Object.MarshalByRefObject. Component.Control.PrintPreviewControl

```
public class System.Windows.Forms.PrintPreviewControl
  ' Constructors
  PrintPreviewControl()
  ' Properties
```

```
  AutoZoom As System.Boolean
  Columns As System.Int32
  Document As System.Drawing.Printing.PrintDocument
  Rows As System.Int32
  StartPage As System.Int32
  Text As System.String
  UseAntiAlias As System.Boolean
  Zoom As System.Double
  ' Methods
  InvalidatePreview()
  ResetBackColor()
  ResetForeColor()
  ' Events
  StartPageChanged As System.EventHandler
```


PrintPreviewDialog Class

Provides the display of a Print Preview dialog box that shows formatted pages to be printed.

Inheritance—Object.MarshalByRefObject. Component.Control.ScrollableControl. ContainerControl.Form.PrintPreviewDialog

```
public class System.Windows.Forms.PrintPreviewDialog
  ' Constructors
  PrintPreviewDialog()
  ' Properties
  AcceptButton As System.Windows.Forms.IButtonControl
  AccessibleDescription As System.String
  AccessibleName As System.String
  AccessibleRole As System.Windows.Forms.AccessibleRole
  AllowDrop As System.Boolean
  Anchor As System.Windows.Forms.AnchorStyles
  AutoScale As System.Boolean
  AutoScaleBaseSize As System.Drawing.Size
  AutoScroll As System.Boolean
  AutoScrollMargin As System.Drawing.Size
  AutoScrollMinSize As System.Drawing.Size
  BackColor As System.Drawing.Color
  BackgroundImage As System.Drawing.Image
  CancelButton As System.Windows.Forms.IButtonControl
  CausesValidation As System.Boolean
  ContextMenu As System.Windows.Forms.ContextMenu
```

```
ControlBox As System.Boolean
Cursor As System.Windows.Forms.Cursor
DataBindings As
  System.Windows.Forms.ControlBindingsCollection
  (read only)
Dock As System.Windows.Forms.DockStyle
DockPadding As System.Windows.Forms.ScrollableControl+
  DockPaddingEdges (read only)
Document As System.Drawing.Printing.PrintDocument
Enabled As System.Boolean
Font As System.Drawing.Font
ForeColor As System.Drawing.Color
FormBorderStyle As System.Windows.Forms.FormBorderStyle
HelpButton As System.Boolean
Icon As System.Drawing.Icon
ImeMode As System.Windows.Forms.ImeMode
IsMdiContainer As System.Boolean
KeyPreview As System.Boolean
Location As System.Drawing.Point
MaximizeBox As System.Boolean
MaximumSize As System.Drawing.Size
Menu As System.Windows.Forms.MainMenu
MinimizeBox As System.Boolean
MinimumSize As System.Drawing.Size
Opacity As System.Double
PrintPreviewControl As
  System.Windows.Forms.PrintPreviewControl (read only)
RightToLeft As System.Windows.Forms.RightToLeft
ShowInTaskbar As System.Boolean
Size As System.Drawing.Size
SizeGripStyle As System.Windows.Forms.SizeGripStyle
StartPosition As System.Windows.Forms.FormStartPosition
TabStop As System.Boolean
Tag As System.Object
Text As System.String
TopMost As System.Boolean
TransparencyKey As System.Drawing.Color
UseAntiAlias As System.Boolean
Visible As System.Boolean
WindowState As System.Windows.Forms.FormWindowState
```

ProgressBar Class

Provides the class used to create an instance of a Windows ProgressBar control. The Value property holds the current value between the range specified by the Minimum and Maximum properties.

Inheritance—Object.MarshalByRefObject. Component.Control.ProgressBar

```
public class System.Windows.Forms.ProgressBar
  ' Constructors
  ProgressBar()
  ' Properties
  AllowDrop As System.Boolean
  BackColor As System.Drawing.Color
  BackgroundImage As System.Drawing.Image
  CausesValidation As System.Boolean
  Font As System.Drawing.Font
  ForeColor As System.Drawing.Color
  ImeMode As System.Windows.Forms.ImeMode
  Maximum As System.Int32
  Minimum As System.Int32
  RightToLeft As System.Windows.Forms.RightToLeft
  Step As System.Int32
  TabStop As System.Boolean
  Text As System.String
  Value As System.Int32
  ' Methods
  Increment(value As Int32)
  PerformStep()
  ToString() As String
  ' Events
  DoubleClick As System.EventHandler
  Enter As System.EventHandler
  KeyDown As System.Windows.Forms.KeyEventHandler
  KeyPress As System.Windows.Forms.KeyPressEventHandler
  KeyUp As System.Windows.Forms.KeyEventHandler
  Leave As System.EventHandler
```

PropertyGrid Class

Provides a class used to create an instance of a Windows PropertyGrid control. This control is not displayed by default in the Visual Studio control toolbox, but is installed with VS and may be added to the toolbox palette.

Inheritance—Object.MarshalByRefObject. Component.Control.ScrollableControl. ContainerControl.PropertyGrid

```
public class System.Windows.Forms.PropertyGrid
  ' Constructors
```

```
PropertyGrid()
' Properties
BackColor As System.Drawing.Color
BackgroundImage As System.Drawing.Image
BrowsableAttributes As
  System.ComponentModel.AttributeCollection
CanShowCommands As System.Boolean (read only)
CommandsBackColor As System.Drawing.Color
CommandsForeColor As System.Drawing.Color
CommandsVisible As System.Boolean (read only)
CommandsVisibleIfAvailable As System.Boolean
ContextMenuDefaultLocation As
  System.Drawing.Point (read only)
Controls As
  System.Windows.Forms.Control+ControlCollection
  (read only)
ForeColor As System.Drawing.Color
HelpBackColor As System.Drawing.Color
HelpForeColor As System.Drawing.Color
HelpVisible As System.Boolean
LargeButtons As System.Boolean
LineColor As System.Drawing.Color
PropertySort As System.Windows.Forms.PropertySort
PropertyTabs As System.Windows.Forms.PropertyGrid+
  PropertyTabCollection (read only)
SelectedGridItem As System.Windows.Forms.GridItem
SelectedObject As System.Object
SelectedObjects As System.Object()
SelectedTab As
  System.Windows.Forms.Design.PropertyTab (read only)
Site As System.ComponentModel.ISite
ToolbarVisible As System.Boolean
ViewBackColor As System.Drawing.Color
ViewForeColor As System.Drawing.Color
' Methods
CollapseAllGridItems()
ExpandAllGridItems()
Refresh()
RefreshTabs(tabScope As PropertyTabScope)
ResetSelectedProperty()
' Events
PropertySortChanged As System.EventHandler
PropertyTabChanged As
  System.Windows.Forms.PropertyTabChangedEventHandler
PropertyValueChanged As
  System.Windows.Forms.PropertyValueChangedEventHandler
SelectedGridItemChanged As
 System.Windows.Forms.SelectedGridItemChangedEventHandler
SelectedObjectsChanged As System.EventHandler
```

PropertyManager Class

Manages the Binding object that creates a relation between an object property and a data control property for binding the control to a data source.

Inheritance—Object.BindingManagerBase.PropertyManager

```
public class System.Windows.Forms.PropertyManager
  ' Constructors
  PropertyManager()
  ' Properties
  Count As System.Int32 (read only)
  Current As System.Object (read only)
  Position As System.Int32
  ' Methods
  AddNew()
  CancelCurrentEdit()
  EndCurrentEdit()
  GetItemProperties() As PropertyDescriptorCollection
  RemoveAt(index As Int32)
  ResumeBinding()
  SuspendBinding()
```

RadioButton Class

Provides the class used to create an instance of a Windows RadioButton control. The Checked property contains the current setting of the control.

Inheritance—Object.MarshalByRefObject.Component.Control.ButtonBase.RadioButton

```
public class System.Windows.Forms.RadioButton
  ' Constructors
  RadioButton()
  ' Properties
```

```
  Appearance As System.Windows.Forms.Appearance
  AutoCheck As System.Boolean
  CheckAlign As System.Drawing.ContentAlignment
  Checked As System.Boolean
  TabStop As System.Boolean
  TextAlign As System.Drawing.ContentAlignment
  ' Methods
  PerformClick()
  ToString() As String
  ' Events
  AppearanceChanged As System.EventHandler
  CheckedChanged As System.EventHandler
```

RichTextBox Class

Provides the class used to create an instance of a Windows RichTextBox control. *See also* the TextBoxBase class.

Inheritance—Object.MarshalByRefObject.Component.Control.TextBoxBase.RichTextBox

```
public class System.Windows.Forms.RichTextBox
  ' Constructors
  RichTextBox()
  ' Properties
  AllowDrop As System.Boolean
  AutoSize As System.Boolean
  AutoWordSelection As System.Boolean
  BackgroundImage As System.Drawing.Image
  BulletIndent As System.Int32
  CanRedo As System.Boolean (read only)
  DetectUrls As System.Boolean
  Font As System.Drawing.Font
  ForeColor As System.Drawing.Color
  MaxLength As System.Int32
  Multiline As System.Boolean
  RedoActionName As System.String (read only)
  RightMargin As System.Int32
  Rtf As System.String
  ScrollBars As System.Windows.Forms.RichTextBoxScrollBars
  SelectedRtf As System.String
  SelectedText As System.String
  SelectionAlignment As
    System.Windows.Forms.HorizontalAlignment
  SelectionBullet As System.Boolean
```

```
SelectionCharOffset As System.Int32
SelectionColor As System.Drawing.Color
SelectionFont As System.Drawing.Font
SelectionHangingIndent As System.Int32
SelectionIndent As System.Int32
SelectionLength As System.Int32
SelectionProtected As System.Boolean
SelectionRightIndent As System.Int32
SelectionTabs As System.Int32()
SelectionType As
  System.Windows.Forms.RichTextBoxSelectionTypes
  (read only)
ShowSelectionMargin As System.Boolean
Text As System.String
UndoActionName As System.String (read only)
ZoomFactor As System.Single
' Methods
CanPaste(clipFormat As Format) As Boolean
Find(characterSet As Char(), start As Int32,
  end As Int32) As Int32
Find(characterSet As Char()) As Int32
Find(str As String) As Int32
Find(str As String, start As Int32, end As Int32,
  options As RichTextBoxFinds) As Int32
Find(str As String, start As Int32,
  options As RichTextBoxFinds) As Int32
Find(str As String, options As RichTextBoxFinds) As Int32
Find(characterSet As Char(), start As Int32) As Int32
GetCharFromPosition(pt As Point) As Char
GetCharIndexFromPosition(pt As Point) As Int32
GetLineFromCharIndex(index As Int32) As Int32
GetPositionFromCharIndex(index As Int32) As Point
LoadFile(data As Stream,
  fileType As RichTextBoxStreamType)
LoadFile(path As String
  [,fileType As RichTextBoxStreamType])
Paste(clipFormat As Format)
Redo()
SaveFile(path As String
  [,fileType As RichTextBoxStreamType])
SaveFile(data As Stream,
  fileType As RichTextBoxStreamType)
' Events
ContentsResized As
  System.Windows.Forms.ContentsResizedEventHandler
DoubleClick As System.EventHandler
DragDrop As System.Windows.Forms.DragEventHandler
DragEnter As System.Windows.Forms.DragEventHandler
DragLeave As System.EventHandler
DragOver As System.Windows.Forms.DragEventHandler
```

```
GiveFeedback As
  System.Windows.Forms.GiveFeedbackEventHandler
HScroll As System.EventHandler
ImeChange As System.EventHandler
LinkClicked As
  System.Windows.Forms.LinkClickedEventHandler
Protected As System.EventHandler
QueryContinueDrag As
  System.Windows.Forms.QueryContinueDragEventHandler
SelectionChanged As System.EventHandler
VScroll As System.EventHandler
```

SaveFileDialog Class

Used to display a Save dialog box for user selection of the path and name of a file to be saved. This class represents one of the common dialog boxes provided by the system. *See also* the ColorDialog, FileDialog, FontDialog, PageSetupDialog, and PrintDialog classes.

Inheritance—Object.MarshalByRefObject. Component.CommonDialog.FileDialog. SaveFileDialog

```
public class System.Windows.Forms.SaveFileDialog
  ' Constructors
  SaveFileDialog()
  ' Properties
  CreatePrompt As System.Boolean
  OverwritePrompt As System.Boolean
  ' Methods
  OpenFile() As Stream
  Reset()
```

Screen Class

Static class that provides access to the information of one or more displays on the current system. An instance of this class is automatically generated implicitly when any of its public methods are called.

Inheritance—Object.Screen

```
public class System.Windows.Forms.Screen
  ' Properties
  AllScreens As System.Windows.Forms.Screen() (read only)
  Bounds As System.Drawing.Rectangle (read only)
  DeviceName As System.String (read only)
  Primary As System.Boolean (read only)
  PrimaryScreen As System.Windows.Forms.Screen (read only)
  WorkingArea As System.Drawing.Rectangle (read only)
  ' Methods
  Equals(obj As Object) As Boolean
  FromControl(control As Control) As Screen
  FromHandle(hwnd As IntPtr) As Screen
  FromPoint(point As Point) As Screen
  FromRectangle(rect As Rectangle) As Screen
  GetBounds(pt As Point) As Rectangle
  GetBounds(rect As Rectangle) As Rectangle
  GetBounds(ctl As Control) As Rectangle
  GetHashCode() As Int32
  GetWorkingArea(pt As Point) As Rectangle
  GetWorkingArea(rect As Rectangle) As Rectangle
  GetWorkingArea(ctl As Control) As Rectangle
  ToString() As String
```

ScrollableControl Class

Provides a foundation class for controls such as Panel, ContainerControl, and ComponentTray that must provide scrolling functionality.

Inheritance—Object.MarshalByRefObject.Component.Control.ScrollableControl

```
public class System.Windows.Forms.ScrollableControl
  ' Constructors
  ScrollableControl()
  ' Properties
  AutoScroll As System.Boolean
  AutoScrollMargin As System.Drawing.Size
  AutoScrollMinSize As System.Drawing.Size
  AutoScrollPosition As System.Drawing.Point
```

```
DisplayRectangle As System.Drawing.Rectangle (read only)
DockPadding As System.Windows.Forms.ScrollableControl+
  DockPaddingEdges (read only)
' Methods
ScrollControlIntoView(activeControl As Control)
SetAutoScrollMargin(x As Int32, y As Int32)
```

ScrollBar Class

Provides a foundation class that defines the functionality of a Windows ScrollBar control. *See also* the HScrollBar and VScrollBar classes.

Inheritance—Object.MarshalByRefObject. Component.Control.ScrollBar

```
public class System.Windows.Forms.ScrollBar
  ' Constructors
  ScrollBar()
  ' Properties
  BackColor As System.Drawing.Color
  BackgroundImage As System.Drawing.Image
  Font As System.Drawing.Font
  ForeColor As System.Drawing.Color
  ImeMode As System.Windows.Forms.ImeMode
  LargeChange As System.Int32
  Maximum As System.Int32
  Minimum As System.Int32
  SmallChange As System.Int32
  TabStop As System.Boolean
  Text As System.String
  Value As System.Int32
  ' Methods
  ToString() As String
  ' Events
  DoubleClick As System.EventHandler
  MouseDown As System.Windows.Forms.MouseEventHandler
  MouseMove As System.Windows.Forms.MouseEventHandler
  MouseUp As System.Windows.Forms.MouseEventHandler
  Scroll As System.Windows.Forms.ScrollEventHandler
  ValueChanged As System.EventHandler
```

SelectionRange Class

Holds a selection range for the MonthCalendar control.

Inheritance—Object.SelectionRange

```
public class System.Windows.Forms.SelectionRange
  ' Constructors
  SelectionRange()
  SelectionRange(range As SelectionRange)
  SelectionRange(lower As DateTime, upper As DateTime)
  ' Properties
  End As System.DateTime
  Start As System.DateTime
  ' Methods
  ToString() As String
```

SelectionRangeConverter Class

Provides conversion for selection ranges between various data types. Found as System.Windows.Forms.**Selection RangeConverter**.

SendKeys Class

Static class that provides functionality to programmatically send keystrokes to an application interface. Use the Send() method to send a keystroke and continue program execution. Use the SendWait() method to halt execution until the keystroke is accepted by the application. Use the curly brackets to specify special keys including: {BACKSPACE}/{BS}/{BKSP}, {BREAK}, {CAPSLOCK}, {DELETE}/{DEL}, {DOWN}, {END}, {ENTER}/~, {ESC}, {HELP}, {HOME}, {INSERT}/{INS}, {LEFT}, {NUMLOCK}, {PGDN}, {PGUP}, {PRTSC}, {RIGHT}, {SCROLLLOCK}, {TAB}, {UP}, {F1}, {F2}, {F3}, {F4}, {F5}, {F6}, {F7}, {F8}, {F9}, {F10}, {F11}, {F12}, {F13}, {F14}, {F15}, {F16}, {ADD}, {SUBTRACT}, {MULTIPLY}, and {DIVIDE}.

Special modifiers include + (for the shift key), ^ (for the control key), and % (for the ALT key). To send the modifiers as standard characters, enclose them in curly brackets (i.e. {+}, {^}, and {%}).

Inheritance—Object.SendKeys

```
public class System.Windows.Forms.SendKeys
   ' Methods
   Flush()
   Send(keys As String)
   SendWait(keys As String)
```

Splitter Class

Provides functionality to access and modify the size of docked controls at runtime.

Inheritance—Object.MarshalByRefObject.Component.Control.Splitter

```
public class System.Windows.Forms.Splitter
   ' Constructors
   Splitter()
   ' Properties
   AllowDrop As System.Boolean
   Anchor As System.Windows.Forms.AnchorStyles
   BackgroundImage As System.Drawing.Image
   BorderStyle As System.Windows.Forms.BorderStyle
   Dock As System.Windows.Forms.DockStyle
   Font As System.Drawing.Font
   ForeColor As System.Drawing.Color
   ImeMode As System.Windows.Forms.ImeMode
   MinExtra As System.Int32
   MinSize As System.Int32
   SplitPosition As System.Int32
   TabStop As System.Boolean
   Text As System.String
   ' Methods
   PreFilterMessage(m As Message&) As Boolean
   ToString() As String
   ' Events
   Enter As System.EventHandler
   KeyDown As System.Windows.Forms.KeyEventHandler
```

```
KeyPress As System.Windows.Forms.KeyPressEventHandler
KeyUp As System.Windows.Forms.KeyEventHandler
Leave As System.EventHandler
SplitterMoved As
  System.Windows.Forms.SplitterEventHandler
SplitterMoving As
  System.Windows.Forms.SplitterEventHandler
```


StatusBar Class

The class used to create an instance of a Windows StatusBar control. By default, the control is empty and StatusBarPanel objects must be added to populate the status bar.

Inheritance—Object.MarshalByRefObject.Component.Control.StatusBar

```
public class System.Windows.Forms.StatusBar
  ' Constructors
  StatusBar()
  ' Properties
  BackColor As System.Drawing.Color
  BackgroundImage As System.Drawing.Image
  Dock As System.Windows.Forms.DockStyle
  Font As System.Drawing.Font
  ForeColor As System.Drawing.Color
  ImeMode As System.Windows.Forms.ImeMode
  Panels As System.Windows.Forms.StatusBar+
    StatusBarPanelCollection (read only)
  ShowPanels As System.Boolean
  SizingGrip As System.Boolean
  TabStop As System.Boolean
  Text As System.String
  ' Methods
  ToString() As String
  ' Events
  DrawItem As
    System.Windows.Forms.StatusBarDrawItemEventHandler
  PanelClick As
    System.Windows.Forms.StatusBarPanelClickEventHandler
```

StatusBarPanel Class

Holds the information of a StatusBar control panel. *See also* the StatusBar class.

Inheritance—Object.MarshalByRefObject.Component.StatusBarPanel

```
public class System.Windows.Forms.StatusBarPanel
  ' Constructors
  StatusBarPanel()
  ' Properties
  Alignment As System.Windows.Forms.HorizontalAlignment
  AutoSize As System.Windows.Forms.StatusBarPanelAutoSize
  BorderStyle As
    System.Windows.Forms.StatusBarPanelBorderStyle
  Icon As System.Drawing.Icon
  MinWidth As System.Int32
  Parent As System.Windows.Forms.StatusBar (read only)
  Style As System.Windows.Forms.StatusBarPanelStyle
  Text As System.String
  ToolTipText As System.String
  Width As System.Int32
  ' Methods
  BeginInit()
  EndInit()
  ToString() As String
```

SystemInformation Class

Static class that provides information on the current system, including OS settings, display settings, network availability, and installed hardware.

Inheritance—Object.SystemInformation

```
public class System.Windows.Forms.SystemInformation
  ' Properties
  ArrangeDirection As
    System.Windows.Forms.ArrangeDirection (read only)
  ArrangeStartingPosition As
   System.Windows.Forms.ArrangeStartingPosition (read only)
```

BootMode As System.Windows.Forms.BootMode (read only)
Border3DSize As System.Drawing.Size (read only)
BorderSize As System.Drawing.Size (read only)
CaptionButtonSize As System.Drawing.Size (read only)
CaptionHeight As System.Int32 (read only)
ComputerName As System.String (read only)
CursorSize As System.Drawing.Size (read only)
DbcsEnabled As System.Boolean (read only)
DebugOS As System.Boolean (read only)
DoubleClickSize As System.Drawing.Size (read only)
DoubleClickTime As System.Int32 (read only)
DragFullWindows As System.Boolean (read only)
DragSize As System.Drawing.Size (read only)
FixedFrameBorderSize As System.Drawing.Size (read only)
FrameBorderSize As System.Drawing.Size (read only)
HighContrast As System.Boolean (read only)
HorizontalScrollBarArrowWidth As System.Int32 (read only)
HorizontalScrollBarHeight As System.Int32 (read only)
HorizontalScrollBarThumbWidth As System.Int32 (read only)
IconSize As System.Drawing.Size (read only)
IconSpacingSize As System.Drawing.Size (read only)
KanjiWindowHeight As System.Int32 (read only)
MaxWindowTrackSize As System.Drawing.Size (read only)
MenuButtonSize As System.Drawing.Size (read only)
MenuCheckSize As System.Drawing.Size (read only)
MenuFont As System.Drawing.Font (read only)
MenuHeight As System.Int32 (read only)
MidEastEnabled As System.Boolean (read only)
MinimizedWindowSize As System.Drawing.Size (read only)
MinimizedWindowSpacingSize As System.Drawing.Size (read only)
MinimumWindowSize As System.Drawing.Size (read only)
MinWindowTrackSize As System.Drawing.Size (read only)
MonitorCount As System.Int32 (read only)
MonitorsSameDisplayFormat As System.Boolean (read only)
MouseButtons As System.Int32 (read only)
MouseButtonsSwapped As System.Boolean (read only)
MousePresent As System.Boolean (read only)
MouseWheelPresent As System.Boolean (read only)
MouseWheelScrollLines As System.Int32 (read only)
NativeMouseWheelSupport As System.Boolean (read only)
Network As System.Boolean (read only)
PenWindows As System.Boolean (read only)
PrimaryMonitorMaximizedWindowSize As System.Drawing.Size (read only)

```
PrimaryMonitorSize As System.Drawing.Size (read only)
RightAlignedMenus As System.Boolean (read only)
Secure As System.Boolean (read only)
ShowSounds As System.Boolean (read only)
SmallIconSize As System.Drawing.Size (read only)
ToolWindowCaptionButtonSize As
  System.Drawing.Size (read only)
ToolWindowCaptionHeight As System.Int32 (read only)
UserDomainName As System.String (read only)
UserInteractive As System.Boolean (read only)
UserName As System.String (read only)
VerticalScrollBarArrowHeight As System.Int32 (read only)
VerticalScrollBarThumbHeight As System.Int32 (read only)
VerticalScrollBarWidth As System.Int32 (read only)
VirtualScreen As System.Drawing.Rectangle (read only)
WorkingArea As System.Drawing.Rectangle (read only)
' Methods
GetFolderPath(folder As SpecialFolder) As String
GetFolderPath(folder As SpecialFolder) As String
```

TabControl Class

Provides a class used to create an instance of a Windows TabControl control that displays a set of tabbed pages within a window. Each tab is represented by a TabPage object held in the collection stored in the TabPages property.

Inheritance—Object.MarshalByRefObject.Component.Control.TabControl

```
public class System.Windows.Forms.TabControl
  ' Constructors
  TabControl()
  ' Properties
  Alignment As System.Windows.Forms.TabAlignment
  Appearance As System.Windows.Forms.TabAppearance
  BackColor As System.Drawing.Color
  BackgroundImage As System.Drawing.Image
  DisplayRectangle As System.Drawing.Rectangle (read only)
  DrawMode As System.Windows.Forms.TabDrawMode
  ForeColor As System.Drawing.Color
  HotTrack As System.Boolean
```

```
ImageList As System.Windows.Forms.ImageList
ItemSize As System.Drawing.Size
Multiline As System.Boolean
Padding As System.Drawing.Point
RowCount As System.Int32 (read only)
SelectedIndex As System.Int32
SelectedTab As System.Windows.Forms.TabPage
ShowToolTips As System.Boolean
SizeMode As System.Windows.Forms.TabSizeMode
TabCount As System.Int32 (read only)
TabPages As System.Windows.Forms.TabControl+
  TabPageCollection (read only)
Text As System.String
' Methods
GetControl(index As Int32) As Control
GetTabRect(index As Int32) As Rectangle
ToString() As String
' Events
Click As System.EventHandler
DrawItem As System.Windows.Forms.DrawItemEventHandler
SelectedIndexChanged As System.EventHandler
```

TabPage Class

Represents a single tabbed page within a TabControl control.

Inheritance—Object.MarshalByRefObject.Component.Control.ScrollableControl.Panel.TabPage

```
public class System.Windows.Forms.TabPage
  ' Constructors
  TabPage(text As String)
  TabPage()
  ' Properties
  Anchor As System.Windows.Forms.AnchorStyles
  Dock As System.Windows.Forms.DockStyle
  Enabled As System.Boolean
  ImageIndex As System.Int32
  TabIndex As System.Int32
  TabStop As System.Boolean
  Text As System.String
```

```
ToolTipText As System.String
Visible As System.Boolean
' Methods
GetTabPageOfComponent(comp As Object) As TabPage
ToString() As String
```

TextBox Class

Provides a class used to create an instance of a Windows TextBox control. *See also* the TextBoxBase and DataGridTextBox classes.

Inheritance—Object.MarshalByRefObject. Component.Control.TextBoxBase.TextBox

```
public class System.Windows.Forms.TextBox
  ' Constructors
  TextBox()
  ' Properties
  AcceptsReturn As System.Boolean
  CharacterCasing As System.Windows.Forms.CharacterCasing
  PasswordChar As System.Char
  ScrollBars As System.Windows.Forms.ScrollBars
  TextAlign As System.Windows.Forms.HorizontalAlignment
  ' Events
  TextAlignChanged As System.EventHandler
```

TextBoxBase Class

Provides the foundation class used to provide the functionality of text editing controls such as TextBox and RichTextBox.

Inheritance—Object.MarshalByRefObject. Component.Control.TextBoxBase

```
public class System.Windows.Forms.TextBoxBase
  ' Properties
  AcceptsTab As System.Boolean
  AutoSize As System.Boolean
  BackColor As System.Drawing.Color
  BackgroundImage As System.Drawing.Image
  BorderStyle As System.Windows.Forms.BorderStyle
  CanUndo As System.Boolean (read only)
```

```
ForeColor As System.Drawing.Color
HideSelection As System.Boolean
Lines As System.String()
MaxLength As System.Int32
Modified As System.Boolean
Multiline As System.Boolean
PreferredHeight As System.Int32 (read only)
ReadOnly As System.Boolean
SelectedText As System.String
SelectionLength As System.Int32
SelectionStart As System.Int32
Text As System.String
TextLength As System.Int32 (read only)
WordWrap As System.Boolean
' Methods
AppendText(text As String)
Clear()
ClearUndo()
Copy()
Cut()
Paste()
ScrollToCaret()
Select(start As Int32, length As Int32)
SelectAll()
ToString() As String
Undo()
' Events
AcceptsTabChanged As System.EventHandler
AutoSizeChanged As System.EventHandler
BorderStyleChanged As System.EventHandler
Click As System.EventHandler
HideSelectionChanged As System.EventHandler
ModifiedChanged As System.EventHandler
MultilineChanged As System.EventHandler
ReadOnlyChanged As System.EventHandler
```

Timer Class

Provides a form-based timer that generates events at user-defined intervals. Instances of this class must be used within a Window. Intervals for this control are specified in milliseconds (1/1000 of a second).

Inheritance—Object.MarshalByRefObject.Component.Timer

```
public class System.Windows.Forms.Timer
  ' Constructors
  Timer(container As IContainer)
  Timer()
  ' Properties
  Enabled As System.Boolean
  Interval As System.Int32
  ' Methods
  Start()
  Stop()
  ToString() As String
  ' Events
  Tick As System.EventHandler
```

ToolBar Class

The class used to create an instance of a Windows ToolBar control that displays a row of ToolBarButton objects as standard, toggle, or drop-down buttons.

Inheritance—Object.MarshalByRefObject.Component.Control.ToolBar

```
public class System.Windows.Forms.ToolBar
  ' Constructors
  ToolBar()
  ' Properties
  Appearance As System.Windows.Forms.ToolBarAppearance
  AutoSize As System.Boolean
  BackColor As System.Drawing.Color
  BackgroundImage As System.Drawing.Image
  BorderStyle As System.Windows.Forms.BorderStyle
  Buttons As System.Windows.Forms.ToolBar+
    ToolBarButtonCollection (read only)
  ButtonSize As System.Drawing.Size
  Divider As System.Boolean
  Dock As System.Windows.Forms.DockStyle
  DropDownArrows As System.Boolean
  ForeColor As System.Drawing.Color
  ImageList As System.Windows.Forms.ImageList
```

```
  ImageSize As System.Drawing.Size (read only)
  ImeMode As System.Windows.Forms.ImeMode
  RightToLeft As System.Windows.Forms.RightToLeft
  ShowToolTips As System.Boolean
  TabStop As System.Boolean
  Text As System.String
  TextAlign As System.Windows.Forms.ToolBarTextAlign
  Wrappable As System.Boolean
  ' Methods
  ToString() As String
  ' Events
  ButtonClick As
    System.Windows.Forms.ToolBarButtonClickEventHandler
  ButtonDropDown As
    System.Windows.Forms.ToolBarButtonClickEventHandler
```


ToolBarButton Class

Provides a class used to create an instance of a Windows ToolBarButton control for use within a ToolBar control.

Inheritance—Object.MarshalByRefObject.Component.ToolBarButton

```
public class System.Windows.Forms.ToolBarButton
  ' Constructors
  ToolBarButton()
  ToolBarButton(text As String)
  ' Properties
  DropDownMenu As System.Windows.Forms.Menu
  Enabled As System.Boolean
  ImageIndex As System.Int32
  ItemData As System.Object
  Parent As System.Windows.Forms.ToolBar (read only)
  PartialPush As System.Boolean
  Pushed As System.Boolean
  Rectangle As System.Drawing.Rectangle (read only)
  Style As System.Windows.Forms.ToolBarButtonStyle
  Tag As System.Object
  Text As System.String
  ToolTipText As System.String
  Visible As System.Boolean
  ' Methods
  ToString() As String
```

ToolTip Class

Provides tool-tip functionality (display of a small text popup description) when the user moves the mouse over the control associated with the ToolTip object.

Inheritance—Object.MarshalByRefObject. Component.ToolTip

```
public class System.Windows.Forms.ToolTip
  ' Constructors
  ToolTip()
  ToolTip(cont As IContainer)
  ' Properties
  Active As System.Boolean
  AutomaticDelay As System.Int32
  AutoPopDelay As System.Int32
  InitialDelay As System.Int32
  ReshowDelay As System.Int32
  ShowAlways As System.Boolean
  ' Methods
  CanExtend(target As Object) As Boolean
  GetToolTip(control As Control) As String
  RemoveAll()
  SetToolTip(control As Control, caption As String)
  ToString() As String
```

TrackBar Class

Provides a class used to create an instance of a Windows TrackBar control.

Inheritance—Object.MarshalByRefObject. Component.Control.TrackBar

```
public class System.Windows.Forms.TrackBar
  ' Constructors
  TrackBar()
  ' Properties
  AutoSize As System.Boolean
```

```
BackgroundImage As System.Drawing.Image
Font As System.Drawing.Font
ForeColor As System.Drawing.Color
ImeMode As System.Windows.Forms.ImeMode
LargeChange As System.Int32
Maximum As System.Int32
Minimum As System.Int32
Orientation As System.Windows.Forms.Orientation
SmallChange As System.Int32
Text As System.String
TickFrequency As System.Int32
TickStyle As System.Windows.Forms.TickStyle
Value As System.Int32
' Methods
BeginInit()
EndInit()
SetRange(minValue As Int32, maxValue As Int32)
ToString() As String
' Events
Click As System.EventHandler
DoubleClick As System.EventHandler
Scroll As System.EventHandler
ValueChanged As System.EventHandler
```


TreeNode Class

Represents a node of a TreeView control. Each TreeNode can hold a collection of other TreeNode objects. The FullPath property holds the absolute path of the individual node within the entire tree.

Inheritance—Object.MarshalByRefObject.TreeNode

```
public class System.Windows.Forms.TreeNode
  ' Constructors
  TreeNode(text As String, children As TreeNode())
  TreeNode(text As String, imageIndex As Int32,
    selectedImageIndex As Int32)
  TreeNode()
  TreeNode(text As String)
  TreeNode(text As String, imageIndex As Int32,
    selectedImageIndex As Int32, children As TreeNode())
  ' Properties
```

```
BackColor As System.Drawing.Color
Bounds As System.Drawing.Rectangle (read only)
Checked As System.Boolean
FirstNode As System.Windows.Forms.TreeNode (read only)
ForeColor As System.Drawing.Color
FullPath As System.String (read only)
Handle As System.IntPtr (read only)
ImageIndex As System.Int32
Index As System.Int32 (read only)
IsEditing As System.Boolean (read only)
IsExpanded As System.Boolean (read only)
IsSelected As System.Boolean (read only)
IsVisible As System.Boolean (read only)
LastNode As System.Windows.Forms.TreeNode (read only)
NextNode As System.Windows.Forms.TreeNode (read only)
NextVisibleNode As
  System.Windows.Forms.TreeNode (read only)
NodeFont As System.Drawing.Font
Nodes As
  System.Windows.Forms.TreeNodeCollection (read only)
Parent As System.Windows.Forms.TreeNode (read only)
PrevNode As System.Windows.Forms.TreeNode (read only)
PrevVisibleNode As
  System.Windows.Forms.TreeNode (read only)
SelectedImageIndex As System.Int32
Tag As System.Object
Text As System.String
TreeView As System.Windows.Forms.TreeView (read only)
' Methods
BeginEdit()
Clone() As Object
Collapse()
EndEdit(cancel As Boolean)
EnsureVisible()
Expand()
ExpandAll()
FromHandle(tree As TreeView, handle As IntPtr)
  As TreeNode
GetNodeCount(includeSubTrees As Boolean) As Int32
Remove()
Toggle()
ToString() As String
```

TreeNodeCollection Class

Holds the collection of TreeNode objects that represent each node displayed in a TreeView control. Found as System.Windows.Forms.**TreeNodeCollection**.

TreeNodeConverter Class

Provides conversion for TreeNode objects between various data types. Retrieve an instance of this class using the GetConverter() method of the TypeDescriptor object. Found as System.Windows.Forms.**TreeNodeConverter**.

TreeView Class

Provides a class used to create an instance of a Windows TreeView control. A Treeview control displays a list of hierarchical items, each represented by TreeNode objects held in the collection in the Nodes property.

Inheritance—Object.MarshalByRefObject.Component.Control.TreeView

```
public class System.Windows.Forms.TreeView
  ' Constructors
  TreeView()
  ' Properties
  BackColor As System.Drawing.Color
  BackgroundImage As System.Drawing.Image
  BorderStyle As System.Windows.Forms.BorderStyle
  CheckBoxes As System.Boolean
  ForeColor As System.Drawing.Color
  FullRowSelect As System.Boolean
  HideSelection As System.Boolean
  HotTracking As System.Boolean
  ImageIndex As System.Int32
```

```
ImageList As System.Windows.Forms.ImageList
Indent As System.Int32
ItemHeight As System.Int32
LabelEdit As System.Boolean
Nodes As
  System.Windows.Forms.TreeNodeCollection (read only)
PathSeparator As System.String
Scrollable As System.Boolean
SelectedImageIndex As System.Int32
SelectedNode As System.Windows.Forms.TreeNode
ShowLines As System.Boolean
ShowPlusMinus As System.Boolean
ShowRootLines As System.Boolean
Sorted As System.Boolean
Text As System.String
TopNode As System.Windows.Forms.TreeNode (read only)
VisibleCount As System.Int32 (read only)
' Methods
BeginUpdate()
CollapseAll()
EndUpdate()
ExpandAll()
GetNodeAt(x As Int32, y As Int32) As TreeNode
GetNodeAt(pt As Point) As TreeNode
GetNodeCount(includeSubTrees As Boolean) As Int32
ToString() As String
' Events
AfterCheck As System.Windows.Forms.TreeViewEventHandler
AfterCollapse As
  System.Windows.Forms.TreeViewEventHandler
AfterExpand As System.Windows.Forms.TreeViewEventHandler
AfterLabelEdit As
  System.Windows.Forms.NodeLabelEditEventHandler
AfterSelect As System.Windows.Forms.TreeViewEventHandler
BeforeCheck As
  System.Windows.Forms.TreeViewCancelEventHandler
BeforeCollapse As
  System.Windows.Forms.TreeViewCancelEventHandler
BeforeExpand As
  System.Windows.Forms.TreeViewCancelEventHandler
BeforeLabelEdit As
  System.Windows.Forms.NodeLabelEditEventHandler
BeforeSelect As
  System.Windows.Forms.TreeViewCancelEventHandler
ItemDrag As System.Windows.Forms.ItemDragEventHandler
```

TreeViewImageIndexConverter Class

Provides conversion for TreeView images between various data types. Found as System.Windows.Forms.**TreeViewImage IndexConverter**.

UpDownBase Class

Provides a foundation class that provides functionality to controls such as DomainUpDown and NumericUpDown controls.

Inheritance—Object.MarshalByRefObject. Component.Control.ScrollableControl. ContainerControl.UpDownBase

```
public class System.Windows.Forms.UpDownBase
  ' Constructors
  UpDownBase()
  ' Properties
  AutoScroll As System.Boolean
  AutoScrollMargin As System.Drawing.Size
  AutoScrollMinSize As System.Drawing.Size
  BackColor As System.Drawing.Color
  BackgroundImage As System.Drawing.Image
  BorderStyle As System.Windows.Forms.BorderStyle
  ContextMenu As System.Windows.Forms.ContextMenu
  DockPadding As System.Windows.Forms.ScrollableControl+
    DockPaddingEdges (read only)
  Focused As System.Boolean (read only)
  ForeColor As System.Drawing.Color
  InterceptArrowKeys As System.Boolean
  PreferredHeight As System.Int32 (read only)
  ReadOnly As System.Boolean
  Text As System.String
  TextAlign As System.Windows.Forms.HorizontalAlignment
  UpDownAlign As System.Windows.Forms.LeftRightAlignment
  ' Methods
  DownButton()
  Select(start As Int32, length As Int32)
  UpButton()
```

UserControl Class

Provides a foundation class for the creation of custom controls.

Inheritance—Object.MarshalByRefObject. Component.Control.ScrollableControl. ContainerControl.UserControl

```
public class System.Windows.Forms.UserControl
  ' Constructors
  UserControl()
  ' Properties
  Text As System.String
  ' Events
  Load As System.EventHandler
```

VScrollBar Class

The class used to create an instance of a Windows vertical ScrollBar control. Most methods, properties, and events for this control are inherited from the ScrollBar class. *See also* the HScrollBar and ScrollBar classes.

Inheritance—Object.MarshalByRefObject. Component.Control.ScrollBar.VScrollBar

```
public class System.Windows.Forms.VScrollBar
  ' Constructors
  VScrollBar()
  ' Properties
  RightToLeft As System.Windows.Forms.RightToLeft
```

Chapter 3
Drawing

3

The .NET Framework contains a comprehensive set of classes available for graphics, drawing, imaging, and printing. To use the graphics system properly, a thorough understanding of the Graphics Device Interface (GDI+) is recommended. All of the classes for these areas of functionality are found under the System.Drawing namespace.

NOTE: Many of the converters in this chapter require that the TypeDescriptor class be used to obtain an instance of the appropriate converter object (such as FontConvert, IconConverter, etc.). The TypeDescriptor class can be found in the System .ComponentModel namespace.

Demonstrated in the following example is some simple drawing through the .NET graphics classes. The code draws a pair of eyes using two filled ovals (eyes), two gradient-filled ovals (pupils), and two lines (eyebrows). To create this example application, start a new VB Windows project in Visual Studio and place these Imports statements at the beginning of the form code:

```
Imports System.Drawing
Imports System.Drawing.Drawing2D
```

In the form's painting event, place the following code:

```
Sub Form1_Paint()
  Dim myPen As Pen, myGraphics As Drawing.Graphics
  Dim myBlend As LinearGradientBrush, myRect As Rectangle

  myGraphics = e.Graphics
  ' Turn on anti-alias
  myGraphics.SmoothingMode = _
    Drawing2D.SmoothingMode.AntiAlias
  ' Draw brows
  myPen = New Pen(Color.Brown, 3)
  myGraphics.DrawLine(myPen, 20, 40, 110, 10)
  myGraphics.DrawLine(myPen, 150, 10, 240, 40)
  ' Draw eyes
  myGraphics.FillEllipse(Brushes.White, 25, 50, 80, 80)
  myGraphics.DrawEllipse(myPen, 25, 50, 80, 80)
  myGraphics.FillEllipse(Brushes.White, 150, 50, 80, 80)
  myGraphics.DrawEllipse(myPen, 150, 50, 80, 80)
  ' Draw pupils
```

```
  myRect = New Rectangle(60, 90, 30, 30)
  myBlend = New LinearGradientBrush(myRect, Color.Blue, _
    Color.Black, LinearGradientMode.Horizontal)
  myGraphics.FillEllipse(myBlend, myRect)
  myRect = New Rectangle(185, 90, 30, 30)
  myBlend = New LinearGradientBrush(myRect, Color.Blue, _
    Color.Black, LinearGradientMode.ForwardDiagonal)
  myGraphics.FillEllipse(myBlend, myRect)
End Sub
```

Executing the application will draw the simple face on the body of the form.

AdjustableArrowCap Class

Holds the settings for the arrow cap that will be drawn on the end of a line by a Pen object. This class is not inheritable.

Inheritance—Object.MarshalByRefObject. CustomLineCap.AdjustableArrowCap

```
public class System.Drawing.Drawing2D.AdjustableArrowCap
  ' Constructors
  AdjustableArrowCap(width As Single,height As Single
    [,isFilled As Boolean])
  ' Properties
  Filled As System.Boolean
  Height As System.Single
  MiddleInset As System.Single
  Width As System.Single
```

Bitmap Class

Represents a GDI+ bitmap image. A bitmap includes the pixel data and the attributes (size, bit depth, transparency, etc.) that define it.

Inheritance—Object.MarshalByRefObject. Image.Bitmap

```
public class System.Drawing.Bitmap
  ' Constructors
```

```
Bitmap(original As Image [,newSize As Size])
Bitmap(original As Image, width As Int32,
  height As Int32)
Bitmap(width As Int32, height As Int32, stride As Int32,
  format As PixelFormat, scan0 As IntPtr)
Bitmap(filename As String [, useIcm As Boolean])
Bitmap(stream As Stream [, useIcm As Boolean])
Bitmap(type As Type, resource As String)
Bitmap(width As Int32, height As Int32
  [, format As PixelFormat])
Bitmap(width As Int32, height As Int32, g As Graphics)
' Methods
Clone(rect As Rectangle, format As PixelFormat) As Bitmap
Clone(rect As RectangleF, format As PixelFormat)
  As Bitmap
FromHicon(hicon As IntPtr) As Bitmap
FromResource(hinstance As IntPtr, bitmapName As String)
  As Bitmap
GetHbitmap() As IntPtr
GetHbitmap(background As Color) As IntPtr
GetHicon() As IntPtr
GetPixel(x As Int32, y As Int32) As Color
LockBits(rect As Rectangle, flags As ImageLockMode,
  format As PixelFormat) As BitmapData
MakeTransparent( [transparentColor As Color] )
SetPixel(x As Int32, y As Int32, color As Color)
SetResolution(xDpi As Single, yDpi As Single)
UnlockBits(bitmapdata As BitmapData)
```

3

BitmapData Class

Holds the properties of the bitmap. This class is not inheritable.

Inheritance—Object.BitmapData

```
public class System.Drawing.Imaging.BitmapData
  ' Constructors
  BitmapData()
  ' Properties
  Height As System.Int32
  PixelFormat As System.Drawing.Imaging.PixelFormat
  Reserved As System.Int32
  Scan0 As System.IntPtr
  Stride As System.Int32
  Width As System.Int32
```

Blend Class

Holds the gradient pattern for the LinearGradientBrush class. Each blend consists of two arrays (held in properties of the corresponding names) of Single data type values: Positions and Factors. The items in the Positions array indicate the proportion of distance along the gradient line, held as a decimal percentage such as .21 (indicating 21 percent). The Factors array holds the ratio (also a decimal percent) of the beginning and the ending colors for the Position item with the same ordinal value. Found as System.Drawing.Drawing2D.**Blend**.

Brush Class

Provides an abstract foundation class for Brush objects that are used to fill the interiors of graphic shapes such as rectangles and polygons. This class cannot be instantiated. Children of this class include HatchBrush, LinearGradientBrush, PathGradientBrush, SolidBrush, and TextureBrush. Found as System.Drawing.**Brush**.

Brushes Class

Holds definitions of Brush objects for all the standard colors. This class is not inheritable.

Inheritance—Object.Brushes

```
public class System.Drawing.Brushes
  ' Properties
  AliceBlue As System.Drawing.Brush (read only)
  ' Also available as
  ' System.Drawing.Brush (read only) properties:
  AntiqueWhite, Aqua, Aquamarine, Azure, Beige, Bisque,
  Black, BlanchedAlmond, Blue, BlueViolet, Brown,
  BurlyWood, CadetBlue, Chartreuse, Chocolate, Coral,
  CornflowerBlue, Cornsilk, Crimson, Cyan, DarkBlue,
  DarkCyan, DarkGoldenrod, DarkGray, DarkGreen, DarkKhaki,
  DarkMagenta, DarkOliveGreen, DarkOrange, DarkOrchid,
```

```
DarkRed, DarkSalmon, DarkSeaGreen, DarkSlateBlue,
DarkSlateGray, DarkTurquoise, DarkViolet, DeepPink,
DeepSkyBlue, DimGray, DodgerBlue, Firebrick, FloralWhite,
ForestGreen, Fuchsia, Gainsboro, GhostWhite, Gold,
Goldenrod, Gray, Green, GreenYellow, Honeydew, HotPink,
IndianRed, Indigo, Ivory, Khaki, Lavender, LavenderBlush,
LawnGreen, LemonChiffon, LightBlue, LightCoral,
LightCyan, LightGoldenrodYellow, LightGray, LightGreen,
LightPink, LightSalmon, LightSeaGreen, LightSkyBlue,
LightSlateGray, LightSteelBlue, LightYellow, Lime,
LimeGreen, Linen, Magenta, Maroon, MediumAquamarine,
MediumBlue, MediumOrchid, MediumPurple, MediumSeaGreen,
MediumSlateBlue, MediumSpringGreen, MediumTurquoise,
MediumVioletRed, MidnightBlue, MintCream, MistyRose,
Moccasin, NavajoWhite, Navy, OldLace, Olive, OliveDrab,
Orange, OrangeRed, Orchid, PaleGoldenrod, PaleGreen,
PaleTurquoise, PaleVioletRed, PapayaWhip, PeachPuff,
Peru, Pink, Plum, PowderBlue, Purple, Red, RosyBrown,
RoyalBlue, SaddleBrown, Salmon, SandyBrown, SeaGreen,
SeaShell, Sienna, Silver, SkyBlue, SlateBlue, SlateGray,
Snow, SpringGreen, SteelBlue, Tan, Teal, Thistle, Tomato,
Transparent, Turquoise, Violet, Wheat, White, WhiteSmoke,
Yellow, YellowGreen As System.Drawing.Brush (read only)
```

3

ColorBlend Class

Provides blending similar to the Blend class but offers a multicolor gradient. In this class, the two arrays Colors (Color type) and Positions (Single type) specify the values to create the gradient. Found as System.Drawing.Drawing2D.**ColorBlend**.

ColorConverter Class

Provides conversion functionality to change a color to a different data type. Use the TypeDescriptor to access this class.

Inheritance—Object.TypeConverter.ColorConverter

```
public class System.Drawing.ColorConverter
  ' Constructors
  ColorConverter()
  ' Methods
  CanConvertFrom(context As ITypeDescriptorContext,
    sourceType As Type) As Boolean
```

```
CanConvertTo(context As ITypeDescriptorContext,
  destinationType As Type) As Boolean
ConvertFrom(context As ITypeDescriptorContext,
  culture As CultureInfo, value As Object) As Object
ConvertTo(context As ITypeDescriptorContext,
  culture As CultureInfo, value As Object,
  destinationType As Type) As Object
GetStandardValues(context As ITypeDescriptorContext)
  As StandardValuesCollection
GetStandardValuesSupported(context As
  ITypeDescriptorContext) As Boolean
```

ColorMap Class

Hold a color map for a conversion where the current pixel color will be converted to a new color. The properties OldColor and NewColor provide the mapping settings. Found as System.Drawing.Imaging.**ColorMap**.

ColorMatrix class

Holds a 5 × 5 linear transformation matrix for coordinates in RGBA (red-green-blue-alpha) space. This class is not inheritable.

Inheritance—Object.ColorMatrix

```
public class System.Drawing.Imaging.ColorMatrix
  ' Constructors
  ColorMatrix( [newColorMatrix As Single()()] )
  ' Properties
  Item As System.Single
  Matrix00 As System.Single
  ' Also available as a System.Single value:
  Matrix01, Matrix02, Matrix03, Matrix04, Matrix10,
  Matrix11, Matrix12, Matrix13, Matrix14, Matrix20,
  Matrix21, Matrix22, Matrix23, Matrix24, Matrix30,
  Matrix31, Matrix32, Matrix33, Matrix34, Matrix40,
  Matrix41, Matrix42, Matrix43, and Matrix44
```

ColorPalette Class

Holds the values of a color palette limited to 32-bit RGBA values. For a 32-bit value, the lowest 8 bits are blue and the other channels follow in the order green, red, and alpha. This class is not inheritable.

Inheritance—Object.ColorPalette

```
public class System.Drawing.Imaging.ColorPalette
  ' Properties
  Entries As System.Drawing.Color() (read only)
  Flags As System.Int32 (read only)
```

ColorTranslator Class

Provides translation between GDI+ colors (Color data type) and HTML, OLE, and Win32 colors. The methods FromHtml(), FromOle(), and FromWin32() convert to a Color object. The methods ToHtml(), ToOle(), and ToWin32() convert from a Color type. Found as System.Drawing.**ColorTranslator**.

CustomLineCap Class

Provides settings to allow the creation of a custom line cap to be drawn by a Pen object. Found as System.Drawing .Drawing2D.**CustomLineCap**.

Encoder Class

Holds the parameters for an image to be passed to a codec (compression/decompression) plug-in. Found as System.Drawing .Imaging.**Encoder**.

Font Class

Provides a representation of a font, including font face, style, and size. This class is not inheritable.

Inheritance—Object.MarshalByRefObject.Font

```
public class System.Drawing.Font
  ' Constructors
  Font(family As FontFamily, emSize As Single)
  Font(familyName As String, emSize As Single,
    style As FontStyle, unit As GraphicsUnit)
  Font(prototype As Font, newStyle As FontStyle)
  Font(familyName As String, emSize As Single
    [, unit As GraphicsUnit])
  Font(familyName As String, emSize As Single,
    style As FontStyle [,unit As GraphicsUnit
    [,gdiCharSet As Byte,gdiVerticalFont As Boolean]])
  Font(family As FontFamily, emSize As Single,
    unit As GraphicsUnit)
  Font(family As FontFamily, emSize As Single,
    style As FontStyle [,unit As GraphicsUnit,
    gdiCharSet As Byte [,gdiVerticalFont As Boolean]])
  Font(familyName As String, emSize As Single,
    style As FontStyle, unit As GraphicsUnit,
    gdiCharSet As Byte)
  ' Properties
  Bold As System.Boolean (read only)
  FontFamily As System.Drawing.FontFamily (read only)
  GdiCharSet As System.Byte (read only)
  GdiVerticalFont As System.Boolean (read only)
  Height As System.Int32 (read only)
  Italic As System.Boolean (read only)
  Name As System.String (read only)
  Size As System.Single (read only)
  SizeInPoints As System.Single (read only)
  Strikeout As System.Boolean (read only)
  Style As System.Drawing.FontStyle (read only)
  Underline As System.Boolean (read only)
  Unit As System.Drawing.GraphicsUnit (read only)
  ' Methods
  Clone() As Object
  Dispose()
  Equals(obj As Object) As Boolean
  FromHdc(hdc As IntPtr) As Font
  FromHfont(hfont As IntPtr) As Font
  FromLogFont(lf As Object [,hdc As IntPtr] ) As Font
```

```
GetHashCode() As Int32
GetHeight( [graphics As Graphics] ) As Single
GetHeight(dpi As Single) As Single
ToHfont() As IntPtr
ToLogFont(logFont As Object [,graphics As Graphics])
ToString() As String
```


FontConverter Class

Provides functionality to convert a font from one type to another. Access this class through the TypeDescriptor object. Found as System.Drawing.**FontConverter**.

FontFamily Class

Holds a grouping of similar fonts that share a basic design. This class is not inheritable. Found as System.Drawing.**FontFamily**.

Graphics Class

Provides a representation of a GDI+ drawing surface to draw graphic objects on the display. Each instance of a Graphics object is linked with a specific device context.

Inheritance—Object.MarshalByRefObject.Graphics

```
public class System.Drawing.Graphics
  ' Properties
  Clip As System.Drawing.Region
  ClipBounds As System.Drawing.RectangleF (read only)
  CompositingMode As
    System.Drawing.Drawing2D.CompositingMode
  CompositingQuality As
    System.Drawing.Drawing2D.CompositingQuality
  DpiX As System.Single (read only)
  DpiY As System.Single (read only)
  InterpolationMode As
    System.Drawing.Drawing2D.InterpolationMode
```

```
  IsClipEmpty As System.Boolean (read only)
  IsVisibleClipEmpty As System.Boolean (read only)
  PageScale As System.Single
  PageUnit As System.Drawing.GraphicsUnit
  PixelOffsetMode As
    System.Drawing.Drawing2D.PixelOffsetMode
  RenderingOrigin As System.Drawing.Point
  SmoothingMode As System.Drawing.Drawing2D.SmoothingMode
  TextContrast As System.Int32
  TextRenderingHint As
    System.Drawing.Text.TextRenderingHint
  Transform As System.Drawing.Drawing2D.Matrix
  VisibleClipBounds As
    System.Drawing.RectangleF (read only)
  ' Methods
  AddMetafileComment(data As Byte())
  BeginContainer() As GraphicsContainer
  TranslateTransform(dx As Single, dy As Single)
```

GraphicsContainer Class

Holds the internal data of a container created using the BeginContainer() and EndContainer() methods of a Graphics object. Found as System.Drawing.Drawing2D.**GraphicsContainer**.

GraphicsPath Class

Provides a representation of a path made up of connected lines, curves, and geometric objects.

Inheritance—Object.MarshalByRefObject. GraphicsPath

```
public class System.Drawing.Drawing2D.GraphicsPath
   ' Constructors
   GraphicsPath( [fillMode As FillMode] )
   GraphicsPath(pts As PointF(), types As Byte()
     [,fillMode As FillMode])
   GraphicsPath(pts As Point(), types As Byte()
     [,fillMode As FillMode])
   ' Properties
```

```
FillMode As System.Drawing.Drawing2D.FillMode
PathData As System.Drawing.Drawing2D.PathData (read only)
PathPoints As System.Drawing.PointF() (read only)
PathTypes As System.Byte() (read only)
PointCount As System.Int32 (read only)
' Methods
AddArc(x As Int32, y As Int32, width As Int32,
  height As Int32, startAngle As Single,
  sweepAngle As Single)
AddArc(rect As Rectangle, startAngle As Single,
  sweepAngle As Single)
AddArc(x As Single, y As Single, width As Single,
  height As Single, startAngle As Single,
  sweepAngle As Single)
AddArc(rect As RectangleF, startAngle As Single,
  sweepAngle As Single)
AddBezier(x1 As Single, y1 As Single, x2 As Single,
  y2 As Single, x3 As Single, y3 As Single,
  x4 As Single, y4 As Single)
AddBezier(pt1 As PointF, pt2 As PointF, pt3 As PointF,
  pt4 As PointF)
AddBezier(pt1 As Point, pt2 As Point, pt3 As Point,
  pt4 As Point)
AddBezier(x1 As Int32, y1 As Int32, x2 As Int32,
  y2 As Int32, x3 As Int32, y3 As Int32, x4 As Int32,
  y4 As Int32)
AddBeziers(points As PointF())
AddBeziers(points As Point())
AddClosedCurve(points As Point() [,tension As Single])
AddClosedCurve(points As PointF() [,tension As Single])
AddCurve(points As Point() [,tension As Single])
AddCurve(points As PointF() [,tension As Single])
AddCurve(points As Point(), offset As Int32,
  numberOfSegments As Int32, tension As Single)
AddCurve(points As PointF(), offset As Int32,
  numberOfSegments As Int32, tension As Single)
AddEllipse(rect As Rectangle)
AddEllipse(rect As RectangleF)
AddEllipse(x As Int32, y As Int32, width As Int32,
  height As Int32)
AddEllipse(x As Single, y As Single, width As Single,
  height As Single)
AddLine(pt1 As Point, pt2 As Point)
AddLine(pt1 As PointF, pt2 As PointF)
AddLine(x1 As Int32, y1 As Int32, x2 As Int32,
  y2 As Int32)
AddLine(x1 As Single, y1 As Single, x2 As Single,
  y2 As Single)
AddLines(points As Point())
AddLines(points As PointF())
```

3

```
AddPath(addingPath As GraphicsPath, connect As Boolean)
AddPie(rect As Rectangle, startAngle As Single,
  sweepAngle As Single)
AddPie(x As Int32, y As Int32, width As Int32,
  height As Int32, startAngle As Single,
  sweepAngle As Single)
AddPie(x As Single, y As Single, width As Single,
  height As Single, startAngle As Single,
  sweepAngle As Single)
AddPolygon(points As Point())
AddPolygon(points As PointF())
AddRectangle(rect As Rectangle)
AddRectangle(rect As RectangleF)
AddRectangles(rects As Rectangle())
AddRectangles(rects As RectangleF())
AddString(s As String, family As FontFamily, style As
  Int32, emSize As Single, origin As PointF,
  format As StringFormat)
AddString(s As String, family As FontFamily, style As
  Int32, emSize As Single, origin As Point,
  format As StringFormat)
AddString(s As String, family As FontFamily, style As
  Int32, emSize As Single, layoutRect As Rectangle,
  format As StringFormat)
AddString(s As String, family As FontFamily, style As
  Int32, emSize As Single, layoutRect As RectangleF,
  format As StringFormat)
ClearMarkers()
Clone() As Object
CloseAllFigures()
CloseFigure()
Dispose()
Flatten( [matrix As Matrix [,flatness As Single] )
GetBounds( [matrix As Matrix [,pen As Pen]] )
  As RectangleF
GetLastPoint() As PointF
IsOutlineVisible(x As Int32, y As Int32, pen As Pen)
  As Boolean
IsOutlineVisible(pt As Point, pen As Pen,
  graphics As Graphics) As Boolean
IsOutlineVisible(x As Int32, y As Int32, pen As Pen,
  graphics As Graphics) As Boolean
IsOutlineVisible(x As Single, y As Single, pen As Pen)
  As Boolean
IsOutlineVisible(point As PointF, pen As Pen) As Boolean
IsOutlineVisible(pt As PointF, pen As Pen,
  graphics As Graphics) As Boolean
IsOutlineVisible(x As Single, y As Single, pen As Pen,
  graphics As Graphics) As Boolean
```

```
IsOutlineVisible(point As Point, pen As Pen) As Boolean
IsVisible(x As Single, y As Single) As Boolean
IsVisible(point As PointF) As Boolean
IsVisible(pt As PointF, graphics As Graphics) As Boolean
IsVisible(x As Int32, y As Int32) As Boolean
IsVisible(pt As Point, graphics As Graphics) As Boolean
IsVisible(x As Single, y As Single, graphics As Graphics)
  As Boolean
IsVisible(point As Point) As Boolean
IsVisible(x As Int32, y As Int32, graphics As Graphics)
  As Boolean
Reset()
Reverse()
SetMarkers()
StartFigure()
Transform(matrix As Matrix)
Warp(destPoints As PointF(), srcRect As RectangleF
  [,matrix As Matrix [,warpMode As WarpMode
  [,flatness As Single]]])
Widen(pen As Pen [,matrix As Matrix
  [,flatness As Single]])
```


GraphicsPathIterator Class

Provides functionality to step through the subpaths of a GraphicsPath object and test each subpath type. The properties Count and SubpathCount and methods NewMarker(), NextPathType(), NextSubpath(), and Rewind() are used to navigate the subpath list. This class is not inheritable. Found as System.Drawing.Drawing2D.**GraphicsPathIterator**.

GraphicsState Class

Holds the current state of the Graphics object. This object is automatically created by a Graphics object and returned when the BeginContainer() method is called. Found as System.Drawing .Drawing2D.**GraphicsState**.

HatchBrush Class

Provides a representation of a hatched brush used to fill rectangular outlines with the settings found in the properties HatchStyle, ForegroundColor, and BackgroundColor. Found as System.Drawing.Drawing2D.**HatchBrush**.

Icon Class

Holds a Windows icon as a small bitmap with transparency capabilities.

Inheritance—Object.MarshalByRefObject.Icon

```
public class System.Drawing.Icon
  ' Constructors
  Icon(fileName As String)
  Icon(stream As Stream)
  Icon(original As Icon, size As Size)
  Icon(original As Icon, width As Int32, height As Int32)
  Icon(stream As Stream, width As Int32, height As Int32)
  Icon(type As Type, resource As String)
  ' Properties
  Handle As System.IntPtr (read only)
  Height As System.Int32 (read only)
  Size As System.Drawing.Size (read only)
  Width As System.Int32 (read only)
  ' Methods
  Clone() As Object
  Dispose()
  FromHandle(handle As IntPtr) As Icon
  Save(outputStream As Stream)
  ToBitmap() As Bitmap
  ToString() As String
```

IconConverter Class

Provides conversion for icons from one data type to another. Retrieve an instance of this class from the TypeDescriptor object. Found as System.Drawing.**IconConverter**.

Image Class

Provides an abstract foundation class for the Bitmap, Icon, and Metafile child classes.

3

Inheritance—Object.MarshalByRefObject.Image

```
public class System.Drawing.Image
  ' Properties
  Flags As System.Int32 (read only)
  FrameDimensionsList As System.Guid() (read only)
  Height As System.Int32 (read only)
  HorizontalResolution As System.Single (read only)
  Palette As System.Drawing.Imaging.ColorPalette
  PhysicalDimension As System.Drawing.SizeF (read only)
  PixelFormat As
    System.Drawing.Imaging.PixelFormat (read only)
  PropertyIdList As System.Int32() (read only)
  PropertyItems As
    System.Drawing.Imaging.PropertyItem() (read only)
  RawFormat As
    System.Drawing.Imaging.ImageFormat (read only)
  Size As System.Drawing.Size (read only)
  VerticalResolution As System.Single (read only)
  Width As System.Int32 (read only)
  ' Methods
  Clone() As Object
  Dispose()
  FromFile(filename As String
    [,useEmbeddedColorManagement As Boolean]) As Image
  FromHbitmap(hbitmap As IntPtr [,hpalette As IntPtr])
    As Bitmap
  FromStream(stream As Stream
    [,useEmbeddedColorManagement As Boolean]) As Image
  GetBounds(pageUnit As GraphicsUnit&) As RectangleF
  GetEncoderParameterList(encoder As Guid) As
    EncoderParameters
  GetFrameCount(dimension As FrameDimension) As Int32
  GetPixelFormatSize(pixfmt As PixelFormat) As Int32
  GetPropertyItem(propid As Int32) As PropertyItem
  GetThumbnailImage(thumbWidth As Int32, thumbHeight As
    Int32, callback As GetThumbnailImageAbort,
    callbackData As IntPtr) As Image
  IsAlphaPixelFormat(pixfmt As PixelFormat) As Boolean
  IsCanonicalPixelFormat(pixfmt As PixelFormat) As Boolean
  IsExtendedPixelFormat(pixfmt As PixelFormat) As Boolean
  RemovePropertyItem(propid As Int32)
  RotateFlip(rotateFlipType As RotateFlipType)
```

```
Save(filename As String [, format As ImageFormat])
Save(stream As Stream, format As ImageFormat)
Save(stream As Stream, encoder As ImageCodecInfo,
  encoderParams As EncoderParameters)
Save(filename As String, encoder As ImageCodecInfo,
  encoderParams As EncoderParameters)
SaveAdd(encoderParams As EncoderParameters)
SaveAdd(image As Image, encoderParams As
  EncoderParameters)
SelectActiveFrame(dimension As FrameDimension,
  frameIndex As Int32) As Int32
SetPropertyItem(propitem As PropertyItem)
```

ImageAnimator Class

Provides animation functionality for multiframe images and includes access to the animation thread. Found as System.Drawing .**ImageAnimator**.

ImageAttributes Class

Holds the settings that determine how colors of an image are modified during rendering, including gamma correction, color remapping, palette adjustment, and so on. This class is not inheritable. Found as System.Drawing.Imaging.**ImageAttributes**.

ImageCodecInfo Class

Holds information about the codecs currently installed and available on the system. Properties describing the codecs include Clsid, CodecName, DllName, FilenameExtension, Flags, FormatDescription, FormatID, MimeType, SignatureMasks,

SignaturePatterns, and Version. Found as System.Drawing .Imaging.**ImageCodecInfo**.

ImageConverter Class

Provides conversion between Image objects and other data types. Retrieve an instance of this class from the TypeDescriptor object. Found as System.Drawing.**ImageConverter**.

ImageFormat Class

Holds the format of the Image object. This class is not inheritable.

Inheritance—Object.ImageFormat

```
public class System.Drawing.Imaging.ImageFormat
  ' Constructors
  ImageFormat(guid As Guid)
  ' Properties
  Guid As System.Guid (read only)
  Bmp As System.Drawing.Imaging.ImageFormat (read only)
  ' Other properties available as
  ' System.Drawing.Imaging.ImageFormat:
  Emf, Exif, Gif, Icon, Jpeg, MemoryBmp, Png, Tiff, Wmf
  ' Methods
  Equals(o As Object) As Boolean
  GetHashCode() As Int32
  ToString() As String
```

ImageFormatConverter Class

Provides functionality to convert colors to other data types. Use the TypeDescriptor object to obtain an instance of this class. Found as System.Drawing.**ImageFormatConverter**.

InstalledFontCollection Class

Holds a reference collection of all the fonts installed on the system at the time an instance is created. This class is not inheritable. Found as System.Drawing.Text.**InstalledFontCollection**.

LinearGradientBrush Class

Provides a Brush object with either a two-color gradient or a custom multicolor gradient. The gradient pattern can show progress as a line, sigma bell shape, triangle, or a custom shape defined with the Blend class. Found as System.Drawing .Drawing2D.**LinearGradientBrush**.

Margins Class

Holds the margins for the printing page in the properties Top, Bottom, Left, and Right. Values are stored in hundredths of an inch. Used with the PageSettings and PrintController classes. Found as System.Drawing.Printing.**Margins**.

MarginsConverter Class

Provides functionality to convert Margin objects to other data types. Use the TypeDescriptor object to obtain an instance of this class. Found as System.Drawing.Printing.**MarginsConverter**.

Matrix Class

Holds a 3 × 3 affine matrix that is used for geometric transformations. In the matrix, the first column represents x, the second y, and the third w. This class is not inheritable.

Inheritance—Object.MarshalByRefObject.Matrix

```
public class System.Drawing.Drawing2D.Matrix
  ' Constructors
  Matrix( [rect As Rectangle, plgpts As Point()] )
  Matrix(rect As RectangleF, plgpts As PointF())
  Matrix(m11 As Single, m12 As Single, m21 As Single,
    m22 As Single, dx As Single, dy As Single)
  ' Properties
  Elements As System.Single() (read only)
  IsIdentity As System.Boolean (read only)
  IsInvertible As System.Boolean (read only)
  OffsetX As System.Single (read only)
  OffsetY As System.Single (read only)
  ' Methods
  Clone() As Matrix
  Dispose()
  Equals(obj As Object) As Boolean
  GetHashCode() As Int32
  Invert()
  Multiply(matrix As Matrix [,order As MatrixOrder])
  Reset()
  Rotate(angle As Single [,order As MatrixOrder])
  RotateAt(angle As Single, point As PointF
    [,order As MatrixOrder])
  Scale(scaleX As Single, scaleY As Single
    [,order As MatrixOrder])
  Shear(shearX As Single, shearY As Single
    [,order As MatrixOrder])
  TransformPoints(pts As PointF())
  TransformPoints(pts As Point())
  TransformVectors(pts As Point())
  TransformVectors(pts As PointF())
  Translate(offsetX As Single, offsetY As Single
    [,order As MatrixOrder])
  VectorTransformPoints(pts As Point())
```

Metafile Class

Holds a graphics metafile, which is a series of graphic instructions (draw rectangle, fill circle, etc.) that can be recorded and played back. This class is not inheritable.

Inheritance—Object.MarshalByRefObject.Image.Metafile

```
public class System.Drawing.Imaging.Metafile
  ' Constructors
  Metafile(fileName As String [,referenceHdc As IntPtr
    [,frameRect As RectangleF, frameUnit As
    MetafileFrameUnit, type As EmfType,
    description As String]])
  Metafile(fileName As String, referenceHdc As IntPtr,
    frameRect As Rectangle, frameUnit As MetafileFrameUnit,
    type As EmfType [,description As String])
  Metafile(fileName As String, referenceHdc As IntPtr,
    frameRect As RectangleF [, frameUnit As
    MetafileFrameUnit, desc As String])
  Metafile(fileName As String, referenceHdc As IntPtr,
    frameRect As RectangleF, frameUnit As MetafileFrameUnit
    [, type As EmfType])
  Metafile(fileName As String, referenceHdc As IntPtr,
    type As EmfType [,description As String])
  Metafile(henhmetafile As IntPtr, deleteEmf As Boolean)
  Metafile(hmetafile As IntPtr, wmfHeader As
    WmfPlaceableFileHeader [,deleteWmf As Boolean])
  Metafile(referenceHdc As IntPtr, emfType As EmfType
    [, description As String])
  Metafile(referenceHdc As IntPtr, frameRect As Rectangle
    [,frameUnit As MetafileFrameUnit [,type As EmfType
    [,desc As String]]])
  Metafile(referenceHdc As IntPtr, frameRect As RectangleF
    [,frameUnit As MetafileFrameUnit [,type As EmfType
    [,description As String]]])
  Metafile(stream As Stream [,referenceHdc As IntPtr
    [,frameRect As Rectangle [,frameUnit As
    MetafileFrameUnit [,type As EmfType
    [,description As String]]]]])
  Metafile(stream As Stream, referenceHdc As IntPtr,
    frameRect As RectangleF [,frameUnit As
    MetafileFrameUnit [,type As EmfType
    [,description As String]]])
```

```
Metafile(stream As Stream, referenceHdc As IntPtr,
  type As EmfType [,description As String])
Metafile(fileName As String, referenceHdc As IntPtr,
  frameRect As Rectangle  [,frameUnit As
  MetafileFrameUnit [,description As String]])
' Methods
GetHenhmetafile() As IntPtr
GetMetafileHeader(fileName As String) As MetafileHeader
GetMetafileHeader(henhmetafile As IntPtr) As
  MetafileHeader
GetMetafileHeader(hmetafile As IntPtr,
  wmfHeader As WmfPlaceableFileHeader) As MetafileHeader
GetMetafileHeader() As MetafileHeader
GetMetafileHeader(stream As Stream) As MetafileHeader
PlayRecord(recordType As EmfPlusRecordType,
  flags As Int32, dataSize As Int32, data As Byte())
```


MetafileHeader Class

Holds the settings of a metafile. Properties that hold the settings include Bounds, DpiX, DpiY, EmfPlusHeaderSize, LogicalDpiX, LogicalDpiY, MetafileSize, Type, Version, and WmfHeader. This class is not inheritable. Found as System.Drawing.Imaging .**MetafileHeader**.

MetaHeader Class

Holds information about the metaheader in properties such as HeaderSize, MaxRecord, NoObjects, NoParamters, Size, Type, and Version. This class is not inheritable. Found as System .Drawing.Imaging.**MetaHeader**.

PageSettings Class

Holds the settings for printing a single-page document.

Inheritance—Object.PageSettings

```
public class System.Drawing.Printing.PageSettings
  ' Constructors
  PageSettings()
  PageSettings(printerSettings As PrinterSettings)
  ' Properties
  Bounds As System.Drawing.Rectangle (read only)
  Color As System.Boolean
  Landscape As System.Boolean
  Margins As System.Drawing.Printing.Margins
  PaperSize As System.Drawing.Printing.PaperSize
  PaperSource As System.Drawing.Printing.PaperSource
  PrinterResolution As
    System.Drawing.Printing.PrinterResolution
  PrinterSettings As
    System.Drawing.Printing.PrinterSettings
  ' Methods
  Clone() As Object
  CopyToHdevmode(hdevmode As IntPtr)
  SetHdevmode(hdevmode As IntPtr)
  ToString() As String
```

PaperSize Class

Holds information about the size of the current print page in properties such as Height, Kind, PaperName, and Width. Kind may be set to one of the PaperKind values: A2, A3, A3Extra, A3ExtraTransverse, A3Rotated, A3Transverse, A4, A4Extra, A4Plus, A4Rotated, A4Small, A4Transverse, A5, A5Extra, A5Rotated, A5Transverse, A6, A6Rotated, APlus, B4, B4 Envelope, B4JisRotated, B5, B5Envelope, B5Extra, B5JisRotated, B5Transverse, B6Envelope, B6Jis, B6JisRotated, BPlus, C3Envelope, C4Envelope, C5Envelope, C65Envelope, C6Envelope, CSheet, Custom, DLEnvelope, DSheet, ESheet, Executive, Folio, GermanLegalFanfold, GermanStandardFanfold, InviteEnvelope, IsoB4, ItalyEnvelope, JapaneseDoublePostcard, JapaneseDoublePostcardRotated, JapaneseEnvelope ChouNumber3, JapaneseEnvelopeChouNumber3Rotated, JapaneseEnvelopeChouNumber4, JapaneseEnvelope ChouNumber4Rotated, JapaneseEnvelopeKakuNumber2, JapaneseEnvelopeKakuNumber2Rotated,

JapaneseEnvelopeKakuNumber3, JapaneseEnvelope KakuNumber3Rotated, JapaneseEnvelopeYouNumber4, JapaneseEnvelopeYouNumber4Rotated, JapanesePostcard, JapanesePostcardRotated, Ledger, Legal, LegalExtra, Letter, LetterExtra, LetterExtraTransverse, LetterPlus, LetterRotated, LetterSmall, LetterTransverse, MonarchEnvelope, Note, Number10Envelope, Number11Envelope, Number12Envelope, Number14Envelope, Number9Envelope, PersonalEnvelope, Prc16K, Prc16KRotated, Prc32K, Prc32KBig, Prc32KBigRotated, Prc32KRotated, PrcEnvelopeNumber1, PrcEnvelopeNumber10, PrcEnvelopeNumber10Rotated, PrcEnvelopeNumber1Rotated, PrcEnvelopeNumber2, PrcEnvelopeNumber2Rotated, PrcEnvelopeNumber3, PrcEnvelopeNumber3Rotated, PrcEnvelopeNumber4, PrcEnvelopeNumber4Rotated, PrcEnvelopeNumber5, PrcEnvelopeNumber5Rotated, PrcEnvelopeNumber6, PrcEnvelopeNumber6Rotated, PrcEnvelopeNumber7, PrcEnvelopeNumber7Rotated, PrcEnvelopeNumber8, PrcEnvelopeNumber8Rotated, PrcEnvelopeNumber9, PrcEnvelopeNumber9Rotated, Quarto, Standard10x11, Standard10x14, Standard11x17, Standard12x11, Standard15x11, Standard9x11, Statement, Tabloid, TabloidExtra, or USStandardFanfold. Found as System.Drawing.Printing.**PaperSize**.

PaperSource Class

Holds the settings that indicate which paper tray will be used through the read-only properties Kind and SourceName. Kind may be set to one of the PaperSourceKind values: AutomaticFeed, Cassette, Custom, Envelope, FormSource, LargeCapacity, LargeFormat, Lower, Manual, ManualFeed, Middle, SmallFormat, TractorFeed, or Upper. Found as System.Drawing.Printing .**PaperSource**.

PathData Class

Holds the actual data that makes up a GraphicsPath object or subpath. This class is not inheritable.

Inheritance—Object.PathData

```
public class System.Drawing.Drawing2D.PathData
  ' Constructors
  PathData()
  ' Properties
  Points As System.Drawing.PointF()
  Types As System.Byte()
```

PathGradientBrush Class

Provides a gradient Brush object that can fill the inside of a GraphicsPath. This class is not inheritable. Found as System.Drawing.Drawing2D.**PathGradientBrush**.

Pen Class

Provides a pen used to draw lines and curves in a specified width and style. The area encapsulated by a pen object can be filled with a number of fill styles including brushes, colors, and textures.

Inheritance—Object.MarshalByRefObject.Pen

```
public class System.Drawing.Pen
  ' Constructors
  Pen(brush As Brush)
  Pen(color As Color)
  Pen(color As Color, width As Single)
  Pen(brush As Brush, width As Single)
  ' Properties
  Alignment As System.Drawing.Drawing2D.PenAlignment
  Brush As System.Drawing.Brush
  Color As System.Drawing.Color
  CompoundArray As System.Single()
  CustomEndCap As System.Drawing.Drawing2D.CustomLineCap
  CustomStartCap As System.Drawing.Drawing2D.CustomLineCap
  DashCap As System.Drawing.Drawing2D.DashCap
  DashOffset As System.Single
  DashPattern As System.Single()
  DashStyle As System.Drawing.Drawing2D.DashStyle
```

```
EndCap As System.Drawing.Drawing2D.LineCap
LineJoin As System.Drawing.Drawing2D.LineJoin
MiterLimit As System.Single
PenType As System.Drawing.Drawing2D.PenType (read only)
StartCap As System.Drawing.Drawing2D.LineCap
Transform As System.Drawing.Drawing2D.Matrix
Width As System.Single
' Methods
Clone() As Object
Dispose()
MultiplyTransform(matrix As Matrix
  [,order As MatrixOrder])
ResetTransform()
RotateTransform(angle As Single [,order As MatrixOrder])
ScaleTransform(sx As Single, sy As Single
  [,order As MatrixOrder])
SetLineCap(startCap As LineCap, endCap As LineCap,
  dashCap As DashCap)
TranslateTransform(dx As Single, dy As Single
  [,order As MatrixOrder])
```


Pens Class

Provides system pens for all common colors as Pen objects. This class is not inheritable.

Inheritance—Object.Pens

```
public class System.Drawing.Pens
  ' Properties
  AliceBlue As System.Drawing.Pen (read only)
  ' Also available as System.Drawing.Pen colors,
  ' see the color list of the Brushes class.
```

PointConverter Class

Provides functionality to convert Point objects to other data types. Use the TypeDescriptor object to obtain an instance of this class. Found as System.Drawing.**PointConverter**.

PreviewPageInfo Class

Holds the settings to preview a single page and used primarily by the PreviewPrintController class. These settings are held in the Image and PhysicalSize properties, which are the same parameters passed to the constructor. This class is not inheritable. Found as System.Drawing.Printing.**PreviewPageInfo**.

PreviewPrintController Class

Provides a preview window that displays the print pages on the screen one at a time.

Inheritance—Object.PrintController. PreviewPrintController

```
public class System.Drawing.Printing.PreviewPrintController
  ' Constructors
  PreviewPrintController()
  ' Properties
  UseAntiAlias As System.Boolean
  ' Methods
  GetPreviewPageInfo() As PreviewPageInfo()
  OnEndPage(document As PrintDocument,
    e As PrintPageEventArgs)
  OnEndPrint(document As PrintDocument,
    e As PrintEventArgs)
  OnStartPage(document As PrintDocument,
    e As PrintPageEventArgs) As Graphics
  OnStartPrint(document As PrintDocument,
    e As PrintEventArgs)
```

PrintController Class

Provides a foundation class that determines how a document is printed. Children of this class include PreviewPrintController, StandardPrintController, and PrintControllerWithStatusDialog.

Inheritance—Object.PrintController

```
public class System.Drawing.Printing.PrintController
  ' Constructors
  PrintController()
  ' Methods
  OnEndPage(document As PrintDocument,
    e As PrintPageEventArgs)
  OnEndPrint(document As PrintDocument,
    e As PrintEventArgs)
  OnStartPage(document As PrintDocument,
    e As PrintPageEventArgs) As Graphics
  OnStartPrint(document As PrintDocument,
    e As PrintEventArgs)
```


PrintDocument Class

Provides a reusable object that allows content to be sent to the printer. This object sits at the core of most application printing implementations. To print a document, a new PrintDocument object should be created, its properties configured, and the Print() method called to send the contents to the printer.

Inheritance—Object.MarshalByRefObject.Component.PrintDocument

```
public class System.Drawing.Printing.PrintDocument
  ' Constructors
  PrintDocument()
  ' Properties
  DefaultPageSettings As
    System.Drawing.Printing.PageSettings
  DocumentName As System.String
  PrintController As
    System.Drawing.Printing.PrintController
  PrinterSettings As
    System.Drawing.Printing.PrinterSettings
  ' Methods
  Print()
  ToString() As String
  ' Events
  BeginPrint As System.Drawing.Printing.PrintEventHandler
  EndPrint As System.Drawing.Printing.PrintEventHandler
```

```
  PrintPage As
    System.Drawing.Printing.PrintPageEventHandler
  QueryPageSettings As
    System.Drawing.Printing.QueryPageSettingsEventHandler
```

PrinterResolution Class

Holds the resolution of the current printer in the properties Kind, X, and Y. Kind may be set to one of the PrintResolutionKind values: Draft, Low, Medium, High, and Custom. If set to Custom, the X and Y properties are used to determine, in dots per inch, the horizontal and vertical resolutions, respectively. Found as System.Drawing .Printing.**PrinterResolution**.

PrinterSettings Class

Holds information about the printer, including which printer to use and how a document is printed.

Inheritance—Object.PrinterSettings

```
public class System.Drawing.Printing.PrinterSettings
  ' Constructors
  PrinterSettings()
  ' Properties
  CanDuplex As System.Boolean (read only)
  Collate As System.Boolean
  Copies As System.Int16
  DefaultPageSettings As
    System.Drawing.Printing.PageSettings (read only)
  Duplex As System.Drawing.Printing.Duplex
  FromPage As System.Int32
  InstalledPrinters As
    System.Drawing.Printing.PrinterSettings+
    StringCollection (read only)
  IsDefaultPrinter As System.Boolean (read only)
  IsPlotter As System.Boolean (read only)
  IsValid As System.Boolean (read only)
  LandscapeAngle As System.Int32 (read only)
  MaximumCopies As System.Int32 (read only)
```

```
MaximumPage As System.Int32
MinimumPage As System.Int32
PaperSizes As
  System.Drawing.Printing.PrinterSettings+
  PaperSizeCollection (read only)
PaperSources As
  System.Drawing.Printing.PrinterSettings+
  PaperSourceCollection (read only)
PrinterName As System.String
PrinterResolutions As
  System.Drawing.Printing.PrinterSettings+
  PrinterResolutionCollection (read only)
PrintRange As System.Drawing.Printing.PrintRange
PrintToFile As System.Boolean
SupportsColor As System.Boolean (read only)
ToPage As System.Int32
' Methods
Clone() As Object
CreateMeasurementGraphics() As Graphics
GetHdevmode(pageSettings As PageSettings) As IntPtr
GetHdevmode() As IntPtr
GetHdevmodeInternal() As IntPtr
GetHdevnames() As IntPtr
SetHdevmode(hdevmode As IntPtr)
SetHdevnames(hdevnames As IntPtr)
ToString() As String
```

PrinterUnitConvert Class

Used by the system to provide conversion capabilities when interoperating with the printing functions of the Win32 API. This class may not be created directly and is not inheritable. Found as System.Drawing.Printing.**PrinterUnitConvert**.

PrintingPermission Class

Specifies the permissions that restrict access to the printer. This class is not inheritable. Found as System.Drawing.Printing .**PrintingPermission**.

PrintingPermissionAttribute Class

Holds the actual printing permission attributes. This class is not inheritable. Found as System.Drawing.Printing .**PrintingPermissionAttribute**.

PrivateFontCollection Class

A collection of private fonts that may be installed without replacing system fonts of the same name. Perfect for temporary use by applications such as printed form layout that require known font widths. Found as System.Drawing.Text.**PrivateFontCollection**.

PropertyItem Class

Holds a metadata property that will be included in the image file to which it is linked. This class is not inheritable.

Inheritance—Object.PropertyItem

```
public class System.Drawing.Imaging.PropertyItem
  ' Properties
  Id As System.Int32
  Len As System.Int32
  Type As System.Int16
  Value As System.Byte()
```

PropertyValueUIItem Class

Provides information related to the user interface for a property displayed in the Properties window of the Visual Studio environment. This class contains data on the invocation handler, the ToolTip, and the icon associated with the property. Found as System.Drawing.Design.**PropertyValueUIItem**.

RectangleConverter Class

Provides conversion between Rectangle objects and other data types. Retrieve an instance of this class from the TypeDescriptor object. Found as System.Drawing.**RectangleConverter**.

Region Class

Provides a representation of the inside of a region that consists of rectangles and paths specified in world coordinates. A Brush object may be used to fill the area specified by a Region object.

Inheritance—Object.MarshalByRefObject.Region

```
public class System.Drawing.Region
  ' Constructors
  Region()
  Region(rect As Rectangle)
  Region(rect As RectangleF)
  Region(rgnData As RegionData)
  Region(path As GraphicsPath)
  ' Methods
  Clone() As Region
  Complement(path As GraphicsPath)
  Complement(region As Region)
  Complement(rect As RectangleF)
  Complement(rect As Rectangle)
  Dispose()
  Equals(region As Region, g As Graphics) As Boolean
  Exclude(rect As Rectangle)
  Exclude(rect As RectangleF)
  Exclude(region As Region)
  Exclude(path As GraphicsPath)
  FromHrgn(hrgn As IntPtr) As Region
  GetBounds(g As Graphics) As RectangleF
  GetHrgn(g As Graphics) As IntPtr
  GetRegionData() As RegionData
  GetRegionScans(matrix As Matrix) As RectangleF()
  Intersect(region As Region)
  Intersect(rect As Rectangle)
  Intersect(rect As RectangleF)
  Intersect(path As GraphicsPath)
  IsEmpty(g As Graphics) As Boolean
  IsInfinite(g As Graphics) As Boolean
```

```
IsVisible(x As Single, y As Single, g As Graphics)
  As Boolean
IsVisible(rect As RectangleF, g As Graphics) As Boolean
IsVisible(x As Int32, y As Int32, g As Graphics)
  As Boolean
IsVisible(point As Point) As Boolean
IsVisible(x As Single, y As Single, width As Single,
  height As Single, g As Graphics) As Boolean
IsVisible(point As PointF, g As Graphics) As Boolean
IsVisible(x As Single, y As Single, width As Single,
  height As Single) As Boolean
IsVisible(rect As RectangleF) As Boolean
IsVisible(point As PointF) As Boolean
IsVisible(rect As Rectangle) As Boolean
IsVisible(x As Int32, y As Int32, width As Int32,
  height As Int32, g As Graphics) As Boolean
IsVisible(rect As Rectangle, g As Graphics) As Boolean
IsVisible(point As Point, g As Graphics) As Boolean
IsVisible(x As Single, y As Single) As Boolean
IsVisible(x As Int32, y As Int32, width As Int32,
  height As Int32) As Boolean
MakeEmpty()
MakeInfinite()
Transform(matrix As Matrix)
Translate(dx As Single, dy As Single)
Translate(dx As Int32, dy As Int32)
Union(path As GraphicsPath)
Union(region As Region)
Union(rect As RectangleF)
Union(rect As Rectangle)
Xor(path As GraphicsPath)
Xor(region As Region)
Xor(rect As RectangleF)
Xor(rect As Rectangle)
```

RegionData Class

Holds the Region object data in a Byte array referenced through the Data property. Found as System.Drawing.Drawing2D.**RegionData**.

SizeConverter Class

Provides conversion between Size objects and other data types. Retrieve an instance of this class from the TypeDescriptor object. Found as System.Drawing.**SizeConverter**.

SolidBrush Class

Provides a brush that is created from a single solid color. Simply pass the constructor a Color data type and the brush will be created from it. The color of a SolidBrush is available through the Color property. This class is not inheritable. Found as System.Drawing.**SolidBrush**.

StandardPrintController Class

Provides the setting that determines the printer controller that will be used to send content to the printer. An instance of this class is used by the PrintDocument class.

Inheritance—Object.PrintController.StandardPrintController

```
public class
  System.Drawing.Printing.StandardPrintController
  ' Constructors
  StandardPrintController()
  ' Methods
  OnEndPage(document As PrintDocument,
    e As PrintPageEventArgs)
  OnEndPrint(document As PrintDocument,
    e As PrintEventArgs)
```

```
OnStartPage(document As PrintDocument,
  e As PrintPageEventArgs) As Graphics
OnStartPrint(document As PrintDocument,
  e As PrintEventArgs)
```

StringFormat Class

Holds text drawing settings such as alignment, line spacing, hotkey prefix display, ellipses insertion, national digit substitution, and OpenType features.

Inheritance—Object.MarshalByRefObject.StringFormat

```
public class System.Drawing.StringFormat
  ' Constructors
  StringFormat(format As StringFormat)
  StringFormat( [options As StringFormatFlags
    [,language As Int32]] )
  ' Properties
  Alignment As System.Drawing.StringAlignment
  DigitSubstitutionLanguage As System.Int32 (read only)
  DigitSubstitutionMethod As
    System.Drawing.StringDigitSubstitute (read only)
  FormatFlags As System.Drawing.StringFormatFlags
  GenericDefault As
    System.Drawing.StringFormat (read only)
  GenericTypographic As
    System.Drawing.StringFormat (read only)
  HotkeyPrefix As System.Drawing.Text.HotkeyPrefix
  LineAlignment As System.Drawing.StringAlignment
  Trimming As System.Drawing.StringTrimming
  ' Methods
  Clone() As Object
  Dispose()
  GetTabStops(firstTabOffset As Single&) As Single()
  SetDigitSubstitution(language As Int32,
    substitute As StringDigitSubstitute)
  SetMeasurableCharacterRanges(ranges As CharacterRange())
  SetTabStops(firstTabOffset As Single, tabStops
    As Single())
  ToString() As String
```

SystemBrushes Class

Holds the system brushes defined as read-only SolidBrush objects.

Inheritance—Object.SystemBrushes

```
public class System.Drawing.SystemBrushes
  ' Properties
  ActiveBorder As System.Drawing.Brush (read only)
  ' Also available as System.Drawing.Brush properties:
  ActiveCaption, ActiveCaptionText, AppWorkspace, Control,
  ControlDark, ControlDarkDark, ControlLight,
  ControlLightLight, ControlText, Desktop, Highlight,
  HighlightText, HotTrack, InactiveBorder, InactiveCaption,
  Info, Menu, ScrollBar, Window, WindowText
  ' Methods
  FromSystemColor(c As Color) As Brush
```

SystemColors Class

Holds the system colors defined as read-only Color objects.

Inheritance—Object.SystemColors

```
public class System.Drawing.SystemColors
  ' Properties
  ActiveBorder As System.Drawing.Color (read only)
  ' Also available as System.Drawing.Color properties:
  ActiveCaption, ActiveCaptionText, AppWorkspace, Control,
  ControlDark, ControlDarkDark, ControlLight,
  ControlLightLight, ControlText, Desktop, GrayText,
  Highlight, HighlightText, HotTrack, InactiveBorder,
  InactiveCaption, InactiveCaptionText, Info, InfoText,
  Menu, MenuText, ScrollBar, Window, WindowFrame,
  WindowText
```

SystemIcons Class

Holds the system icons defined as read-only Icon objects.

Inheritance—Object.SystemIcons

```
public class System.Drawing.SystemIcons
  ' Properties
  Application As System.Drawing.Icon (read only)
  ' Also available as System.Drawing.Icon properties:
  Asterisk, Error, Exclamation, Hand, Information,
  Question, Warning, WinLogo
```

SystemPens Class

Holds the system pens defined as read-only Pen objects that contain a system color and a width of 1.

Inheritance—Object.SystemPens

```
public class System.Drawing.SystemPens
  ' Properties
  ActiveCaptionText As System.Drawing.Pen (read only)
  ' Also available as System.Drawing.Pen properties:
  Control, ControlDark, ControlDarkDark, ControlLight,
  ControlLightLight, ControlText, GrayText, Highlight,
  HighlightText, InactiveCaptionText, InfoText, MenuText,
  WindowFrame, WindowText
  ' Methods
  FromSystemColor(c As Color) As Pen
```

TextureBrush Class

Provides a texture Brush object defined by an Image object passed as an argument. This class is not inheritable.

Inheritance—Object.MarshalByRefObject.Brush.TextureBrush

```
public class System.Drawing.TextureBrush
  ' Constructors
  TextureBrush(bitmap As Image)
  TextureBrush(image As Image, dstRect As Rectangle
    [,imageAttr As ImageAttributes] )
  TextureBrush(image As Image, wrapMode As WrapMode
    [,dstRect As Rectangle])
```

```
TextureBrush(image As Image, dstRect As RectangleF
  [,imageAttr As ImageAttributes] )
TextureBrush(image As Image, wrapMode As WrapMode,
  dstRect As RectangleF)
' Properties
Image As System.Drawing.Image (read only)
Transform As System.Drawing.Drawing2D.Matrix
WrapMode As System.Drawing.Drawing2D.WrapMode
' Methods
Clone() As Object
MultiplyTransform(matrix As Matrix
  [,order As MatrixOrder])
ResetTransform()
RotateTransform(angle As Single [,order As MatrixOrder])
ScaleTransform(sx As Single, sy As Single
  [,order As MatrixOrder])
TranslateTransform(dx As Single, dy As Single
  [,order As MatrixOrder] )
```


ToolboxBitmapAttribute Class

Holds the image linked with a specified component for display in the Toolbox window of the Visual Studio environment. The attribute represented by this object must include a reference to a small icon and may contain an optional large icon. Found as System.Drawing.**ToolboxBitmapAttribute**.

ToolboxItem Class

Provides a foundation class implementation of a toolbox item that may apply to a single component or encapsulate several. Found as System.Drawing.Design.**ToolboxItem**.

UITypeEditor Class

Provides a foundation class for presenting a user interface (in the Visual Studio environment) to allow editing the values of objects of supported data types. A custom editor would be needed where the single textbox value editor in the Properties window is insufficient to provide the needed editing capabilities. Children of this class include CollectionEditor, FontEditor, ImageEditor, DataBindingCollectionEditor, UrlEditor, DataGridColumnCollectionEditor, RegexTypeEditor, XmlFileEditor, AnchorEditor, FileNameEditor, and FolderNameEditor. Found as System.Drawing.Design.**UITypeEditor**.

WmfPlaceableFileHeader Class

Holds a metafile placeable header with settings available through the properties BboxBottom, BboxLeft, BboxRight, BboxTop, Checksum, Hmf, Inch, Key, and Reserved. This class is not inheritable. Found as System.Drawing.Imaging .**WmfPlaceableFileHeader**.

Chapter 4
Input and Output

There are a number of ways the .NET framework provides for accessing files. Specialized file capabilities are found in the DataSet functionality, object serialization classes, XML library classes, and so on. For traditional file input and output functions, the System.IO classes provide the principal access to file stores.

The three primary types of I/O objects include

- **Text** The TextReader and TextWriter classes perform the highest level of file abstraction for reading, writing, and parsing files stored as a series of characters such as text or INI files.
- **Stream** A stream is used to access individual bytes within a file. Despite the implications given by the name of the class, a stream can be used for random access in both reading and writing operations.
- **Binary** For the lowest level of data, the BinaryReader and BinaryWriter classes give access to binary data such as that used to store images or structured data formats.

Each of these three forms has a number of classes for file access. Additionally, the System.IO classes provide file- and directory-related services such as path string parsing, directory creation and manipulation, and I/O-related event trapping.

The following examples provide simple usage cases of the System.IO classes for reference. Note that because System.IO is not a commonly used assembly, all of the examples have included full class extension (namespace hierarchy) references to instantiate the class objects. This allows you to type the examples from the chapter directory into the VS environment without any confusion (or requiring an Imports statement in the file header). For example, here is an example of addressing the DirectoryInfo class:

```
Dim myNewDir As New System.IO.DirectoryInfo("c:\TestDir")
```

However, for a true programming project, you would likely instead include a reference to the entire class at the opening of your file, such as:

```
Imports System.IO
```

With this reference, the DirectoryInfo class example would be simplified to this:

```
Dim myNewDir As New DirectoryInfo("c:\TestDir")
```

Creating a New Directory

To create a form button that would use the Directory class to generate a new directory, only a single line of code would be necessary:

```
Sub cmdCreateDir1_Click()
  System.IO.Directory.CreateDirectory("c:\TestDir")
End Sub
```

Security authentication is performed each time an abstract method accesses a directory. For multiples uses of a directory, instantiating a DirInfo object can save some of the security overhead to increase performance. To use the DirInfo class to mirror the functionality presented by the CreateDirectory command, simply make a new object instance and use the Create() method like this:

```
Sub cmdCreateDirInfo_Click()
  Dim myNewDir As New System.IO.DirectoryInfo("c:\TestDir")
  myNewDir.Create()
End Sub
```

Be aware that when a new directory is created, by default complete read and write access is granted to all users. Therefore, be sure any folder creation routines fall within the purview of your security policy.

Examining a Path

The Path class included in the System.IO framework makes examining individual parts of a file or directory path a simple operation. The Path class understands all of the particulars of path construction that traditionally made constructing a string-parsing algorithm to disassemble paths so tedious.

The following code provides a simple presentation of disassembling a created path into its component parts. Each part is output to the Console window for examination.

```
Sub cmdExaminePath_Click()
  Dim myPath As String = "c:\WINNT\Win.INI"
  Console.WriteLine( _
    System.IO.Path.GetDirectoryName(myPath))
  Console.WriteLine(System.IO.Path.GetFileName(myPath))
  Console.WriteLine( _
    System.IO.Path.GetFileNameWithoutExtension(myPath))
  Console.WriteLine(System.IO.Path.GetExtension(myPath))
End Sub
```


Writing to a File

The primary use of the System.IO classes will be file access. This example provides code that demonstrates writing to a simple text file. The file is first opened as a FileStream object, and then a StreamWriter object is created to accept the actual output to the file. A sample of text is written into a file called *Test.htm* and then the file is closed.

Note that since input and output of any stream is buffered, the data is not immediately written into the file. Only when the Flush() or Close() methods have been called is the data sent to the disk. By placing the following text inside the Click event of a button, a click will execute this code:

```
Sub cmdWriteStream_Click()
  ' Open file stream to destination file
  Dim myFS As New IO.FileStream("c:\Test.htm", _
    IO.FileMode.OpenOrCreate, IO.FileAccess.Write)
  ' Open StreamWriter to output to stream
  Dim w As New IO.StreamWriter(myfs)
  Dim i As Integer

  ' Write line HTML header line
  w.WriteLine("<HTML><BODY>")
  For i = 0 To 10
    ' Write without a carriage return so next written text
    ' will appear on the same line.
    w.Write("This is line #")
    w.Write(i.ToString())
```

```
    w.WriteLine("<hr>")
  Next
  w.WriteLine("</BODY></HTML>")
  ' Close StreamWriter and stream.
  w.Close()
  myFS.Close()
End Sub
```

Reading a Text File Using a Stream

The sample code below will read and display in the Console window the *Test.htm* file written by the routine in the "Writing to a File" section. Simply place the following code in the Click event of a button and execute it:

```
Sub cmdReadText_Click()
  ' Open file stream to destination file
  Dim myFS As New IO.FileStream("c:\Test.htm", _
    IO.FileMode.Open, IO.FileAccess.Read)
  ' Open StreamReader for input
  Dim r As New IO.StreamReader(myFS)
  Dim i As Integer, myLine As String
  myLine = r.ReadLine
  Do While Not (myLine Is Nothing)
    Console.WriteLine(myLine)
    myLine = r.ReadLine
  Loop
End Sub
```

Processing a String

Input and output aren't limited to file manipulation. The StringReader and StringWriter classes are available to process text contained in a string as if it were located inside a file. This functionality is particularly useful when you need to load parts of a file for later processing or create a single routine to process both a file-based format as well as a memory format (such as processing information from the clipboard).

The following code creates a simple string and then uses the Read() method to load a piece of that string into an array of characters. Those characters are then output into the Console window. Execute the following code to demonstrate the StringReader object:

```
Sub cmdReadChars_Click()
  Dim myStr = _
    "<HTML><BODY>The weather will be warmer.</BODY><HTML>"
  Dim myStream As New System.IO.StringReader(myStr)
  Dim myHeader(6) As Char, i As Integer

  ' Read the stream of 6 characters into the array
  ' starting at array index 0
  myStream.Read(myHeader, 0, 6)
  For i = 0 To 5
    Console.Write(myHeader(i))
  Next
End Sub
```


BinaryReader Class

Provides a way to read information (such as image or structured data) that is stored as a sequence of binary values.

Inheritance—Object.BinaryReader

```
public class System.IO.BinaryReader
  ' Constructors
  BinaryReader(input As Stream [,encoding As Encoding])
  ' Properties
  BaseStream As System.IO.Stream (read only)
  ' Methods
  Close()
  PeekChar() As Int32
  Read() As Int32
  Read(buffer As Byte(), index As Int32, count As Int32)
    As Int32
  Read(buffer As Char(), index As Int32, count As Int32)
    As Int32
  ReadBoolean() As Boolean
  ReadByte() As Byte
  ReadBytes(count As Int32) As Byte()
  ReadChar() As Char
  ReadChars(count As Int32) As Char()
  ReadDecimal() As Decimal
```

```
ReadDouble() As Double
ReadInt16() As Int16
ReadInt32() As Int32
ReadInt64() As Int64
ReadSByte() As SByte
ReadSingle() As Single
ReadString() As String
ReadUInt16() As UInt16
ReadUInt32() As UInt32
ReadUInt64() As UInt64
```

BinaryWriter class

Provides a method of writing information, such as that found in images and structured data, as a sequence of binary values.

Inheritance—Object.BinaryWriter

```
public class System.IO.BinaryWriter
  ' Constructors
  BinaryWriter(output As Stream [,encoding As Encoding])
  ' Properties
  BaseStream As System.IO.Stream (read only)
  ' Methods
  Close()
  Flush()
  Seek(offset As Int32, origin As SeekOrigin) As Int64
  Write(value As SByte)
  Write(value As Boolean)
  Write(value As Byte)
  Write(ch As Char)
  Write(value As Int64)
  Write(value As UInt32)
  Write(value As Int32)
  Write(value As String)
  Write(value As Single)
  Write(value As UInt64)
  Write(value As Double)
  Write(value As UInt16)
  Write(value As Int16)
  Write(value As Decimal)
  Write(buffer As Byte() [,index As Int32, count As Int32])
  Write(chars As Char() [,index As Int32, count As Int32])
```

BufferedStream Class

Provides data buffering for read and write operations performed by the stream objects such as FileStream, MemoryStream, NetworkStream, and CryptoStream.

Inheritance—Object.MarshalByRefObject.Stream.BufferedStream

```
public class System.IO.BufferedStream
  ' Constructors
  BufferedStream(stream As Stream)
  BufferedStream(stream As Stream,bufferSize As Int32)
  ' Properties
  CanRead As System.Boolean (read only)
  CanSeek As System.Boolean (read only)
  CanWrite As System.Boolean (read only)
  Length As System.Int64 (read only)
  Position As System.Int64
  ' Methods
  Close()
  Flush()
  Read(array As Byte(), offset As Int32, count As Int32)
    As Int32
  ReadByte() As Int32
  Seek(offset As Int64, origin As SeekOrigin) As Int64
  SetLength(value As Int64)
  Write(array As Byte(), offset As Int32, count As Int32)
  WriteByte(value As Byte)
```

Directory Class

Static class used to manage directory and subdirectory operations, including moving a directory, deleting a directory, and querying and setting directory properties.

Inheritance—Object.Directory

```
public class System.IO.Directory
  ' Methods
```

4

```
CreateDirectory(path As String) As DirectoryInfo
Delete(path As String [,recursive As Boolean])
Exists(path As String) As Boolean
GetCreationTime(path As String) As DateTime
GetCurrentDirectory() As String
GetDirectories(path As String
  [,searchPattern As String]) As String()
GetDirectoryRoot(path As String) As String
GetFiles(path As String [,searchPattern As String])
  As String()
GetFileSystemEntries(path As String
  [,searchPattern As String]) As String()
GetLastAccessTime(path As String) As DateTime
GetLastWriteTime(path As String) As DateTime
GetLogicalDrives() As String()
GetParent(path As String) As DirectoryInfo
Move(sourceDirName As String, destDirName As String)
SetCreationTime(path As String, creationTime As DateTime)
SetCurrentDirectory(path As String)
SetLastAccessTime(path As String,
  lastAccessTime As DateTime)
SetLastWriteTime(path As String,
  lastWriteTime As DateTime)
```

DirectoryInfo Class

Provides functionality to manage directory operations, including moving a directory, deleting a directory, and querying and setting directory properties. In contrast to the Directory class, which is static, DirectoryInfo provides an instance of a directory access object. Creating an instance provides better performance for multiple directory operations since security checks can be established for the object rather than being reconfirmed with each new call.

Inheritance—Object.MarshalByRefObject. FileSystemInfo.DirectoryInfo

```
public class System.IO.DirectoryInfo
  ' Constructors
  DirectoryInfo(path As String)
  ' Properties
  Exists As System.Boolean (read only)
  Name As System.String (read only)
  Parent As System.IO.DirectoryInfo (read only)
  Root As System.IO.DirectoryInfo (read only)
  ' Methods
  Create()
```

```
CreateSubdirectory(path As String) As DirectoryInfo
Delete()
Delete(recursive As Boolean)
GetDirectories() As DirectoryInfo()
GetDirectories(searchPattern As String)
  As DirectoryInfo()
GetFiles() As FileInfo()
GetFiles(searchPattern As String) As FileInfo()
GetFileSystemInfos( [searchPattern As String] )
  As FileSystemInfo()
MoveTo(destDirName As String)
ToString() As String
```


DirectoryNotFoundException Class

Activated when an attempt is made to access a directory that cannot be found. Note that most of the functionality of this class is inherited from the IOException class. Found as System.IO.**DirectoryNotFoundException**.

EndOfStreamException Class

Activated when an attempt is made to access data beyond the current end of stream. Note that most of the functionality of this class is inherited from the IOException class.

Inheritance—Object.Exception.IOException. EndOfStreamException

```
public class System.IO.EndOfStreamException
  ' Constructors
  EndOfStreamException( [message As String
    [,innerException As Exception]])
```

File Class

Static class that provides file operations such as file copying, file deleting, file moving, and appending a text file to a stream object.

Inheritance—Object.File

```
public class System.IO.File
  ' Methods
  AppendText(path As String) As StreamWriter
  Copy(sourceFileName As String, destFileName As String
    [,overwrite As Boolean])
  Create(path As String [,bufferSize As Int32])
    As FileStream
  CreateText(path As String) As StreamWriter
  Delete(path As String)
  Exists(path As String) As Boolean
  GetAttributes(path As String) As FileAttributes
  GetCreationTime(path As String) As DateTime
  GetLastAccessTime(path As String) As DateTime
  GetLastWriteTime(path As String) As DateTime
  Move(sourceFileName As String, destFileName As String)
  Open(path As String, mode As FileMode
    [,access As FileAccess [,share As FileShare]])
    As FileStream
  OpenRead(path As String) As FileStream
  OpenText(path As String) As StreamReader
  OpenWrite(path As String) As FileStream
  SetAttributes(path As String,
    fileAttributes As FileAttributes)
  SetCreationTime(path As String, creationTime As DateTime)
  SetLastAccessTime(path As String,
    lastAccessTime As DateTime)
  SetLastWriteTime(path As String,
    lastAccessTime As DateTime)
```

FileInfo Class

Provides functionality to manage file operations, including reading a file, moving a file, deleting a file, and querying and setting file properties. In contrast to the File class, which is static, FileInfo provides an instance of a file access object. Creating an instance provides better performance for multiple file operations since security checks can be established for the object rather than being reconfirmed with each new call.

Inheritance—Object.MarshalByRefObject.FileSystemInfo.FileInfo

```
public class System.IO.FileInfo
  ' Constructors
  FileInfo(fileName As String)
  ' Properties
```

```
Directory As System.IO.DirectoryInfo (read only)
DirectoryName As System.String (read only)
Exists As System.Boolean (read only)
Length As System.Int64 (read only)
Name As System.String (read only)
' Methods
AppendText() As StreamWriter
CopyTo(destFileName As String) As FileInfo
CopyTo(destFileName As String, overwrite As Boolean)
  As FileInfo
Create() As FileStream
CreateText() As StreamWriter
Delete()
MoveTo(destFileName As String)
Open(mode As FileMode) As FileStream
Open(mode As FileMode, access As FileAccess)
  As FileStream
Open(mode As FileMode, access As FileAccess,
  share As FileShare) As FileStream
OpenRead() As FileStream
OpenText() As StreamReader
OpenWrite() As FileStream
ToString() As String
```


FileLoadException Class

Activated when the file requested for access is located but cannot be loaded. Found as System.IO.**FileLoadException**.

FileNotFoundException Class

Activated when an attempt is made to access a file that cannot be found. Found as System.IO.**FileNotFoundException**.

FileStream Class

Provides random access read and write operations on information sources as varied as files, pipes, standard input, etc. All FileStream operations are buffered, and either synchronous or asynchronous methods of access may be selected.

Inheritance—Object.MarshalByRefObject.Stream.FileStream

```
public class System.IO.FileStream
  ' Constructors
  FileStream(path As String, mode As FileMode
    [,access As FileAccess [,share As FileShare
    [,bufferSize As Int32 [,useAsync As Boolean]]]])
  FileStream(handle As IntPtr,access As FileAccess
    [,ownsHandle As Boolean [,bufferSize As Int32
    [,isAsync As Boolean]]])
  ' Properties
  CanRead As System.Boolean (read only)
  CanSeek As System.Boolean (read only)
  CanWrite As System.Boolean (read only)
  Handle As System.IntPtr (read only)
  IsAsync As System.Boolean (read only)
  Length As System.Int64 (read only)
  Name As System.String (read only)
  Position As System.Int64
  ' Methods
  BeginRead(array As Byte(), offset As Int32,
    numBytes As Int32, userCallback As AsyncCallback,
    stateObject As Object) As IAsyncResult
  BeginWrite(array As Byte(), offset As Int32,
    numBytes As Int32, userCallback As AsyncCallback,
    stateObject As Object) As IAsyncResult
  Close()
  EndRead(asyncResult As IAsyncResult) As Int32
  EndWrite(asyncResult As IAsyncResult)
  Flush()
  Lock(position As Int64, length As Int64)
  Read(array As Byte(), offset As Int32, count As Int32)
    As Int32
  ReadByte() As Int32
  Seek(offset As Int64, origin As SeekOrigin) As Int64
  SetLength(value As Int64)
  Unlock(position As Int64, length As Int64)
  Write(array As Byte(), offset As Int32, count As Int32)
  WriteByte(value As Byte)
```

FileSystemInfo Class

Provides a foundation class for system information access to classes such as DirectoryInfo and FileInfo.

Inheritance—Object.MarshalByRefObject.FileSystemInfo

```
public class System.IO.FileSystemInfo
  ' Properties
  Attributes As System.IO.FileAttributes
  CreationTime As System.DateTime
  Exists As System.Boolean (read only)
  Extension As System.String (read only)
  FullName As System.String (read only)
  LastAccessTime As System.DateTime
  LastWriteTime As System.DateTime
  Name As System.String (read only)
  ' Methods
  Delete()
  Refresh()
```


FileSystemWatcher Class

Provides functionality to watch the file system and raises events when changes occur in a file or directory. Watches may be specified to raise events when a change is made to the directory itself or to particular files within that directory.

Inheritance—Object.MarshalByRefObject.Component.FileSystemWatcher

```
public class System.IO.FileSystemWatcher
  ' Constructors
  FileSystemWatcher( [path As String [,filter As String]] )
  ' Properties
```

```
EnableRaisingEvents As System.Boolean
Filter As System.String
IncludeSubdirectories As System.Boolean
InternalBufferSize As System.Int32
NotifyFilter As System.IO.NotifyFilters
Path As System.String
Site As System.ComponentModel.ISite
SynchronizingObject As
  System.ComponentModel.ISynchronizeInvoke
' Methods
BeginInit()
Dispose()
EndInit()
WaitForChanged(changeType As WatcherChangeTypes
  [,timeout As Int32]) As WaitForChangedResult
' Events
Changed As System.IO.FileSystemEventHandler
Created As System.IO.FileSystemEventHandler
Deleted As System.IO.FileSystemEventHandler
Error As System.IO.ErrorEventHandler
Renamed As System.IO.RenamedEventHandler
```

InternalBufferOverflowException Class

Activated when the internal file changes buffer overflows. The file changes buffer is filled by API calls stored by the FileSystemWatcher class. The size of the internal buffer is determined by the InternalBufferSize property of the FileSystemWatcher class. If overflow occurs frequently, changes to the NotifyFilter and IncludeSubdirectories properties of the FileSystemWatcher class will prevent some of the unwanted change events from being stored to the internal buffer. Found as System.IO.**InternalBufferOverflowException**.

IODescriptionAttribute Class

Holds the description of an event, extender, or property that can be accessed by a visual designer in the Visual Studio environment. The description is set through the constructor, and thereafter the property is read-only.

Inheritance—Object.Attribute.DescriptionAttribute.IODescriptionAttribute

```
public class System.IO.IODescriptionAttribute
  ' Constructors
  IODescriptionAttribute(description As String)
  ' Properties
  Description As System.String (read only)
```

IOException Class

Activated when an input/output error occurs and provides the base class of other exceptions, including DirectoryNotFoundException, EndOfStreamException, FileLoadException, and FileNotFoundException. Found as System.IO.**IOException**.

MemoryStream Class

Holds a random access memory store that allows read and write operations in much the same way as a file is accessed through the FileStream object.

Inheritance—Object.MarshalByRefObject.Stream.MemoryStream

```
public class System.IO.MemoryStream
  ' Constructors
  MemoryStream()
  MemoryStream(capacity As Int32)
  MemoryStream(buffer As Byte() [,index As Int32
    [,count As Int32 [,writable As Boolean
    [,publiclyVisible As Boolean]]]])
  MemoryStream(buffer As Byte(),writable As Boolean)
  ' Properties
  CanRead As System.Boolean (read only)
  CanSeek As System.Boolean (read only)
  CanWrite As System.Boolean (read only)
  Capacity As System.Int32
  Length As System.Int64 (read only)
  Position As System.Int64
  ' Methods
  Close()
```

```
Flush()
GetBuffer() As Byte()
Read(buffer As Byte(), offset As Int32, count As Int32)
  As Int32
ReadByte() As Int32
Seek(offset As Int64, loc As SeekOrigin) As Int64
SetLength(value As Int64)
ToArray() As Byte()
Write(buffer As Byte(), offset As Int32, count As Int32)
WriteByte(value As Byte)
WriteTo(stream As Stream)
```

Path Class

Provides path deconstruction functionality that allows easy parsing of a path string for directory, filename, extension, and other parameters.

Inheritance—Object.Path

```
public class System.IO.Path
  ' Methods
  ChangeExtension(path As String, extension As String)
    As String
  Combine(path1 As String, path2 As String) As String
  GetDirectoryName(path As String) As String
  GetExtension(path As String) As String
  GetFileName(path As String) As String
  GetFileNameWithoutExtension(path As String) As String
  GetFullPath(path As String) As String
  GetPathRoot(path As String) As String
  GetTempFileName() As String
  GetTempPath() As String
  HasExtension(path As String) As Boolean
  IsPathRooted(path As String) As Boolean
```

PathTooLongException Class

Activated when a specified path or filename exceeds the system character limits. Found as System.IO.**PathTooLongException**.

Stream Class

Base class that provides functionality to the stream classes, including BufferedStream, FileStream, MemoryStream, NetworkStream, and CryptoStream.

Inheritance—Object.MarshalByRefObject.Stream

```
public class System.IO.Stream
  ' Properties
  CanRead As System.Boolean (read only)
  CanSeek As System.Boolean (read only)
  CanWrite As System.Boolean (read only)
  Length As System.Int64 (read only)
  Position As System.Int64
  ' Methods
  BeginRead(buffer As Byte(), offset As Int32,
    count As Int32, callback As AsyncCallback,
    state As Object) As IAsyncResult
  BeginWrite(buffer As Byte(), offset As Int32,
    count As Int32, callback As AsyncCallback,
    state As Object) As IAsyncResult
  Close()
  EndRead(asyncResult As IAsyncResult) As Int32
  EndWrite(asyncResult As IAsyncResult)
  Flush()
  Read(buffer As Byte(), offset As Int32, count As Int32)
    As Int32
  ReadByte() As Int32
  Seek(offset As Int64, origin As SeekOrigin) As Int64
  SetLength(value As Int64)
  Write(buffer As Byte(), offset As Int32, count As Int32)
  WriteByte(value As Byte)
```

StreamReader Class

As a subclass of the TextReader class, provides text reading capabilities for specific byte formats such as ASCIIEncoding, UnicodeEncoding, UTF7Encoding, and UTF8Encoding.

4

Inheritance—Object.MarshalByRefObject. TextReader.StreamReader

```
public class System.IO.StreamReader
  ' Constructors
  StreamReader(path As String [,encoding As Encoding
    [,detectEncodingFromByteOrderMarks As Boolean
    [,bufferSize As Int32]]])
  StreamReader(path As String,
    detectEncodingFromByteOrderMarks As Boolean)
  StreamReader(stream As Stream [,encoding As Encoding
    [,detectEncodingFromByteOrderMarks As Boolean
    [,bufferSize As Int32]]])
  StreamReader(stream As Stream,
    detectEncodingFromByteOrderMarks As Boolean)
  ' Properties
  BaseStream As System.IO.Stream (read only)
  CurrentEncoding As System.Text.Encoding (read only)
  ' Methods
  Close()
  DiscardBufferedData()
  Peek() As Int32
  Read( [buffer As Char(), index As Int32,
    count As Int32] ) As Int32
  ReadLine() As String
  ReadToEnd() As String
```

StreamWriter Class

As a subclass of TextWriter, this class provides text writing capabilities for specific byte formats such as ASCIIEncoding, UnicodeEncoding, UTF7Encoding, and UTF8Encoding.

Inheritance—Object.MarshalByRefObject. TextWriter.StreamWriter

```
public class System.IO.StreamWriter
  ' Constructors
  StreamWriter(path As String [,append As Boolean
    [,encoding As Encoding [,bufferSize As Int32]]])
  StreamWriter(stream As Stream [,encoding As Encoding
    [,bufferSize As Int32]])
  ' Properties
  AutoFlush As System.Boolean
  BaseStream As System.IO.Stream (read only)
```

```
Encoding As System.Text.Encoding (read only)
' Methods
Close()
Flush()
Write(value As Char)
Write(value As String)
Write(buffer As Char() [,index As Int32, count As Int32])
```

StringReader Class

Provides a subclass of TextReader that can be used on individual string variables.

Inheritance—Object.MarshalByRefObject. TextReader.StringReader

```
public class System.IO.StringReader
  ' Constructors
  StringReader(s As String)
  ' Methods
  Close()
  Peek() As Int32
  Read() As Int32
  Read(buffer As Char(), index As Int32, count As Int32)
    As Int32
  ReadLine() As String
  ReadToEnd() As String
```

StringWriter Class

Provides a subclass of TextWriter that can be used on individual string variables.

Inheritance—Object.MarshalByRefObject. TextWriter.StringWriter

```
public class System.IO.StringWriter
  ' Constructors
  StringWriter()
  StringWriter(formatProvider As IFormatProvider)
  StringWriter(sb As StringBuilder
    [,formatProvider As IFormatProvider])
  ' Properties
```

```
Encoding As System.Text.Encoding (read only)
' Methods
Close()
GetStringBuilder() As StringBuilder
ToString() As String
Write(value As String)
Write(value As Char)
Write(buffer As Char(), index As Int32, count As Int32)
```

TextReader Class

Provides text reading functionality for a file consisting of a series of sequential characters.

Inheritance—Object.MarshalByRefObject.TextReader

```
public class System.IO.TextReader
  ' Methods
  Close()
  Peek() As Int32
  Read( [buffer As Char(), index As Int32,
    count As Int32] ) As Int32
  ReadBlock(buffer As Char(), index As Int32,
    count As Int32) As Int32
  ReadLine() As String
  ReadToEnd() As String
  Synchronized(reader As TextReader) As TextReader
```

TextWriter Class

Provides text writing functionality for a file consisting of a series of sequential characters.

Inheritance—Object.MarshalByRefObject.TextWriter

```
public class System.IO.TextWriter
  ' Properties
  Encoding As System.Text.Encoding (read only)
  FormatProvider As System.IFormatProvider (read only)
```

```
NewLine As System.String
' Methods
Close()
Flush()
Synchronized(writer As TextWriter) As TextWriter
Write(value As Single)
Write(value As UInt64)
Write(value As Int64)
Write(value As String)
Write(value As Decimal)
Write(value As Double)
Write(buffer As Char())
Write(value As Char)
Write(value As UInt32)
Write(value As Int32)
Write(value As Boolean)
Write(value As Object)
Write(buffer As Char(), index As Int32, count As Int32)
Write(format As String, arg0 As Object
  [,arg1 As Object [,arg2 As Object]])
Write(format As String, arg As Object())
WriteLine()
WriteLine(value As Decimal)
WriteLine(value As String)
WriteLine(value As Single)
WriteLine(value As Double)
WriteLine(value As Object)
WriteLine(format As String, arg0 As Object
  [,arg1 As Object [,arg2 As Object]])
WriteLine(format As String, arg As Object())
WriteLine(buffer As Char() [,index As Int32,
  count As Int32])
WriteLine(value As Char)
WriteLine(value As Boolean)
WriteLine(value As Int64)
WriteLine(value As UInt64)
WriteLine(value As Int32)
WriteLine(value As UInt32)
```

Chapter 5
Networking

Before the astonishing growth of the Internet, networking functionality had been largely an afterthought for most operating systems and development projects. With the .NET framework, network technology has been embraced from the ground up. Objects available through the framework make it efficient to send data over a network to create peer-to-peer solutions, distributed architecture, or client/server systems.

5

The classes in the System.Net namespace supply programming constructs to build lower-level (nonobject) network applications. The features of the System.Net classes include data transfer, socket control, encryption, authentication, chunking, proxy support, pipelining, certificate validation, connection pooling, asynchronous communication, and connection management. Like the foundation of the IO namespace and the capabilities found in XML, the networking classes embrace the *stream* as a standard method of interaction with data.

Network Communication

Network communication is organized into three logical layers of network implementation:

- **Transport layer** The lowest level of implementation uses sockets to communicate over the network. The Socket classes allow direct access to the WinSock interface in the same way the Win32 API was programmed for network services.
- **Application protocol layer** This layer provides a substantially abstracted communication interface and provides support for the HTTP, TCP, and UDP protocols. Most low-level applications will use the TcpClient or UdpClient classes instead of the Socket class for best performance. Applications such as "instant messaging" or Napster would use this layer for implementation.
- **Request and response layer** This layer adopts the WebRequest and WebResponse classes to provide protocol-independent

communication over a network. In the future, code that uses these classes can utilize new protocols without rewriting or redesigning.

There are several facets of using the System.Net classes that depend on the type of network application that is needed—for example, the .NET framework including *chunking*, a useful technology that speeds data transmission when the exact size of the data is unknown when the transfer begins.

Pipelining is another useful technology because it sends multiple simultaneous HTTP requests to a server, which can enhance performance over sequential requests from the same client. The .NET classes perform pipelining by default. If you don't want to expend the resources required for a persistent connection for each user (needed for pipelining), setting the Pipelined property of the HttpWebRequest class to False will disable the pipelining feature.

NOTE: When the user needs to repeatedly access a secure Web application, the most optimized performance can be obtained by using the CredentialCache class. The CredentialCache class caches credentials based on the URL address, making every interaction after the initial authorization much more efficient. Client authentication may occur through these client mechanisms: digest, basic, Kerberos, NTLM, and custom. SSL support is handled by the .NET framework and is transparent to the application.

By default, .NET opens two connections per application per host when an Internet resource is accessed. If you have a large amount of data exchange, you may want to increase the number of connections for better performance. The ConnectionLimit property of the ServicePoint object holds the modifiable value.

One of the most advanced capabilities included in the System.Net classes is the availability of pluggable protocols. Pluggable protocols may be used with the WebRequest and WebResponse classes and allow additional protocols to be added to the network system. Through this pluggable interface, protocols may be utilized much as additional printer drivers can allow an application to use a new type of printer without any customization. The RegisterPrefix() method of the WebRequest class activates a particular pluggable protocol. It will remain active for the duration of the life of the executed application. The HTTP protocol is registered by default, while other protocols require explicit registration.

Getting a Request

The WebRequest and WebResponse objects make interacting with the Internet easy. If you create a new VB Windows application for networking, these imports should be included at the beginning of the header:

```
Imports System.Net
Imports System.Net.Sockets
```

If you place the following code in a button's click event, it will demonstrate a simple Web page response retrieval:

```
Sub txtGetRequest_Click()
  Dim myWebRequest As WebRequest
  Dim myWebResponse As WebResponse

  myWebRequest = WebRequest.Create(_
    "http://www.microsoft.com/default.htm")
  myWebResponse = myWebRequest.GetResponse()
End Sub
```

Sending a Response

The WebResponse object can be used to send client data to the Web, such as the information posted to a form or a file that would be uploaded. In the following example, a basic string is converted into an array of bytes and sent to the Web site in the form of an HTTP Post operation. Enter the following code into another button on the same form created in the last section and make sure to change the coded URI (a refined but compatible version of a URL that is backwards compatible) to a site where you have upload permission:

```
Sub cmdPostResponse_Click()
  Dim myWebRequest As WebRequest
  Dim myStream As System.IO.Stream
  Dim uploadData() As Byte
  Dim uploadStr As String

  myWebRequest = WebRequest.Create( _
    "http://www.microsoft.com/public")
  uploadStr = "Data to be sent to the server"
  ' Convert string into proper upload format
```

```
  uploadData = _
    System.Text.Encoding.ASCII.GetBytes(uploadStr)
  myWebRequest.Method = "POST"
  myWebRequest.ContentType = _
    "application/x-www-form-urlencoded"
  myWebRequest.ContentLength = uploadData.Length

  myStream = myWebRequest.GetRequestStream
  myStream.Write(uploadData, 0, uploadData.Length)
  myStream.Close()
End Sub
```

AuthenticationManager Class

Provides a static class for management of authentication services. Client authentication methods, represented as modules, are available for authentication types: basic, digest, negotiate, NTLM, and Kerberos. Found as System.Net.**AuthenticationManager**.

Authorization Class

Holds an authentication message that is sent to the Internet server to indicate that the client has authorization. Instances of this class are created automatically by the authentication manager class to pass to a server.

Inheritance—Object.Authorization

```
public class System.Net.Authorization
  ' Constructors
  Authorization(token As String [,finished _
    As Boolean [,connectionGroupId As String]])
  ' Properties
  Complete As System.Boolean (read only)
  ConnectionGroupId As System.String (read only)
  Message As System.String (read only)
  ProtectionRealm As System.String()
```

Cookie Class

Provides methods and properties for managing the reading and writing of cookies. This class is not inheritable.

Inheritance—Object.Cookie

```
public class System.Net.Cookie
  ' Constructors
  Cookie([name As String [,value As String [,path _
    As String [,domain As String]]]])
  ' Properties
  Comment As System.String
  CommentUri As System.Uri
  Discard As System.Boolean
  Domain As System.String
  Expired As System.Boolean
  Expires As System.DateTime
  Name As System.String
  Path As System.String
  Port As System.String
  Secure As System.Boolean
  TimeStamp As System.DateTime (read only)
  Value As System.String
  Version As System.Int32
  ' Methods
  Equals(comparand As Object) As Boolean
  GetHashCode() As Int32
  ToString() As String
```

5

CookieCollection Class

Holds a collection of Cookie objects that represent the cookies available for a session. Found as System.Net.**CookieCollection**.

CookieContainer Class

Provides a representation of a Cookie container that holds the cookies for the specified URI. Found as System.Net.**CookieContainer**.

CredentialCache Class

Provides a cache for acknowledged credentials, enabling fast authorization on repeated access to multiple Internet resources. For client applications, a credential set is represented by a username, a password, and a login domain. For ASP.NET applications, a credential set is represented by the credentials of the logged-in user or the user the Web server is impersonating.

Inheritance—Object.CredentialCache

```
public class System.Net.CredentialCache
  ' Constructors
  CredentialCache()
  ' Properties
  DefaultCredentials As System.Net.ICredentials (read only)
  ' Methods
  Add(uriPrefix As Uri, authType As String, _
    cred As NetworkCredential)
  GetCredential(uriPrefix As Uri, authType As _
    String) As NetworkCredential
  GetEnumerator() As IEnumerator
  Remove(uriPrefix As Uri, authType As String)
```

Dns Class

Provides a static class that can attempt domain name resolution through the Internet Domain Name System (DNS) configured for the current machine. The results are returned as an IPHostEntry object that may contain one or more IPs and aliases if there is more than one entry in the DNS database.

Inheritance—Object.Dns

```
public class System.Net.Dns
  ' Methods
  BeginGetHostByName(hostName As String, _
    requestCallback As AsyncCallback, _
    stateObject As Object) As IAsyncResult
  BeginResolve(hostName As String, _
    requestCallback As AsyncCallback, _
    stateObject As Object) As IAsyncResult
  EndGetHostByName(asyncResult As IAsyncResult) _
    As IPHostEntry
  EndResolve(asyncResult As IAsyncResult) _
    As IPHostEntry
  GetHostByAddress(address As IPAddress) As IPHostEntry
  GetHostByAddress(address As String) As IPHostEntry
  GetHostByName(hostName As String) As IPHostEntry
  GetHostName() As String
  IpToString(address As Int32) As String
  Resolve(hostName As String) As IPHostEntry
```


DnsPermission Class

Represents control of the permissions to the DNS servers of the network. The default allows access to the DNS by local traffic and forbids permission to Internet zone applications. Found as System.Net.**DnsPermissionAttribute**.

Inheritance—Object.CodeAccessPermission. DnsPermission

```
public class System.Net.DnsPermission
  ' Constructors
  DnsPermission(state As PermissionState)
  ' Methods
  Copy() As IPermission
  FromXml(securityElement As SecurityElement)
  Intersect(target As IPermission) As IPermission
  IsSubsetOf(target As IPermission) As Boolean
  IsUnrestricted() As Boolean
  ToXml() As SecurityElement
  Union(target As IPermission) As IPermission
```

DnsPermissionAttribute Class

Provides the security actions for instances of the DnsPermission class. This class is not inheritable.

EndPoint Class

Provides an abstract foundation class for the identification of a network address. Found as System.Net.**EndPoint**.

EndpointPermission Class

Provides a representation of a network endpoint. Each object created from this class contains the hostname, network port number, and transport type to be used for a connection.

Inheritance—Object.EndpointPermission

```
public class System.Net.EndpointPermission
  ' Properties
  Hostname As System.String (read only)
  Port As System.Int32 (read only)
  Transport As System.Net.TransportType (read only)
  ' Methods
  Equals(obj As Object) As Boolean
  GetHashCode() As Int32
  ToString() As String
```

FileWebRequest Class

Provides a file implementation of the WebRequest class to request local files. Do not directly create an instance of this class. Instead, use the Create() method of the WebRequest class and pass a URI that begins with the *file://* prefix, and the instance returned will be created from this class. To write to a file with the FileWebRequest class, use the GetRequestStream() method [for asynchronous file access, use the BeginGetRequestStream() and EndGetRequestStream() methods] to retrieve a Stream object with write access.

Inheritance—Object.MarshalByRefObject.WebRequest.FileWebRequest

```
public class System.Net.FileWebRequest
  ' Properties
  ConnectionGroupName As System.String
  ContentLength As System.Int64
  ContentType As System.String
  Credentials As System.Net.ICredentials
  Headers As System.Net.WebHeaderCollection (read only)
  Method As System.String
  PreAuthenticate As System.Boolean
  Proxy As System.Net.IWebProxy
  RequestUri As System.Uri (read only)
  Timeout As System.Int32
  ' Methods
  BeginGetRequestStream(callback As AsyncCallback, _
    state As Object) As IAsyncResult
  BeginGetResponse(callback As AsyncCallback, _
    state As Object) As IAsyncResult
  EndGetRequestStream(asyncResult As IAsyncResult) _
    As Stream
  EndGetResponse(asyncResult As IAsyncResult) _
    As WebResponse
  GetRequestStream() As Stream
  GetResponse() As WebResponse
```

FileWebResponse Class

Provides a file implementation of the WebResponse class to retrieve file resources. Do not directly create an instance of this class. Instead, use the GetResponse() method of the FileWebRequest class. To obtain read-only access to a file with the FileWebResponse class, use the GetResponseStream() method to retrieve a Stream object.

5

Inheritance—Object.MarshalByRefObject.WebResponse.FileWebResponse

```
public class System.Net.FileWebResponse
  ' Properties
  ContentLength As System.Int64 (read only)
  ContentType As System.String (read only)
  Headers As System.Net.WebHeaderCollection (read only)
  ResponseUri As System.Uri (read only)
  ' Methods
  Close()
  GetResponseStream() As Stream
```

GlobalProxySelection Class

Provides a global proxy for all HTTP requests. Instances of this class hold the settings for the default proxy used by WebRequest objects to access the Internet. Although the object is initialized with the settings of the default proxy, settings may be overridden for individual requests or disabled altogether. Found as System.Net.**GlobalProxySelection**.

HttpVersion Class

Holds information about the current version of the HTTP protocol used by the HttpWebRequest and HttpWebResponse classes.

Inheritance—Object.HttpVersion

```
public class System.Net.HttpVersion
  ' Constructors
  HttpVersion()
```

HttpWebRequest Class

Provides an HTTP implementation of the WebRequest class. Do not directly create an instance of this class. Instead, use the Create() method of the WebRequest class and pass a URI that begins with the http:// or https:// prefix. The instance returned will be created from the HttpWebRequest class.

Inheritance—Object.MarshalByRefObject. WebRequest.HttpWebRequest

```
public class System.Net.HttpWebRequest
  ' Properties
  Accept As System.String
  Address As System.Uri (read only)
  AllowAutoRedirect As System.Boolean
  AllowWriteStreamBuffering As System.Boolean
  ClientCertificates As System.Security._
    Cryptography.X509Certificates._
    X509CertificateCollection (read only)
  Connection As System.String
  ConnectionGroupName As System.String
  ContentLength As System.Int64
  ContentType As System.String
  ContinueDelegate As System.Net.HttpContinueDelegate
  CookieContainer As System.Net.CookieContainer
  Credentials As System.Net.ICredentials
  EnableCookies As System.Boolean
  Expect As System.String
  HaveResponse As System.Boolean (read only)
  Headers As System.Net.WebHeaderCollection
  IfModifiedSince As System.DateTime
  KeepAlive As System.Boolean
  MaximumAutomaticRedirections As System.Int32
  MediaType As System.String
  Method As System.String
  Pipelined As System.Boolean
  PreAuthenticate As System.Boolean
  ProtocolVersion As System.Version
  Proxy As System.Net.IWebProxy
  Referer As System.String
  RequestUri As System.Uri (read only)
  SendChunked As System.Boolean
  ServicePoint As System.Net.ServicePoint (read only)
  Timeout As System.Int32
  TransferEncoding As System.String
  UserAgent As System.String
  ' Methods
  Abort()
  AddRange(rangeSpecifier As String, _
    from As Int32, to As Int32)
```

```
AddRange(rangeSpecifier As String, range As Int32)
AddRange(from As Int32, to As Int32)
AddRange(range As Int32)
BeginGetRequestStream(callback As AsyncCallback, _
  state As Object) As IAsyncResult
BeginGetResponse(callback As AsyncCallback, _
  state As Object) As IAsyncResult
EndGetRequestStream(asyncResult As IAsyncResult) _
  As Stream
EndGetResponse(asyncResult As IAsyncResult) _
  As WebResponse
GetHashCode() As Int32
GetRequestStream() As Stream
GetResponse() As WebResponse
```

HttpWebResponse Class

Provides an HTTP implementation of the WebResponse class. Do not directly create an instance of this class. Instead, use the GetResponse() method of the HttpWebRequest class. The instance returned will be created from the HttpWebResponse class.

Inheritance—Object.MarshalByRefObject. WebResponse.HttpWebResponse

```
public class System.Net.HttpWebResponse
  ' Properties
  CharacterSet As System.String (read only)
  ContentEncoding As System.String (read only)
  ContentLength As System.Int64 (read only)
  ContentType As System.String (read only)
  Cookies As System.Net.CookieCollection
  Headers As System.Net.WebHeaderCollection (read only)
  LastModified As System.DateTime (read only)
  Method As System.String (read only)
  ProtocolVersion As System.Version (read only)
  ResponseUri As System.Uri (read only)
  Server As System.String (read only)
  StatusCode As System.Net.HttpStatusCode (read only)
  StatusDescription As System.String (read only)
  ' Methods
  Close()
```

```
GetHashCode() As Int32
GetResponseHeader(headerName As String) As String
GetResponseStream() As Stream
```

IPAddress Class

Holds an Internet Protocol (IP) address.

Inheritance—Object.IPAddress

```
public class System.Net.IPAddress
  ' Constructors
  IPAddress(newAddress As Int64)
  ' Properties
  Address As System.Int32
  AddressFamily As _
    System.Net.Sockets.AddressFamily (read only)
  ' Methods
  Equals(comparand As Object) As Boolean
  GetHashCode() As Int32
  HostToNetworkOrder(host As Int32) As Int32
  HostToNetworkOrder(host As Int16) As Int16
  HostToNetworkOrder(host As Int64) As Int64
  IsLoopback(address As IPAddress) As Boolean
  NetworkToHostOrder(network As Int16) As Int16
  NetworkToHostOrder(network As Int32) As Int32
  NetworkToHostOrder(network As Int64) As Int64
  Parse(ipString As String) As IPAddress
  ToString() As String
```


IPEndPoint Class

Holds the IP address and the port number of an IP network endpoint.

Inheritance—Object.EndPoint.IPEndPoint

```
public class System.Net.IPEndPoint
  ' Constructors
  IPEndPoint(address As IPAddress, port As Int32)
```

```
  IPEndPoint(address As Int64, port As Int32)
  ' Properties
  Address As System.Net.IPAddress
  AddressFamily As _
    System.Net.Sockets.AddressFamily (read only)
  Port As System.Int32
  ' Methods
  Create(socketAddress As SocketAddress) As EndPoint
  Equals(comparand As Object) As Boolean
  GetHashCode() As Int32
  Serialize() As SocketAddress
  ToString() As String
```

IPHostEntry Class

Holds one or more IP addresses or alias entries in the AddressList or Aliases arrays. This class is used by the DNS class to represent IP mappings to DNS entries. Found as System.Net.**IPHostEntry**.

LingerOption Class

Holds the amount of time (linger time) in seconds that a socket, marked to close, will remain open to send remaining data. If the Enabled property is set to False or the LingerTime property is set to 0, the socket will close immediately, and unsent data will not be transmitted. Disabling the linger time can be useful for implementing a transfer or connection abort feature.

Inheritance—Object.LingerOption

```
public class System.Net.Sockets.LingerOption
  ' Constructors
  LingerOption(enable As Boolean, seconds As Int32)
  ' Properties
  Enabled As System.Boolean
  LingerTime As System.Int32
```

MulticastOption Class

Sets the IP address or addresses for multicast packets when joining or leaving a multicast group.

Inheritance—Object.MulticastOption

```
public class System.Net.Sockets.MulticastOption
  ' Constructors
  MulticastOption(group As IPAddress)
  MulticastOption(group As IPAddress, mcint As IPAddress)
  ' Properties
  Group As System.Net.IPAddress
  LocalAddress As System.Net.IPAddress
```


NetworkCredential Class

Provides a foundation class that holds the credentials for password-based authentication to provide users with access to Internet resources. This class is used by the basic, digest, Kerberos, and NTLM authentication routines, but does not support public key systems (such as SSL).

Inheritance—Object.NetworkCredential

```
public class System.Net.NetworkCredential
  ' Constructors
  NetworkCredential([userName As String, _
    password As String [, domain As String]])
  ' Properties
  Domain As System.String
  Password As System.String
  UserName As System.String
  ' Methods
  GetCredential(uri As Uri, authType As String) _
    As NetworkCredential
```

NetworkStream Class

Provides a foundation class for all network-based stream access to send and receive data through sockets. Both synchronous and asynchronous protocols are supported. This class does not support random access, so the CanSeek property is set to False, and reading the Position property or calling the Seek() method will cause an exception to be thrown.

Inheritance—Object.MarshalByRefObject.Stream.NetworkStream

```
public class System.Net.Sockets.NetworkStream
  ' Constructors
  NetworkStream(socket As Socket [,access As _
    FileAccess [,ownsSocket As Boolean ]])
  NetworkStream(socket As Socket, ownsSocket As Boolean)
  ' Properties
  CanRead As System.Boolean (read only)
  CanSeek As System.Boolean (read only)
  CanWrite As System.Boolean (read only)
  DataAvailable As System.Boolean (read only)
  Length As System.Int64 (read only)
  Position As System.Int64
  ' Methods
  BeginRead(buffer As Byte(), offset As Int32, _
    size As Int32, callback As AsyncCallback, _
    state As Object) As IAsyncResult
  BeginWrite(buffer As Byte(), offset As Int32, _
    size As Int32, callback As AsyncCallback, _
    state As Object) As IAsyncResult
  Close()
  EndRead(asyncResult As IAsyncResult) As Int32
  EndWrite(asyncResult As IAsyncResult)
  Flush()
  Read(buffer As Byte(), offset As Int32, _
    size As Int32) As Int32
  Seek(offset As Int64, origin As SeekOrigin) As Int64
  SetLength(value As Int64)
  Write(buffer As Byte(), offset As Int32, size As Int32)
```

ServicePoint Class

Provides connection management to Internet resources for the HTTP protocol. Instances of this class are created and used by ServicePointManager objects.

Inheritance—Object.ServicePoint

```
public class System.Net.ServicePoint
  ' Properties
  Address As System.Uri (read only)
  Certificate As System.Security.Cryptography._
    X509Certificates.X509Certificate (read only)
  ClientCertificate As System.Security.Cryptography._
    X509Certificates.X509Certificate (read only)
  ConnectionLimit As System.Int32
  ConnectionName As System.String (read only)
  CurrentConnections As System.Int32 (read only)
  IdleSince As System.DateTime (read only)
  MaxIdleTime As System.Int32
  ProtocolVersion As System.Version (read only)
  SupportsPipelining As System.Boolean (read only)
  ' Methods
  GetHashCode() As Int32
```


ServicePointManager Class

Provides a static foundation class that manages the collection of ServicePoint object instances. Instances of the ServicePoint class can be created, modified, and deleted from the collection. If an application requests access to an Internet resource, this class passes an existing ServicePoint instance (if available) or creates a new one.

Inheritance—Object.ServicePointManager

```
public class System.Net.ServicePointManager
  ' Properties
  CertificatePolicy As System.Net.ICertificatePolicy
```

```
DefaultConnectionLimit As System.Int32
MaxServicePointIdleTime As System.Int32
MaxServicePoints As System.Int32
' Methods
FindServicePoint(address As Uri _
  [, proxy As IWebProxy]) As ServicePoint
FindServicePoint(uriString As String, _
  proxy As IWebProxy) As ServicePoint
```

Socket Class

Provides an interface to the Berkeley implementation of sockets. Socket objects are used as a base protocol layer by the TcpClient, UdpClient, and WebRequest classes and their children. Once an instance of the class is created, use the Bind() method to fix the socket to an endpoint and then the Connect() method to open the connection.

Inheritance—Object.Socket

```
public class System.Net.Sockets.Socket
  ' Constructors
  Socket(addressFamily As AddressFamily, _
    socketType As SocketType, protocolType As ProtocolType)
  ' Properties
  AddressFamily As _
    System.Net.Sockets.AddressFamily (read only)
  Available As System.Int32 (read only)
  Blocking As System.Boolean
  Connected As System.Boolean (read only)
  Handle As System.IntPtr (read only)
  LocalEndPoint As System.Net.EndPoint (read only)
  ProtocolType As _
    System.Net.Sockets.ProtocolType (read only)
  RemoteEndPoint As System.Net.EndPoint (read only)
  SocketType As System.Net.Sockets.SocketType (read only)
  ' Methods
  Accept() As Socket
  BeginAccept(callback As AsyncCallback, _
    state As Object) As IAsyncResult
  BeginConnect(remoteEP As EndPoint, callback As _
    AsyncCallback, state As Object) As IAsyncResult
  BeginReceive(buffer As Byte(), offset As Int32, size As _
    Int32, socketFlags As SocketFlags, callback As _
    AsyncCallback, state As Object) As IAsyncResult
```

BeginReceiveFrom(buffer As Byte(), offset As Int32, _
  size As Int32, socketFlags As SocketFlags, remoteEP _
  As EndPoint&, callback As AsyncCallback, state As _
  Object) As IAsyncResult
BeginSend(buffer As Byte(), offset As Int32, size As _
  Int32, socketFlags As SocketFlags, callback As _
  AsyncCallback, state As Object) As IAsyncResult
BeginSendTo(buffer As Byte(), offset As Int32, size As _
  Int32, socketFlags As SocketFlags, remoteEP As _
  EndPoint, callback As AsyncCallback, state As Object) _
  As IAsyncResult
Bind(localEP As EndPoint)
Close()
Connect(remoteEP As EndPoint)
EndAccept(asyncResult As IAsyncResult) As Socket
EndConnect(asyncResult As IAsyncResult)
EndReceive(asyncResult As IAsyncResult) As Int32
EndReceiveFrom(asyncResult As IAsyncResult, _
  endPoint As EndPoint&) As Int32
EndSend(asyncResult As IAsyncResult) As Int32
EndSendTo(asyncResult As IAsyncResult) As Int32
GetHashCode() As Int32
GetSocketOption(optionLevel As SocketOptionLevel, _
  optionName As SocketOptionName) As Object
GetSocketOption(optionLevel As SocketOptionLevel, _
  optionName As SocketOptionName, optionLength _
  As Int32) As Byte()
GetSocketOption(optionLevel As SocketOptionLevel, _
  optionName As SocketOptionName, optionValue As Byte())
IOControl(ioControlCode As Int32, optionInValue _
  As Byte(), optionOutValue As Byte()) As Int32
Listen(backlog As Int32)
Poll(microSeconds As Int32, mode As SelectMode) As Boolean
Receive(buffer As Byte() [, offset As Int32, _
  size As Int32, socketFlags As SocketFlags]) As Int32
Receive(buffer As Byte(), size As Int32, _
  socketFlags As SocketFlags) As Int32
Receive(buffer As Byte(), socketFlags As _
  SocketFlags) As Int32
ReceiveFrom(buffer As Byte(), remoteEP As _
  EndPoint&) As Int32
ReceiveFrom(buffer As Byte(), socketFlags As _
  SocketFlags, remoteEP As EndPoint&) As Int32
ReceiveFrom(buffer As Byte(), offset As Int32, _
  size As Int32, socketFlags As SocketFlags, _
  remoteEP As EndPoint&) As Int32
ReceiveFrom(buffer As Byte(), size As Int32, _
  socketFlags As SocketFlags, remoteEP As _
  EndPoint&) As Int32
Select(checkRead As IList, checkWrite As IList, _
  checkError As IList, microSeconds As Int32)

```
Send(buffer As Byte() [, socketFlags As _
  SocketFlags]) As Int32
Send(buffer As Byte(), size As Int32, socketFlags _
  As SocketFlags) As Int32
Send(buffer As Byte(), offset As Int32, size As _
  Int32, socketFlags As SocketFlags) As Int32
SendTo(buffer As Byte(), socketFlags As _
  SocketFlags, remoteEP As EndPoint) As Int32
SendTo(buffer As Byte(), remoteEP As EndPoint) As Int32
SendTo(buffer As Byte(), offset As Int32, size _
  As Int32, socketFlags As SocketFlags, _
  remoteEP As EndPoint) As Int32
SendTo(buffer As Byte(), size As Int32, socketFlags As _
  SocketFlags, remoteEP As EndPoint) As Int32
SetSocketOption(optionLevel As SocketOptionLevel, _
  optionName As SocketOptionName, optionValue As Object)
SetSocketOption(optionLevel As SocketOptionLevel, _
  optionName As SocketOptionName, optionValue As Int32)
SetSocketOption(optionLevel As SocketOptionLevel, _
  optionName As SocketOptionName, optionValue As Byte())
Shutdown(how As SocketShutdown)
```

SocketAddress Class

Holds a socket address.

Inheritance—Object.SocketAddress

```
public class System.Net.SocketAddress
  ' Constructors
  SocketAddress(family As AddressFamily, size As Int32)
  SocketAddress(family As AddressFamily)
  ' Properties
  Family As System.Net.Sockets.AddressFamily (read only)
  Item As System.Byte
  Size As System.Int32 (read only)
  ' Methods
  Equals(comparand As Object) As Boolean
  GetHashCode() As Int32
  ToString() As String
```

SocketPermission Class

Holds the permission settings for a transport address to connect or accept connections.

Inheritance—Object.CodeAccessPermission.SocketPermission

```
public class System.Net.SocketPermission
  ' Constructors
  SocketPermission(access As NetworkAccess, _
    transport As TransportType, hostName As String, _
    portNumber As Int32)
  SocketPermission(state As PermissionState)
  ' Properties
  AcceptList As System.Collections.IEnumerator (read only)
  ConnectList As System.Collections.IEnumerator (read only)
  ' Methods
  AddPermission(access As NetworkAccess, transport _
    As TransportType, hostName As String, _
    portNumber As Int32)
  Copy() As IPermission
  FromXml(securityElement As SecurityElement)
  Intersect(target As IPermission) As IPermission
  IsSubsetOf(target As IPermission) As Boolean
  IsUnrestricted() As Boolean
  ToXml() As SecurityElement
  Union(target As IPermission) As IPermission
```


SocketPermissionAttribute Class

Holds the actual permission settings such as access, host, port, and transport that are available through the SocketPermission class. This class is not inheritable. Found as System.Net.**SocketPermissionAttribute**.

TcpClient Class

Provides TCP support for connections and data exchange. This class sits atop the Socket class to provide a higher level of network access. The FTP and HTTP protocols are included in this class. Data sent and received by a TcpClient object occurs through a NetworkStream object.

Inheritance—Object.TcpClient

```
public class System.Net.Sockets.TcpClient
  ' Constructors
  TcpClient( [localEP As IPEndPoint] )
  TcpClient(hostname As String, port As Int32)
  ' Properties
  LingerState As System.Net.Sockets.LingerOption
  NoDelay As System.Boolean
  ReceiveBufferSize As System.Int32
  ReceiveTimeout As System.Int32
  SendBufferSize As System.Int32
  SendTimeout As System.Int32
  ' Methods
  Close()
  Connect(address As IPAddress, port As Int32)
  Connect(remoteEP As IPEndPoint)
  Connect(hostname As String, port As Int32)
  GetStream() As NetworkStream
```

TcpListener Class

Listens for connections on the TCP network protocol at a specified endpoint, IP address, or port. This class sits atop the Socket class to provide a higher level of network access. The FTP and HTTP protocols are included in this class. In the constructor, if the passed port number argument is a value of 0, a port number will be randomly selected.

Inheritance—Object.TcpListener

```
public class System.Net.Sockets.TcpListener
  ' Constructors
  TcpListener(localEP As IPEndPoint)
  TcpListener(localaddr As IPAddress, port As Int32)
  TcpListener(port As Int32)
  ' Properties
  LocalEndpoint As System.Net.EndPoint (read only)
  ' Methods
  AcceptSocket() As Socket
  AcceptTcpClient() As TcpClient
  Pending() As Boolean
  Start()
  Stop()
```


UdpClient Class

Provides UDP (User Datagram Protocol) support for connections and data exchange. This class sits atop the Socket class to provide a higher level of network access.

Inheritance—Object.UdpClient

```
public class System.Net.Sockets.UdpClient
  ' Constructors
  UdpClient()
  UdpClient(localEP As IPEndPoint)
  UdpClient(hostname As String, port As Int32)
  UdpClient(port As Int32)
  ' Methods
  Close()
  Connect(endPoint As IPEndPoint)
  Connect(hostname As String, port As Int32)
  Connect(addr As IPAddress, port As Int32)
  DropMulticastGroup(multicastAddr As IPAddress)
  JoinMulticastGroup(multicastAddr As IPAddress, _
    timeToLive As Int32)
  JoinMulticastGroup(multicastAddr As IPAddress)
```

```
Receive(remoteEP As IPEndPoint&) As Byte()
Send(dgram As Byte(), bytes As Int32, endPoint _
  As IPEndPoint) As Int32
Send(dgram As Byte(), bytes As Int32, hostname _
  As String, port As Int32) As Int32
Send(dgram As Byte(), bytes As Int32) As Int32
```

WebClient Class

Provides a high-level interface for transmission and reception of data from a URI resource. By default, this class can process any URI that begins with the http://, https://, or file:// prefix. This class uses the WebRequest class for actual data exchange and is not inheritable.

Inheritance—Object.MarshalByRefObject. Component.WebClient

```
public class System.Net.WebClient
  ' Constructors
  WebClient()
  ' Properties
  BaseAddress As System.String
  Credentials As System.Net.ICredentials
  Headers As System.Net.WebHeaderCollection
  QueryString As _
    System.Collections.Specialized.NameValueCollection
  ResponseHeaders As _
    System.Net.WebHeaderCollection (read only)
  ' Methods
  DownloadData(address As String) As Byte()
  DownloadFile(address As String, fileName As String)
  OpenRead(address As String) As Stream
  OpenWrite(address As String [, method As String]) _
    As Stream
  UploadData(address As String, method As String, _
    data As Byte()) As Byte()
  UploadData(address As String, data As Byte()) As Byte()
  UploadFile(address As String, fileName As String) _
    As Byte()
```

```
  UploadFile(address As String, method As String, _
    fileName As String) As Byte()
  UploadValues(address As String, _
    data As NameValueCollection) As Byte()
  UploadValues(address As String, method As String, _
    data As NameValueCollection) As Byte()
```

WebHeaderCollection Class

Holds a collection of the headers used by the WebRequest and WebResponse classes. Some of the headers are read-only or restricted to direct API access. The restricted headers include Accept, Connection, Content-Length, Content-Type, Date, Expect, Host, Range, Referer, Transfer-Encoding, and UserAgent.

Inheritance—Object.NameObjectCollectionBase.NameValueCollection.WebHeaderCollection

```
public class System.Net.WebHeaderCollection
  ' Constructors
  WebHeaderCollection()
  ' Methods
  Add(header As String)
  Add(name As String, value As String)
  GetValues(header As String) As String()
  IsRestricted(headerName As String) As Boolean
  OnDeserialization(sender As Object)
  Remove(name As String)
  Set(name As String, value As String)
  ToByteArray() As Byte()
  ToString() As String
```

WebPermission Class

Holds the permission settings (such as Accept, AcceptPattern, Connect, and ConnectPattern) for an Internet resource.

Inheritance—Object.CodeAccessPermission. WebPermission

```
public class System.Net.WebPermission
  ' Constructors
  WebPermission( [state As PermissionState] )
  WebPermission(access As NetworkAccess, uriRegex As Regex)
  WebPermission(access As NetworkAccess, _
    uriString As String)
  ' Properties
  AcceptList As System.Collections.IEnumerator (read only)
  ConnectList As System.Collections.IEnumerator (read only)
  ' Methods
  AddPermission(access As NetworkAccess, uriRegex As Regex)
  AddPermission(access As NetworkAccess, _
    uriString As String)
  Copy() As IPermission
  FromXml(securityElement As SecurityElement)
  Intersect(target As IPermission) As IPermission
  IsSubsetOf(target As IPermission) As Boolean
  IsUnrestricted() As Boolean
  ToXml() As SecurityElement
  Union(target As IPermission) As IPermission
```

WebPermissionAttribute Class

Holds the actual settings such as Accept, AcceptPattern, Connect, and ConnectPattern for the WebPermission class. This class is not inheritable. Found as System.Net.**WebPermissionAttribute**.

WebProxy Class

Holds the proxy settings used by the WebRequest class that can override the GlobalProxySelection settings.

Inheritance—Object.WebProxy

```
public class System.Net.WebProxy
  ' Constructors
```

```
WebProxy( [Address As Uri [,BypassOnLocal As Boolean _
  [,BypassList As String() _
  [,Credentials As ICredentials]]]] )
WebProxy(Address As String [,BypassOnLocal As Boolean _
  [,BypassList As String() _
  [,Credentials As ICredentials]]] )
WebProxy(Host As String, Port As Int32)
' Properties
Address As System.Uri
BypassArrayList As _
  System.Collections.ArrayList (read only)
BypassList As System.String()
BypassProxyOnLocal As System.Boolean
Credentials As System.Net.ICredentials
' Methods
GetDefaultProxy() As WebProxy
GetProxy(destination As Uri) As Uri
IsBypassed(host As Uri) As Boolean
```


WebRequest Class

Provides an implementation class of a network request service that can be developed without the need to build around a specific protocol. This class uses a URI that points the location to submit a request. A synchronous request can be initiated with the GetRequestStream() method or asynchronously with the BeginGetRequestStream() and EndGetRequestStream() methods. The response can be obtained with the GetResponse() method or asynchronously with the BeginGetResponse() and EndGetResponse() methods. This class supports the protocols FTP, HTTP, and SMTP. The FileWebRequest and HttpWebRequest classes are children of this class.

Inheritance—Object.MarshalByRefObject.WebRequest

```
public class System.Net.WebRequest
  ' Properties
  ConnectionGroupName As System.String
  ContentLength As System.Int64
  ContentType As System.String
  Credentials As System.Net.ICredentials
  Headers As System.Net.WebHeaderCollection
  Method As System.String
```

```
PreAuthenticate As System.Boolean
Proxy As System.Net.IWebProxy
RequestUri As System.Uri (read only)
Timeout As System.Int32
' Methods
Abort()
BeginGetRequestStream(callback As AsyncCallback, _
  state As Object) As IAsyncResult
BeginGetResponse(callback As AsyncCallback, _
  state As Object) As IAsyncResult
Create(requestUriString As String) As WebRequest
Create(requestUri As Uri) As WebRequest
CreateDefault(requestUri As Uri) As WebRequest
EndGetRequestStream(asyncResult As IAsyncResult) _
  As Stream
EndGetResponse(asyncResult As IAsyncResult) _
  As WebResponse
GetRequestStream() As Stream
GetResponse() As WebResponse
RegisterPrefix(prefix As String, _
  creator As IWebRequestCreate) As Boolean
```

WebResponse Class

Provides an implementation class of a network response service that can be developed without the need to build around a specific protocol. This class uses a URI for the location to submit a response and supports the FTP, HTTP, and SMTP protocols. The FileWebResponse and HttpWebResponse classes are children of this class.

Inheritance—Object.MarshalByRefObject.WebResponse

```
public class System.Net.WebResponse
  ' Properties
  ContentLength As System.Int64
  ContentType As System.String
  Headers As System.Net.WebHeaderCollection (read only)
  ResponseUri As System.Uri (read only)
  ' Methods
  Close()
  GetResponseStream() As Stream
```

Chapter 6
Component Objects

Components play a critical role in modern software development. A component or control can encapsulate program or business logic. By creating a component, logic can be reused within an organization or provided for sale in the large third-party component market.

With the release of Visual Studio.NET, the breadth of component capability has expanded to include both runtime and design-time implementations, the addition of Web controls, and the ability to inherit from existing components. All of this functionality has its foundation in the System.ComponentModel classes.

ComponentModel Overview

The System.ComponentModel classes include the base classes and interfaces necessary for component creation. The classes provided through ComponentModel provide four primary types of functionality:

- **Foundation classes for component definition** Classes such as Component and Container are used to define and contain components, including those that run on the .NET system as well as external COM objects.
- **Component licensing services** Licensing allows you to limit installation and execution of controls to those authorized to use them. Core licensing services are included in the framework as well as the foundation for custom license systems that might be developed.
- **Type conversion services** Data type conversion is included. It is a critical facility for heterogeneous communication between components or between the component and its host container. Conversion is provided for everything from primitive variable types (such as unsigned 16-bit integers, DateTime objects, etc.) to collections and arrays to conversion of the component objects themselves.
- **Data binding capabilities** Properties may be published with the BindableAttribute setting. Once published, the property represented in the component may be bound to an external data source or another control within the object system.

All of the components that are available for the Windows user interface (through the System.Windows.Forms classes) are based on the central System.ComponentModel.Component class. Therefore, even when a new component is created using the UserControl class, the inheritance path will lead back to the Component base class. Any components that use the Windows object system will need to use this class as the root class, if not indirectly.

NOTE: Design-time controls function differently than runtime controls that use the ComponentModel class. These design controls typically require a large number of special implementation details because of each control's dependence on the hosting environment. As such, covering design-time controls is beyond the scope of this book. Classes related to design-time implementation can be found in the .NET library documentation in the System.ComponentModel. Design and System.ComponentModel. Design.Serialization namespaces.

COM Access from Visual Studio

In addition to allowing easy development of components for use with the .NET system, the framework provides complete access to the Component Object Model (COM). COM is the current standard for Windows object sharing, communication, and management. Project code in .NET can access any COM object registered on the system where the program or component is executing. Additionally, components written in .NET can be configured to be published into the COM system.

In either direction—COM to .NET or .NET to COM—object wrappers are necessary to present a recognizable interface to the destination infrastructure. COM objects are handled in .NET as unmanaged entities. This means that while the instance of the component itself will be managed by the memory and garbage collection functionality of the .NET framework, memory operations that occur on the inside of the COM component will not be part of the unified management system of .NET.

In COM, each class uses a globally unique identifier (GUID) for independent unique identification. The .NET framework has supplanted this type of identity with the use of strong names (which in a format similar to a fully qualified path name). A strong name provides context for the assembly within the namespace hierarchy under which the assembly can be located. One clear advantage of the strong name system over the GUID system is that changes to the object interface can be accommodated after the initial strong name is generated. Any changes to a COM interface requires the generation of a new GUID.

To allow the two different object systems to interact, automation to generate the necessary metadata wrappers is included within .NET. For a COM component to be placed in the proper .NET namespace, a strong name is generated based on the component name and other information supplied by the COM registration, the OCX header, a TLB file, or an OLB file. Likewise, a .NET component is given a GUID before it is published into the COM system.

Publishing a .NET Component to COM

A public class can be called by other programs within .NET without any additional processing or metadata generation. If the class is properly constructed for execution in .NET, publishing it into the COM system is a fairly straightforward process. To access any class or library created with .NET through the COM technology, an assembly must be created to hold the component.

An assembly can be defined as either an EXE or DLL file. After the assembly has been compiled, there are two utilities included with the .NET Framework SDK that will take the metadata of the assembly (called the assembly manifest) automatically created by Visual Studio and define an entry for the assembly in the COM registry. Each assembly must include a key pair, which can be generated by VS.NET. Once the assembly is registered, the published assembly can be addressed like any other COM component.

If you have a Visual Studio.NET component ready for compilation and registration, follow these eight steps to publish that control into the COM system:

1. Load the component project into the Visual Studio.NET environment.

2. Right-click on the item representing the assembly in the Solution Explorer and select the Properties option from the context menu.

3. Under the Common Properties folder, select the Strong Name item in the option list.
4. Click the Generate Strong Name Using checkbox to activate the key generation system.
5. Click the Generate Key button. Once the creation of the key is completed, the text box will display the default name of the key file (i.e., KeyFile.snk). A key is required to place an assembly in the Global Assembly Cache so that any program on the system can address it.
6. Under the Configuration Properties folder, select the Build item.
7. Check the Register for COM Interop box.
8. Click the OK button.

When you select the Build | Build menu option, watch the output window of Visual Studio. You'll now notice the last line of the build process will read "Registering project output for COM Interop..." to indicate proper registration has taken place.

Addressing a COM Object from .NET

With the significant investment in COM technology that has been made by organizations over the years, it is critical that .NET be able to effectively address the objects that have been created in the COM environment. The wrapper for the COM object is a set of metadata held in the assembly file that describes the component and allows .NET to understand its members (i.e., methods, properties, etc.).

There are four methods of creating this metadata:

- **Visual Studio** Through the Add Reference dialog box, all of the COM objects on the current system may be accessed.
- **Type Library Importer** An import utility included with the .NET SDK that can read a specified type library and generate the necessary metadata for .NET access. This utility has a filename of TLBIMP.EXE and can be executed from the command line.

- **TypeLibConverter class** By programming the TypeLibConverter class, .NET access to a COM type library may be automated. This class holds the same functions provided by the command line Type Library Importer utility.
- **Custom wrapper** A custom wrapper can be created manually that provides the bridge between a COM object and the .NET system. This option is complicated and rarely chosen.

Although the built-in import functionality included with VS.NET will be used a large majority of the time, the other options are available in case you need more control over the process.

AmbientValueAttribute Class

Contains the value that, when passed to a property, will cause the property to obtain its value from another source. A property that obtains its value from another source is known as an ambient value. This class is not inheritable.

Inheritance—Object.Attribute.AmbientValueAttribute

```
public class System.ComponentModel.AmbientValueAttribute
  ' Constructors
  AmbientValueAttribute(value As Single)
  AmbientValueAttribute(value As Int64)
  AmbientValueAttribute(value As Int32)
  AmbientValueAttribute(value As Double)
  AmbientValueAttribute(value As Object)
  AmbientValueAttribute(value As String)
  AmbientValueAttribute(value As Boolean)
  AmbientValueAttribute(value As Char)
  AmbientValueAttribute(type As Type, value As String)
  AmbientValueAttribute(value As Int16)
  AmbientValueAttribute(value As Byte)
  ' Properties
  Value As System.Object (read only)
  ' Methods
  Equals(obj As Object) As Boolean
  GetHashCode() As Int32
```

ArrayConverter Class

Provides conversions of arrays from one data type to another. This class shouldn't be used directly, but instead accessed through the GetConverter() method of the TypeDescriptor class.

Inheritance—Object.TypeConverter. CollectionConverter.ArrayConverter

```
public class System.ComponentModel.ArrayConverter
  ' Constructors
  ArrayConverter()
  ' Methods
  ConvertTo(context As ITypeDescriptorContext, culture As
    CultureInfo, value As Object, destinationType As Type)
    As Object
  GetProperties(context As ITypeDescriptorContext, value
    As Object, attributes As Attribute())
    As PropertyDescriptorCollection
  GetPropertiesSupported(context As
    ITypeDescriptorContext) As Boolean
```

AttributeCollection Class

Holds a read-only collection of attributes. Found as System.ComponentModel.**AttributeCollection.**

BaseNumberConverter Class

Provides a foundation class for the creation of converter classes that alter nonfloating point numerical types. This class should not be used directly, but as a parent class for a new class definition.

Inheritance—Object.TypeConverter.BaseNumberConverter

```
public class System.ComponentModel.BaseNumberConverter
  ' Methods
  CanConvertFrom(context As ITypeDescriptorContext,
    sourceType As Type) As Boolean
  CanConvertTo(context As ITypeDescriptorContext,
    t As Type) As Boolean
  ConvertFrom(context As ITypeDescriptorContext,
    culture As CultureInfo, value As Object) As Object
  ConvertTo(context As ITypeDescriptorContext,
    culture As CultureInfo, value As Object,
    destinationType As Type) As Object
```

BindableAttribute Class

Indicates whether a specified attribute can be used for binding.

Inheritance—Object.Attribute.BindableAttribute

```
public class System.ComponentModel.BindableAttribute
  ' Constructors
  BindableAttribute(bindable As Boolean)
  BindableAttribute(flags As BindableSupport)
  ' Properties
  Bindable As System.Boolean (read only)
  ' Methods
  Equals(obj As Object) As Boolean
  GetHashCode() As Int32
  IsDefaultAttribute() As Boolean
```

BooleanConverter Class

Converts Boolean value types to other data types. This class shouldn't be used directly, but instead accessed through the GetConverter() method of the TypeDescriptor class.

Inheritance—Object.TypeConverter.BooleanConverter

```
public class System.ComponentModel.BooleanConverter
  ' Constructors
  BooleanConverter()
  ' Methods
  CanConvertFrom(context As ITypeDescriptorContext,
    sourceType As Type) As Boolean
  ConvertFrom(context As ITypeDescriptorContext,
    culture As CultureInfo, value As Object) As Object
  GetStandardValues(context As ITypeDescriptorContext)
    As StandardValuesCollection
  GetStandardValuesExclusive(context As
    ITypeDescriptorContext) As Boolean
  GetStandardValuesSupported(context As
    ITypeDescriptorContext) As Boolean
```

BrowsableAttribute Class

Indicates whether the specified property or event is available for browsing in the Properties window. This attribute is set to False when no design-time examination or modification of the attribute is needed.

Inheritance—Object.Attribute.BrowsableAttribute

```
public class System.ComponentModel.BrowsableAttribute
  ' Constructors
  BrowsableAttribute(browsable As Boolean)
  ' Properties
  Browsable As System.Boolean (read only)
  ' Methods
  Equals(obj As Object) As Boolean
  GetHashCode() As Int32
  IsDefaultAttribute() As Boolean
```

ByteConverter Class

Converts 8-bit unsigned type values to and from a string data type. This class should be accessed through the GetConverter() method of the TypeDescriptor class. Found as System.ComponentModel.**ByteConverter**.

CategoryAttribute Class

Indicates which category the specified property or event is shown under in the Properties window. These common categories are defined by the CategoryAttribute: Action, Appearance, Behavior, Data, Default, Design, DragDrop, Focus, Format, Key, Layout, Mouse, and WindowStyle.

Inheritance—Object.Attribute.CategoryAttribute

```
public class System.ComponentModel.CategoryAttribute
  ' Constructors
  CategoryAttribute(category As String)
  CategoryAttribute()
  ' Properties
  Action As
    System.ComponentModel.CategoryAttribute (read only)
  Appearance As
    System.ComponentModel.CategoryAttribute (read only)
  Behavior As
    System.ComponentModel.CategoryAttribute (read only)
  Category As System.String (read only)
  Data As
    System.ComponentModel.CategoryAttribute (read only)
  Default As
    System.ComponentModel.CategoryAttribute (read only)
  Design As
    System.ComponentModel.CategoryAttribute (read only)
  DragDrop As
    System.ComponentModel.CategoryAttribute (read only)
  Focus As
    System.ComponentModel.CategoryAttribute (read only)
  Format As
    System.ComponentModel.CategoryAttribute (read only)
  Key As
    System.ComponentModel.CategoryAttribute (read only)
  Layout As
    System.ComponentModel.CategoryAttribute (read only)
  Mouse As
    System.ComponentModel.CategoryAttribute (read only)
  WindowStyle As
    System.ComponentModel.CategoryAttribute (read only)
  ' Methods
  Equals(obj As Object) As Boolean
  GetHashCode() As Int32
  IsDefaultAttribute() As Boolean
```

CharConverter Class

Converts a single character Unicode string to other data types. Use the GetConverter() method from the TypeDescriptor class to get an instance reference instead of instantiating objects directly from this class.

Inheritance—Object.TypeConverter.CharConverter

```
public class System.ComponentModel.CharConverter
  ' Constructors
  CharConverter()
  ' Methods
  CanConvertFrom(context As ITypeDescriptorContext,
    sourceType As Type) As Boolean
  ConvertFrom(context As ITypeDescriptorContext,
    culture As CultureInfo, value As Object) As Object
  ConvertTo(context As ITypeDescriptorContext, culture As
    CultureInfo, value As Object, destinationType As Type)
    As Object
```

CollectionConverter Class

Converts the data types of the items contained in a collection.

Inheritance—Object.TypeConverter.CollectionConverter

```
public class System.ComponentModel.CollectionConverter
  ' Constructors
  CollectionConverter()
  ' Methods
  ConvertTo(context As ITypeDescriptorContext, culture As
    CultureInfo, value As Object, destinationType As Type)
    As Object
  GetProperties(context As ITypeDescriptorContext,
    value As Object, attributes As Attribute())
    As PropertyDescriptorCollection
  GetPropertiesSupported(context As ITypeDescriptorContext)
    As Boolean
```

Component Class

The foundation class for all components created for object sharing between applications. Components that inherit from this class will receive the containment and cleanup services included in the automatic resource management capabilities of the .NET system. This class provides the base class for the IComponent interface and all of the system components located in the namespace System.Windows.Forms.

Components created from this class may be hosted by any object that implements the IContainer interface. An IContainer-based object creates a site for each component added to it. This site may be used with the MarshalByValueComponent class to provide remotability for an individual component instance.

6

Inheritance—Object.MarshalByRefObject.Component

```
public class System.ComponentModel.Component
  ' Constructors
  Component()
  ' Properties
  Container As System.ComponentModel.IContainer (read only)
  Site As System.ComponentModel.ISite
  ' Methods
  Dispose()
  ToString() As String
  ' Events
  Disposed As System.EventHandler
```

ComponentCollection Class

Holds the collection of references to the component objects stored in a container.

Inheritance—Object.ReadOnlyCollectionBase.ComponentCollection

```
public class System.ComponentModel.ComponentCollection
  ' Constructors
```

```
ComponentCollection(components As IComponent())
' Properties
Item As System.ComponentModel.IComponent (read only)
Item As System.ComponentModel.IComponent (read only)
' Methods
CopyTo(array As IComponent(), index As Int32)
```

ComponentConverter Class

Converts components to different data types. Use the GetConverter() method from the TypeDescriptor class to get an instance reference instead of instantiating objects directly from this class. Most of the methods available to this important class are overridden versions of methods found in the grandparent class TypeConverter.

Inheritance—Object.TypeConverter.ReferenceConverter.ComponentConverter

```
public class System.ComponentModel.ComponentConverter
  ' Constructors
  ComponentConverter(type As Type)
  ' Methods
  GetProperties(context As ITypeDescriptorContext,
    value As Object, attributes As Attribute())
    As PropertyDescriptorCollection
  GetPropertiesSupported(context As
    ITypeDescriptorContext) As Boolean
```

ComponentEditor Class

Provides the foundation class for implementing a custom user interface for editing component attributes.

Inheritance—Object.ComponentEditor

```
public class System.ComponentModel.ComponentEditor
  ' Methods
  EditComponent(component As Object) As Boolean
  EditComponent(context As ITypeDescriptorContext,
    component As Object) As Boolean
```

Container Class

Provides a container that holds, tracks, and manages one or more components. Components may be of visual and nonvisual types and are held in a first-in-first-out order list.

Inheritance—Object.Container

```
public class System.ComponentModel.Container
  ' Constructors
  Container()
  ' Properties
  Components As
    System.ComponentModel.ComponentCollection (read only)
  ' Methods
  Add(component As IComponent, name As String)
  Add(component As IComponent)
  Dispose()
  Remove(component As IComponent)
```


CultureInfoConverter Class

Converts a CultureInfo object to and from a String data type. Use the GetConverter() method of the TypeDescriptor object to obtain an instance of this class.

Inheritance—Object.TypeConverter.CultureInfoConverter

```
public class System.ComponentModel.CultureInfoConverter
  ' Constructors
  CultureInfoConverter()
  ' Methods
  CanConvertFrom(context As ITypeDescriptorContext,
    sourceType As Type) As Boolean
  CanConvertTo(context As ITypeDescriptorContext,
    destinationType As Type) As Boolean
  ConvertFrom(context As ITypeDescriptorContext, culture
    As CultureInfo, value As Object) As Object
  ConvertTo(context As ITypeDescriptorContext, culture As
    CultureInfo, value As Object, destinationType As Type)
    As Object
```

```
GetStandardValues(context As ITypeDescriptorContext)
  As StandardValuesCollection
GetStandardValuesExclusive(context As
  ITypeDescriptorContext) As Boolean
GetStandardValuesSupported(context As
  ITypeDescriptorContext) As Boolean
```

DateTimeConverter Class

Converts a DateTime object to and from a String data type. While ConvertTo uses the Parse() method of the DateTime object, ConvertFrom takes advantage of the current culture settings unless a specific CultureInfo object is passed to it. Use the GetConverter() method of the TypeDescriptor object to obtain an instance of this class.

Inheritance—Object.TypeConverter.DateTimeConverter

```
public class System.ComponentModel.DateTimeConverter
  ' Constructors
  DateTimeConverter()
  ' Methods
  CanConvertFrom(context As ITypeDescriptorContext,
    sourceType As Type) As Boolean
  CanConvertTo(context As ITypeDescriptorContext,
    destinationType As Type) As Boolean
  ConvertFrom(context As ITypeDescriptorContext, culture
    As CultureInfo, value As Object) As Object
  ConvertTo(context As ITypeDescriptorContext, culture As
    CultureInfo, value As Object, destinationType As Type)
    As Object
```

DecimalConverter Class

Converts a Decimal object to and from a String data type. Use the GetConverter() method of the TypeDescriptor object to obtain an instance of this class.

Inheritance—Object.TypeConverter. BaseNumberConverter.DecimalConverter

```
public class System.ComponentModel.DecimalConverter
  ' Constructors
  DecimalConverter()
  ' Methods
  CanConvertTo(context As ITypeDescriptorContext,
    destinationType As Type) As Boolean
  ConvertTo(context As ITypeDescriptorContext,
    culture As CultureInfo, value As Object,
    destinationType As Type) As Object
```

DefaultEventAttribute Class

Sets the default event for a component and holds the name of that event in the Name property. This event may be set during class definition in both VB *(<DefaultEvent("CollectionChanged")> Public Class MyClass)*and C# *([DefaultEvent("CollectionChanged")] public class MyClass : BaseCollection {}).*

Inheritance—Object.Attribute.DefaultEventAttribute

```
public class System.ComponentModel.DefaultEventAttribute
  ' Constructors
  DefaultEventAttribute(name As String)
  ' Properties
  Name As System.String (read only)
  ' Methods
  Equals(obj As Object) As Boolean
  GetHashCode() As Int32
```

DefaultPropertyAttribute Class

Sets the default property for a component and holds the name of that event in the Name property. This property may be set during class definition in both VB *<DefaultProperty("Text")> Public Class MyClass)* and C# *([DefaultProperty("Text")] public class MyClass : BaseCollection {}).*

Inheritance—Object.Attribute.DefaultPropertyAttribute

```
public class System.ComponentModel.DefaultPropertyAttribute
  ' Constructors
  DefaultPropertyAttribute(name As String)
  ' Properties
  Name As System.String (read only)
  ' Methods
  Equals(obj As Object) As Boolean
  GetHashCode() As Int32
```

DefaultValueAttribute Class

Sets the default value for a property. This value may be specified during property definition in both VB (*<DefaultValue(False)> Public Property MyProperty() As Boolean*) and C# (*[DefaultValue(false)] public bool MyProperty {}*).

Inheritance—Object.Attribute.DefaultValueAttribute

```
public class System.ComponentModel.DefaultValueAttribute
  ' Constructors
  DefaultValueAttribute(value As Single)
  DefaultValueAttribute(value As Int64)
  DefaultValueAttribute(value As Int32)
  DefaultValueAttribute(value As Double)
  DefaultValueAttribute(value As Object)
  DefaultValueAttribute(value As String)
  DefaultValueAttribute(value As Boolean)
  DefaultValueAttribute(value As Char)
  DefaultValueAttribute(type As Type, value As String)
  DefaultValueAttribute(value As Int16)
  DefaultValueAttribute(value As Byte)
  ' Properties
  Value As System.Object (read only)
  ' Methods
  Equals(obj As Object) As Boolean
  GetHashCode() As Int32
```

DescriptionAttribute Class

Sets a description for a property or event that can be displayed in a visual designer environment such as the Visual Studio Properties window. This value may be specified during property definition in both VB (*<Description("My property."), Category("Appearance")> Public Property MyProperty() As Boolean*) and C# (*[Description("My property."), Category("Appearance")] public bool MyProperty {}*).

Inheritance—Object.Attribute.DescriptionAttribute

```
public class System.ComponentModel.DescriptionAttribute
  ' Constructors
  DescriptionAttribute(description As String)
  DescriptionAttribute()
  ' Properties
  Description As System.String (read only)
  ' Methods
  Equals(obj As Object) As Boolean
  GetHashCode() As Int32
```


DesignerAttribute Class

Sets the design-time interface for a component. The DesignerBaseTypeName property is used to specify the class or namespace name of the designer interface. The designer class must implement the IDesigner interface. The interface may be specified during class definition in both VB (*<Designer("System.Windows.Forms.Design.DocumentDesigner, System.Windows.Forms.Design.DLL", GetType(IRootDesigner)), DesignerCategory("Form")> Public Class myClass()*) and C# (*[Designer("System.Windows.Forms.Design.DocumentDesigner, System.Windows.Forms.Design.DLL", typeof(IRootDesigner)), DesignerCategory("Form")] public class myClass : ContainerControl {}*).

Inheritance—Object.Attribute.DesignerAttribute

```
public class System.ComponentModel.DesignerAttribute
  ' Constructors
  DesignerAttribute(designerType As Type)
  DesignerAttribute(designerTypeName As String)
  DesignerAttribute(designerTypeName As String,
    designerBaseTypeName As String)
  DesignerAttribute(designerType As Type,
    designerBaseType As Type)
  DesignerAttribute(designerTypeName As String,
    designerBaseType As Type)
  ' Properties
  DesignerBaseTypeName As System.String (read only)
  DesignerTypeName As System.String (read only)
  TypeId As System.Object (read only)
  ' Methods
  Equals(obj As Object) As Boolean
  GetHashCode() As Int32
```

DesignerCategoryAttribute Class

Sets the category of the designer class. Categories include *Component*, *Form*, *Designer*, and an empty string (""). An empty string is the default. The category may be specified during class definition in both VB (*<Designer("System.Windows.Forms.Design.DocumentDesigner, System.Windows.Forms.Design.DLL", GetType(IRootDesigner)), DesignerCategory("Form")> Public Class myClass()*) and C# (*[Designer("System.Windows.Forms.Design.DocumentDesigner, System.Windows.Forms.Design.DLL", typeof(IRootDesigner)), DesignerCategory("Form")] public class myClass : ContainerControl {}*).

Inheritance—Object.Attribute.DesignerCategoryAttribute

```
public class System.ComponentModel.
    DesignerCategoryAttribute
  ' Constructors
  DesignerCategoryAttribute(category As String)
  DesignerCategoryAttribute()
  ' Properties
  Category As System.String (read only)
```

```
TypeId As System.Object (read only)
' Methods
Equals(obj As Object) As Boolean
GetHashCode() As Int32
IsDefaultAttribute() As Boolean
```

DesignerSerializationVisibilityAttribute Class

Defines how a property is saved (serialized) by a designer. Setting the Visibility property to Hidden will tell the serializing routine to ignore the property when saving. The Content setting will direct the saving routine to store the actual item or items specified by the property (such as items in a collection) rather than the property value (such as the collection reference). The Visible setting, which is the default, allows the saving routine to save the parameter normally.

Inheritance—Object.Attribute. DesignerSerializationVisibilityAttribute

```
public class System.ComponentModel.
    DesignerSerializationVisibilityAttribute
  ' Constructors
  DesignerSerializationVisibilityAttribute(visibility As
    DesignerSerializationVisibility)
  ' Properties
  Visibility As System.ComponentModel.
    DesignerSerializationVisibility (read only)
  ' Methods
  Equals(obj As Object) As Boolean
  GetHashCode() As Int32
  IsDefaultAttribute() As Boolean
```

DesignOnlyAttribute Class

Determines whether a property may be modified only at design time or can be modified at runtime as well. The default setting of False allows a property to be modified at runtime as well as design time.

Inheritance—Object.Attribute.DesignOnlyAttribute

```
public class System.ComponentModel.DesignOnlyAttribute
  ' Constructors
  DesignOnlyAttribute(isDesignOnly As Boolean)
  ' Properties
  IsDesignOnly As System.Boolean (read only)
  ' Methods
  Equals(obj As Object) As Boolean
  GetHashCode() As Int32
  IsDefaultAttribute() As Boolean
```

DesignTimeVisibleAttribute Class

Determines whether a property may be visible only at design time or can be displayed at runtime as well.

Inheritance—Object.Attribute.DesignTimeVisibleAttribute

```
public class System.ComponentModel.
    DesignTimeVisibleAttribute
  ' Constructors
  DesignTimeVisibleAttribute()
  DesignTimeVisibleAttribute(visible As Boolean)
  ' Properties
  Visible As System.Boolean (read only)
  ' Methods
  Equals(obj As Object) As Boolean
  GetHashCode() As Int32
  IsDefaultAttribute() As Boolean
```

DoubleConverter Class

Converts a double-precision floating-point number object to and from a String data type. Use the GetConverter() method of the TypeDescriptor object to obtain an instance of this class.

Inheritance—Object.TypeConverter.BaseNumberConverter.DoubleConverter

```
public class System.ComponentModel.DoubleConverter
  ' Constructors
  DoubleConverter()
```

EditorAttribute Class

Sets the editor to be used for modifying properties. This class is not inheritable.

Inheritance—Object.Attribute.EditorAttribute

```
public class System.ComponentModel.EditorAttribute
  ' Constructors
  EditorAttribute(typeName As String,
    baseTypeName As String)
  EditorAttribute()
  EditorAttribute(type As Type, baseType As Type)
  EditorAttribute(typeName As String, baseType As Type)
  ' Properties
  EditorBaseTypeName As System.String (read only)
  EditorTypeName As System.String (read only)
  TypeId As System.Object (read only)
  ' Methods
  Equals(obj As Object) As Boolean
  GetHashCode() As Int32
```


EditorBrowsableAttribute Class

Determines whether a property or method is available for browsing in an editor.

Inheritance—Object.Attribute.EditorBrowsableAttribute

```
public class System.ComponentModel.
    EditorBrowsableAttribute
  ' Constructors
  EditorBrowsableAttribute(state As EditorBrowsableState)
  EditorBrowsableAttribute()
  ' Properties
  State As
    System.ComponentModel.EditorBrowsableState (read only)
  ' Methods
  Equals(obj As Object) As Boolean
  GetHashCode() As Int32
```

EnumConverter Class

Converts an Enum object to and from a String data type. Use the GetConverter() method of the TypeDescriptor object to obtain an instance of this class.

Inheritance—Object.TypeConverter.EnumConverter

```
public class System.ComponentModel.EnumConverter
  ' Constructors
  EnumConverter(type As Type)
  ' Methods
  CanConvertFrom(context As ITypeDescriptorContext,
    sourceType As Type) As Boolean
  CanConvertTo(context As ITypeDescriptorContext,
    destinationType As Type) As Boolean
  ConvertFrom(context As ITypeDescriptorContext, culture
    As CultureInfo, value As Object) As Object
  ConvertTo(context As ITypeDescriptorContext, culture As
    CultureInfo, value As Object, destinationType As Type)
    As Object
  GetStandardValues(context As ITypeDescriptorContext)
    As StandardValuesCollection
  GetStandardValuesExclusive(context As
    ITypeDescriptorContext) As Boolean
  GetStandardValuesSupported(context As
    ITypeDescriptorContext) As Boolean
  IsValid(context As ITypeDescriptorContext,
    value As Object) As Boolean
```

EventDescriptor Class

Holds information about an event for a component, including the component name, component attributes, reference to the component that will receive the event, the event delegate, the type of event, and its multicast setting.

Inheritance—Object.MemberDescriptor.EventDescriptor

```
public class System.ComponentModel.EventDescriptor
  ' Properties
  ComponentType As System.Type (read only)
  EventType As System.Type (read only)
  IsMulticast As System.Boolean (read only)
  ' Methods
  AddEventHandler(component As Object, value As Delegate)
  RemoveEventHandler(component As Object,
    value As Delegate)
```

EventDescriptorCollection Class

Holds a read-only collection of EventDescriptor objects.

Inheritance—Object.EventDescriptorCollection

```
public class System.ComponentModel.
    EventDescriptorCollection
  ' Constructors
  EventDescriptorCollection(events As EventDescriptor())
  ' Properties
  Count As System.Int32 (read only)
  Item As System.ComponentModel.EventDescriptor (read only)
  Item As System.ComponentModel.EventDescriptor (read only)
  ' Methods
  Add(value As EventDescriptor) As Int32
  Clear()
  Contains(value As EventDescriptor) As Boolean
  Find(name As String, ignoreCase As Boolean)
    As EventDescriptor
  GetEnumerator() As IEnumerator
  IndexOf(value As EventDescriptor) As Int32
  Insert(index As Int32, value As EventDescriptor)
  Remove(value As EventDescriptor)
  RemoveAt(index As Int32)
  Sort() As EventDescriptorCollection
  Sort(names As String()) As EventDescriptorCollection
  Sort(comparer As IComparer) As EventDescriptorCollection
  Sort(names As String(), comparer As IComparer)
    As EventDescriptorCollection
```

EventHandlerList Class

Holds a list of delegates that may be searched for individual entries. The search routine is linear, so searches should only by made on smaller lists; otherwise, performance may become a factor. This class is not inheritable.

Inheritance—Object.EventHandlerList

```
public class System.ComponentModel.EventHandlerList
  ' Constructors
  EventHandlerList()
  ' Properties
  Item As System.Delegate
  ' Methods
  AddHandler(key As Object, value As Delegate)
  Dispose()
  RemoveHandler(key As Object, value As Delegate)
```

ExpandableObjectConverter Class

Converts expandable objects (such as icons, margins, and list view items) to and from other data types. Use the appropriate method on the TypeDescriptor object to obtain an instance of the class.

Inheritance—Object.TypeConverter. ExpandableObjectConverter

```
public class System.ComponentModel.
    ExpandableObjectConverter
  ' Constructors
  ExpandableObjectConverter()
  ' Methods
  GetProperties(context As ITypeDescriptorContext,
    value As Object, attributes As Attribute())
    As PropertyDescriptorCollection
  GetPropertiesSupported(context As ITypeDescriptorContext)
    As Boolean
```

GuidConverter Class

Converts a 128-bit globally unique identifier (GUID) object to and from a String data type.

Inheritance—Object.TypeConverter.GuidConverter

```
public class System.ComponentModel.GuidConverter
  ' Constructors
  GuidConverter()
  ' Methods
  CanConvertFrom(context As ITypeDescriptorContext,
    sourceType As Type) As Boolean
  CanConvertTo(context As ITypeDescriptorContext,
    destinationType As Type) As Boolean
  ConvertFrom(context As ITypeDescriptorContext,
    culture As CultureInfo, value As Object) As Object
  ConvertTo(context As ITypeDescriptorContext,
    culture As CultureInfo, value As Object,
    destinationType As Type) As Object
```


ImmutableObjectAttribute Class

Indicates that the object has no editable subproperties. This property is used by the design time environment.

Inheritance—Object.Attribute.ImmutableObjectAttribute

```
public class Sys-
tem.ComponentModel.ImmutableObjectAttribute
  ' Constructors
  ImmutableObjectAttribute(immutable As Boolean)
  ' Properties
  Immutable As System.Boolean (read only)
  ' Methods
  Equals(obj As Object) As Boolean
  GetHashCode() As Int32
  IsDefaultAttribute() As Boolean
```

InheritanceAttribute Class

Indicates whether the specified class may be used as a parent for inheritance. The InheritanceAttribute class is not inheritable.

Inheritance—Object.Attribute.InheritanceAttribute

```
public class System.ComponentModel.InheritanceAttribute
  ' Constructors
  InheritanceAttribute()
  InheritanceAttribute(
    inheritanceLevel As InheritanceLevel)
  ' Properties
  InheritanceLevel As
    System.ComponentModel.InheritanceLevel (read only)
  ' Methods
  Equals(value As Object) As Boolean
  GetHashCode() As Int32
  IsDefaultAttribute() As Boolean
  ToString() As String
```

InstallerTypeAttribute Class

Specifies the installer to be used for a particular type of component installation. The InstallerType property holds the reference to the installer associated with this attribute.

Inheritance—Object.Attribute.InstallerTypeAttribute

```
public class Sys-
tem.ComponentModel.InstallerTypeAttribute
  ' Constructors
  InstallerTypeAttribute(installerType As Type)
  InstallerTypeAttribute(typeName As String)
  ' Properties
  InstallerType As System.Type (read only)
  ' Methods
  Equals(obj As Object) As Boolean
  GetHashCode() As Int32
```

Int16Converter Class

Converts a 16-bit signed integer object to and from a String data type. The ConvertFrom method uses the Parse method of the Int16 object, while the ConvertTo method returns a string in the general ("G") numeric format. Use the GetConverter() method of the TypeDescriptor object to obtain an instance of this class.

Inheritance—Object.TypeConverter. BaseNumberConverter.Int16Converter

```
public class System.ComponentModel.Int16Converter
  ' Constructors
  Int16Converter()
```


Int32Converter Class

Converts a 32-bit signed integer object to and from a String data type. The ConvertFrom method uses the Parse method of the Int32 object, while the ConvertTo method returns a string in the general ("G") numeric format. Use the GetConverter() method of the TypeDescriptor object to obtain an instance of this class.

Inheritance—Object.TypeConverter. BaseNumberConverter.Int32Converter

```
public class System.ComponentModel.Int32Converter
  ' Constructors
  Int32Converter()
```

Int64Converter Class

Converts a 64-bit signed integer object to and from a String data type. The ConvertFrom method uses the Parse method of the Int64 object, while the ConvertTo method returns a string in the general ("G") numeric format. Use the GetConverter() method of the TypeDescriptor object to obtain an instance of this class.

Inheritance—Object.TypeConverter.BaseNumberConverter.Int64Converter

```
public class System.ComponentModel.Int64Converter
  ' Constructors
  Int64Converter()
```

License Class

Provides an abstract foundation class for the creation of all license classes. This class cannot be used directly, but only as a parent class for a new class definition. A license must be separately granted to each new instance of a component. When the License class is used as a parent, the LicenseKey property and the Dispose() method must be overridden.

Inheritance—Object.License

```
public class System.ComponentModel.License
  ' Properties
  LicenseKey As System.String (read only)
  ' Methods
  Dispose()
```

LicenseContext Class

Specifies the context in which a licensed object may be used. This class provides the default license context that implements runtime-only support and doesn't include the functionality to serialize or save license keys.

Inheritance—Object.LicenseContext

```
public class System.ComponentModel.LicenseContext
  ' Constructors
  LicenseContext()
  ' Properties
  UsageMode As
    System.ComponentModel.LicenseUsageMode (read only)
  ' Methods
```

```
GetSavedLicenseKey(type As Type,
  resourceAssembly As Assembly) As String
GetService(type As Type) As Object
SetSavedLicenseKey(type As Type, key As String)
```

LicenseManager Class

Provides the creation and management of a license provider that may be added to a component. This class is not inheritable.

Inheritance—Object.LicenseManager

```
public class System.ComponentModel.LicenseManager
  ' Properties
  CurrentContext As
    System.ComponentModel.LicenseContext
  UsageMode As
    System.ComponentModel.LicenseUsageMode (read only)
  ' Methods
  CreateWithContext(type As Type, creationContext As
    LicenseContext [,args As Object()] ) As Object
  IsLicensed(type As Type) As Boolean
  IsValid(type As Type, instance As Object,
    license As License&) As Boolean
  IsValid(type As Type) As Boolean
  LockContext(contextUser As Object)
  UnlockContext(contextUser As Object)
  Validate(type As Type)
  Validate(type As Type, instance As Object) As License
```

6

LicenseProvider Class

Provides an abstract class that can be used as a parent for a new license provider class.

Inheritance—Object.LicenseProvider

```
public class System.ComponentModel.LicenseProvider
  ' Methods
  GetLicense(context As LicenseContext, type As Type,
    instance As Object, allowExceptions As Boolean)
    As License
```

LicenseProviderAttribute Class

Indicates the LicenseProvider object to be used with the specified class. This class is required with the creation of a component that is to be licensed. The provider may be specified during class definition in both VB (*<LicenseProvider(GetType(LicFileLicenseProvider))> Public Class myComponent() Inherits Control*) and C# (*[LicenseProvider (typeof(LicFileLicenseProvider))] public class myComponent : Control {}*).

Inheritance—Object.Attribute.LicenseProviderAttribute

```
public class Sys-
tem.ComponentModel.LicenseProviderAttribute
  ' Constructors
  LicenseProviderAttribute(typeName As String)
  LicenseProviderAttribute()
  LicenseProviderAttribute(type As Type)
  ' Properties
  LicenseProvider As System.Type (read only)
  TypeId As System.Object (read only)
  ' Methods
  Equals(value As Object) As Boolean
  GetHashCode() As Int32
```

LicFileLicenseProvider Class

Provides a LicenseProvider implementation that checks for authorization allowing the program or development system to use the control. This provider works similarly to the .NET and .COM standard licensing and uses license files stored as text files.

Inheritance—Object.LicenseProvider.LicFileLicenseProvider

```
public class System.ComponentModel.LicFileLicenseProvider
  ' Constructors
```

```
LicFileLicenseProvider()
' Methods
GetLicense(context As LicenseContext, type As Type,
  instance As Object, allowExceptions As Boolean)
  As License
```

ListBindableAttribute Class

Indicates that a list may be used as a valid data source. In a development environment, this attribute is used to determine whether the databinding picker should be used to display the list.

Inheritance—Object.Attribute.ListBindableAttribute


```
public class Sys-
tem.ComponentModel.ListBindableAttribute
  ' Constructors
  ListBindableAttribute(listBindable As Boolean)
  ListBindableAttribute(flags As BindableSupport)
  ' Properties
  ListBindable As System.Boolean (read only)
  ' Methods
  Equals(obj As Object) As Boolean
  GetHashCode() As Int32
  IsDefaultAttribute() As Boolean
```

LocalizableAttribute Class

Indicates whether the specified property should be localized. If set to True, the property is stored in the resource file of the application so it can be easily modified based on locality without modification of the program code. The default value is False. The value may be specified during property definition in both VB (*<Localizable(True)> Public Property MyProperty() As Boolean*) and C# (*[Localizable(true)] public bool MyProperty {}*).

Inheritance—Object.Attribute.LocalizableAttribute

```
public class System.ComponentModel.LocalizableAttribute
  ' Constructors
  LocalizableAttribute(isLocalizable As Boolean)
  ' Properties
```

```
IsLocalizable As System.Boolean (read only)
' Methods
Equals(obj As Object) As Boolean
GetHashCode() As Int32
IsDefaultAttribute() As Boolean
```

MarshalByValueComponent Class

Provides a foundation class that can be used to create components that can be marshalled by value. In the .NET Framework, the following classes are children of this base class: DataColumn, DataSet, DataTable, DataView, and DataViewManager. If this class is used as a parent class, the child class must override the methods: Dispose(), GetService(), and Site().

Inheritance—Object.MarshalByValueComponent

```
public class System.ComponentModel.MarshalByValueComponent
  ' Constructors
  MarshalByValueComponent()
  ' Properties
  Container As System.ComponentModel.IContainer (read only)
  DesignMode As System.Boolean (read only)
  Site As System.ComponentModel.ISite
  ' Methods
  Dispose()
  GetService(service As Type) As Object
  ' Events
  Disposed As System.EventHandler
```

MemberDescriptor Class

Provides the base class for the classes EventDescriptor and PropertyDescriptor. Holds an array of the attributes of a class member (event or property) as well as the means of accessing items in this array.

Inheritance—Object.MemberDescriptor

```
public class System.ComponentModel.MemberDescriptor
  ' Properties
  Attributes As
    System.ComponentModel.AttributeCollection (read only)
```

```
Category As System.String (read only)
Description As System.String (read only)
DesignTimeOnly As System.Boolean (read only)
DisplayName As System.String (read only)
IsBrowsable As System.Boolean (read only)
Name As System.String (read only)
' Methods
Equals(obj As Object) As Boolean
GetHashCode() As Int32
```

MergablePropertyAttribute Class

Indicates that the specified property can be merged with other properties presented in the Properties window. If False, the property must be displayed separately. The default value for this attribute is True. Setting the value of this property to True or False will actually store the constant values Yes or No, respectively, in the AllowMerge property. The value may be specified during property definition in both VB (*<MergableProperty(True)> Public Property MyProperty() As Boolean*) and C# (*[MergableProperty(true)] public bool MyProperty {}*). This class is not inheritable.

Inheritance—Object.Attribute.MergablePropertyAttribute

```
public class System.ComponentModel.
    MergablePropertyAttribute
  ' Constructors
  MergablePropertyAttribute(allowMerge As Boolean)
  ' Properties
  AllowMerge As System.Boolean (read only)
  ' Methods
  Equals(obj As Object) As Boolean
  GetHashCode() As Int32
  IsDefaultAttribute() As Boolean
```

NotifyParentPropertyAttribute Class

Indicates that the parent of this class will be notified in the event this property is changed. This attribute should be set particularly when the property is one of several nested properties so the parent will be notified of the change. This class cannot be inherited.

Inheritance—Object.Attribute.NotifyParentPropertyAttribute

```
public class System.ComponentModel.
    NotifyParentPropertyAttribute
  ' Constructors
  NotifyParentPropertyAttribute(notifyParent As Boolean)
  ' Properties
  NotifyParent As System.Boolean (read only)
  ' Methods
  Equals(obj As Object) As Boolean
  GetHashCode() As Int32
  IsDefaultAttribute() As Boolean
```

ParenthesizePropertyNameAttribute Class

Indicates that the property, when displayed in the Properties window, will be displayed in parentheses (like the Name property). In alphabetical mode, properties with parentheses will be displayed at the top of the list. In category mode, a property with parentheses is displayed at the top of its category.

Inheritance—Object.Attribute.ParenthesizePropertyNameAttribute

```
public class System.ComponentModel.
    ParenthesizePropertyNameAttribute
  ' Constructors
  ParenthesizePropertyNameAttribute(
    [needParenthesis As Boolean] )
  ' Properties
```

```
NeedParenthesis As System.Boolean (read only)
' Methods
Equals(o As Object) As Boolean
GetHashCode() As Int32
IsDefaultAttribute() As Boolean
```

PropertyDescriptor Class

Holds a description of the property that consists of the property name, type of property, its attributes, and the component class that owns the property.

Inheritance—Object.MemberDescriptor.PropertyDescriptor

```
public class System.ComponentModel.PropertyDescriptor
  ' Properties
  ComponentType As System.Type (read only)
  Converter As
    System.ComponentModel.TypeConverter (read only)
  IsLocalizable As System.Boolean (read only)
  IsReadOnly As System.Boolean (read only)
  PropertyType As System.Type (read only)
  SerializationVisibility As System.ComponentModel.
      DesignerSerializationVisibility (read only)
  ' Methods
  AddValueChanged(component As Object,
    handler As EventHandler)
  CanResetValue(component As Object) As Boolean
  Equals(obj As Object) As Boolean
  GetChildProperties() As PropertyDescriptorCollection
  GetChildProperties(instance As Object,
    filter As Attribute()) As PropertyDescriptorCollection
  GetChildProperties(instance As Object)
    As PropertyDescriptorCollection
  GetChildProperties(filter As Attribute())
    As PropertyDescriptorCollection
  GetEditor(editorBaseType As Type) As Object
  GetHashCode() As Int32
  GetValue(component As Object) As Object
  RemoveValueChanged(component As Object,
    handler As EventHandler)
  ResetValue(component As Object)
  SetValue(component As Object, value As Object)
  ShouldSerializeValue(component As Object) As Boolean
```

6

PropertyDescriptorCollection Class

Holds a collection of PropertyDescriptor objects. Found as System.ComponentModel.**PropertyDescriptorCollection.**

PropertyTabAttribute Class

Indicates which tab or tabs within the Properties window display the specified property.

Inheritance—Object.Attribute.PropertyTabAttribute

```
public class System.ComponentModel.PropertyTabAttribute
  ' Constructors
  PropertyTabAttribute(tabClass As Type)
  PropertyTabAttribute()
  PropertyTabAttribute(tabClassName As String)
  PropertyTabAttribute(tabClassName As String,
    tabScope As PropertyTabScope)
  PropertyTabAttribute(tabClass As Type,
    tabScope As PropertyTabScope)
  ' Properties
  TabClasses As System.Type() (read only)
  TabScopes As
    System.ComponentModel.PropertyTabScope() (read only)
  ' Methods
  Equals(other As Object) As Boolean
  Equals(other As PropertyTabAttribute) As Boolean
  GetHashCode() As Int32
```

ProvidePropertyAttribute Class

Holds a string of the name of the property that will be passed to other components by the IExtenderProvider. If a property is marked with this attribute, the class that contains it must include Get and Set methods that match the property name.

Inheritance—Object.Attribute.ProvidePropertyAttribute

```
public class Sys-
tem.ComponentModel.ProvidePropertyAttribute
  ' Constructors
  ProvidePropertyAttribute(propertyName As String,
    receiverType As Type)
  ProvidePropertyAttribute(propertyName As String,
    receiverTypeName As String)
  ' Properties
  PropertyName As System.String (read only)
  ReceiverTypeName As System.String (read only)
  TypeId As System.Object (read only)
  ' Methods
  Equals(obj As Object) As Boolean
  GetHashCode() As Int32
```


ReadOnlyAttribute Class

Indicates that the specified property is read-only at design time. The default setting is False, which makes the property read and write capable.

Inheritance—Object.Attribute.ReadOnlyAttribute

```
public class System.ComponentModel.ReadOnlyAttribute
  ' Constructors
  ReadOnlyAttribute(isReadOnly As Boolean)
  ' Properties
  IsReadOnly As System.Boolean (read only)
  ' Methods
  Equals(value As Object) As Boolean
  GetHashCode() As Int32
  IsDefaultAttribute() As Boolean
```

RecommendedAsConfigurableAttribute Class

Indicates that the specified property can be used as an application setting. If set to True, the property will be displayed in the Configurable Properties of VS.NET's Properties window. The default setting is False.

Inheritance—Object.Attribute. RecommendedAsConfigurableAttribute

```
public class System.ComponentModel.
    RecommendedAsConfigurableAttribute
  ' Constructors
  RecommendedAsConfigurableAttribute(
    recommendedAsConfigurable As Boolean)
  ' Properties
  RecommendedAsConfigurable As System.Boolean (read only)
  ' Methods
  Equals(obj As Object) As Boolean
  GetHashCode() As Int32
  IsDefaultAttribute() As Boolean
```

ReferenceConverter Class

Converts an object reference to and from various data types. For proper use, this class needs a component site or a usable ITypeDescriptorContext. Use the GetConverter() method of the TypeDescriptor object to obtain an instance of this class.

Inheritance—Object.TypeConverter. ReferenceConverter

```
public class System.ComponentModel.ReferenceConverter
  ' Constructors
  ReferenceConverter(type As Type)
  ' Methods
  CanConvertFrom(context As ITypeDescriptorContext,
    sourceType As Type) As Boolean
  ConvertFrom(context As ITypeDescriptorContext, culture
    As CultureInfo, value As Object) As Object
```

```
ConvertTo(context As ITypeDescriptorContext, culture As
  CultureInfo, value As Object, destinationType As Type)
  As Object
GetStandardValues(context As ITypeDescriptorContext)
  As StandardValuesCollection
GetStandardValuesExclusive(context As
  ITypeDescriptorContext) As Boolean
GetStandardValuesSupported(context As
  ITypeDescriptorContext) As Boolean
```

RefreshPropertiesAttribute Class

Indicates the mode that will be used to refresh the property when a value change occurs. Refresh modes include All (requery and repaint the properties), None (don't refresh), and Repaint (refresh the display of the property). This class is not inheritable.

Inheritance—Object.Attribute.RefreshPropertiesAttribute

```
public class System.ComponentModel.
    RefreshPropertiesAttribute
  ' Constructors
  RefreshPropertiesAttribute(refresh As RefreshProperties)
  ' Properties
  RefreshProperties As
    System.ComponentModel.RefreshProperties (read only)
  ' Methods
  Equals(value As Object) As Boolean
  GetHashCode() As Int32
  IsDefaultAttribute() As Boolean
```

RunInstallerAttribute Class

Indicates whether an installer should be run during the installation of the specified assembly. If set to True, VS.NET's Custom Action Installer or the InstallUtil.exe utility will be execute when the assembly is installed. The default is False.

Inheritance—Object.Attribute.RunInstallerAttribute

```
public class System.ComponentModel.RunInstallerAttribute
  ' Constructors
  RunInstallerAttribute(runInstaller As Boolean)
  ' Properties
  RunInstaller As System.Boolean (read only)
  ' Methods
  Equals(obj As Object) As Boolean
  GetHashCode() As Int32
  IsDefaultAttribute() As Boolean
```

SByteConverter Class

Converts an 8-bit unsigned integer object to and from a String data type. Use the GetConverter() method of the TypeDescriptor object to obtain an instance of this class.

Inheritance—Object.TypeConverter.BaseNumberConverter.SByteConverter

```
public class System.ComponentModel.SByteConverter
  ' Constructors
  SByteConverter()
```

SingleConverter Class

Converts a single-precision floating-point number object to and from a String data type. Use the GetConverter() method of the TypeDescriptor object to obtain an instance of this class.

Inheritance—Object.TypeConverter.BaseNumberConverter.SingleConverter

```
public class System.ComponentModel.SingleConverter
  ' Constructors
  SingleConverter()
```

StringConverter Class

Converts a String object to and from other data types. Use the GetConverter() method of the TypeDescriptor object to obtain an instance of this class.

Inheritance—Object.TypeConverter.StringConverter

```
public class System.ComponentModel.StringConverter
  ' Constructors
  StringConverter()
  ' Methods
  CanConvertFrom(context As ITypeDescriptorContext,
    sourceType As Type) As Boolean
  ConvertFrom(context As ITypeDescriptorContext,
    culture As CultureInfo, value As Object) As Object
```

6

SyntaxCheck Class

Provides methods that can be used to check the syntax of machine names, paths, and rooted paths.

Inheritance—Object.SyntaxCheck

```
public class System.ComponentModel.SyntaxCheck
  ' Methods
  CheckMachineName(value As String) As Boolean
  CheckPath(value As String) As Boolean
  CheckRootedPath(value As String) As Boolean
```

TimeSpanConverter Class

Converts a TimeSpan object to and from a String data type. Use the GetConverter() method of the TypeDescriptor object to obtain an instance of this class.

Inheritance—Object.TypeConverter.TimeSpanConverter

```
public class System.ComponentModel.TimeSpanConverter
  ' Constructors
  TimeSpanConverter()
  ' Methods
  CanConvertFrom(context As ITypeDescriptorContext,
    sourceType As Type) As Boolean
  CanConvertTo(context As ITypeDescriptorContext,
    destinationType As Type) As Boolean
  ConvertFrom(context As ITypeDescriptorContext,
    culture As CultureInfo, value As Object) As Object
  ConvertTo(context As ITypeDescriptorContext,
    culture As CultureInfo, value As Object,
    destinationType As Type) As Object
```

ToolboxItemAttribute Class

Holds the data type and an attribute related to the specified toolbox item object.

Inheritance—Object.Attribute.ToolboxItemAttribute

```
public class System.ComponentModel.ToolboxItemAttribute
  ' Constructors
  ToolboxItemAttribute(toolboxItemTypeName As String)
  ToolboxItemAttribute(defaultType As Boolean)
  ToolboxItemAttribute(toolboxItemType As Type)
  ' Properties
  ToolboxItemType As System.Type (read only)
  ToolboxItemTypeName As System.String (read only)
  ' Methods
  Equals(obj As Object) As Boolean
  GetHashCode() As Int32
  IsDefaultAttribute() As Boolean
```

TypeConverter Class

Converts the value of an object from one data type to another. The provider may be specified during class definition in both VB (*<TypeConverter (GetType(MyClassConverter))> Public Class* *myClass()*) and C# (*[TypeConverter(typeof(MyClassConverter))] public class myClass {}*).

Inheritance—Object.TypeConverter

```
public class System.ComponentModel.TypeConverter
  ' Constructors
  TypeConverter()
  ' Methods
  CanConvertFrom(sourceType As Type) As Boolean
  CanConvertFrom(context As ITypeDescriptorContext,
    sourceType As Type) As Boolean
  CanConvertTo(destinationType As Type) As Boolean
  CanConvertTo(context As ITypeDescriptorContext,
    destinationType As Type) As Boolean
  ConvertFrom(value As Object) As Object
  ConvertFrom(context As ITypeDescriptorContext,
    culture As CultureInfo, value As Object) As Object
  ConvertFromInvariantString(context As
    ITypeDescriptorContext, text As String) As Object
  ConvertFromInvariantString(text As String) As Object
  ConvertFromString(context As ITypeDescriptorContext,
    culture As CultureInfo, text As String) As Object
  ConvertFromString(context As ITypeDescriptorContext,
    text As String) As Object
  ConvertFromString(text As String) As Object
  ConvertTo(value As Object, destinationType As Type)
    As Object
  ConvertTo(context As ITypeDescriptorContext,
    culture As CultureInfo, value As Object,
    destinationType As Type) As Object
  ConvertToInvariantString(context As
    ITypeDescriptorContext, value As Object) As String
  ConvertToInvariantString(value As Object) As String
  ConvertToString(context As ITypeDescriptorContext,
    culture As CultureInfo, value As Object) As String
  ConvertToString(context As ITypeDescriptorContext,
    value As Object) As String
  ConvertToString(value As Object) As String
  CreateInstance(context As ITypeDescriptorContext,
    propertyValues As IDictionary) As Object
  CreateInstance(propertyValues As IDictionary) As Object
  GetCreateInstanceSupported( [context As
    ITypeDescriptorContext] ) As Boolean
  GetProperties(value As Object)
    As PropertyDescriptorCollection
  GetProperties(context As ITypeDescriptorContext,
    value As Object [,attributes As Attribute()] )
    As PropertyDescriptorCollection
```

6

```
  GetPropertiesSupported( [context As
    ITypeDescriptorContext]) As Boolean
  GetStandardValues(context As ITypeDescriptorContext)
    As StandardValuesCollection
  GetStandardValues() As ICollection
  GetStandardValuesExclusive(
    [context As ITypeDescriptorContext] ) As Boolean
  GetStandardValuesSupported( [context As
    ITypeDescriptorContext] ) As Boolean
  IsValid(context As ITypeDescriptorContext,
    value As Object) As Boolean
  IsValid(value As Object) As Boolean
```

TypeConverterAttribute Class

Indicates what type of converter should be used for the specified object. This class is not inheritable.

Inheritance—Object.Attribute.TypeConverterAttribute

```
public class System.ComponentModel.TypeConverterAttribute
  ' Constructors
  TypeConverterAttribute(typeName As String)
  TypeConverterAttribute()
  TypeConverterAttribute(type As Type)
  ' Properties
  ConverterTypeName As System.String (read only)
  ' Methods
  Equals(obj As Object) As Boolean
  GetHashCode() As Int32
```

TypeDescriptor Class

Contains the information descriptions of the events and properties of a component. This class is static or shared, so an instance of this class may not be created by the developer. The GetConverter() method is the source of obtaining instances of most of the converter classes (such as TypeListConverter, UInt16Converter, etc.). This class is not inheritable.

Inheritance—Object.TypeDescriptor

```
public class System.ComponentModel.TypeDescriptor
  ' Properties
  ComNativeDescriptorHandler As
    System.ComponentModel.IComNativeDescriptorHandler
  ' Methods
  AddEditorTable(editorBaseType As Type,
    table As Hashtable)
  CreateDesigner(component As IComponent,
    designerBaseType As Type) As IDesigner
  CreateEvent(componentType As Type, name As String, type
    As Type, attributes As Attribute()) As EventDescriptor
  CreateEvent(componentType As Type, oldEventDescriptor
    As EventDescriptor, attributes As Attribute())
    As EventDescriptor
  CreateProperty(componentType As Type, name As String,
    type As Type, attributes As Attribute())
    As PropertyDescriptor
  CreateProperty(componentType As Type,
    oldPropertyDescriptor As PropertyDescriptor,
    attributes As Attribute()) As PropertyDescriptor
  GetAttributes(component As Object
    [,noCustomTypeDesc As Boolean]) As AttributeCollection
  GetAttributes(componentType As Type)
    As AttributeCollection
  GetClassName(component As Object
    [,noCustomTypeDesc As Boolean]) As String
  GetComponentName(component As Object
    [,noCustomTypeDesc As Boolean]) As String
  GetConverter(component As Object
    [,noCustomTypeDesc As Boolean]) As TypeConverter
  GetConverter(type As Type) As TypeConverter
  GetDefaultEvent(component As Object
    [,noCustomTypeDesc As Boolean]) As EventDescriptor
  GetDefaultEvent(componentType As Type) As EventDescriptor
  GetDefaultProperty(component As Object
    [,noCustomTypeDesc As Boolean]) As PropertyDescriptor
  GetDefaultProperty(componentType As Type)
    As PropertyDescriptor
  GetEditor(component As Object, editorBaseType As Type
    [,noCustomTypeDesc As Boolean]) As Object
  GetEditor(type As Type, editorBaseType As Type) As Object
  GetEvents(componentType As Type
    [,attributes As Attribute()])
    As EventDescriptorCollection
  GetEvents(component As Object, attributes As Attribute()
    [,noCustomTypeDesc As Boolean])
    As EventDescriptorCollection
  GetEvents(component As Object [,noCustomTypeDesc As
    Boolean]) As EventDescriptorCollection
```

```
  GetProperties(componentType As Type [,attributes As
    Attribute()]) As PropertyDescriptorCollection
  GetProperties(component As Object, attributes As
    Attribute() [,noCustomTypeDesc As Boolean])
    As PropertyDescriptorCollection
  GetProperties(component As Object, noCustomTypeDesc
    As Boolean) As PropertyDescriptorCollection
  GetProperties(component As Object)
    As PropertyDescriptorCollection
  Refresh(module As Module)
  Refresh(assembly As Assembly)
  Refresh(type As Type)
  Refresh(component As Object)
  SortDescriptorArray(infos As IList)
  ' Events
  Refreshed As System.ComponentModel.RefreshEventHandler
```

TypeListConverter Class

A foundation class that provides conversion capabilities to transform a list of items into a list in the proper format for display in a ListBox control. A list of types to be converted must be passed to the constructor when this class is instantiated. Use the GetConverter() method of the TypeDescriptor object to obtain an instance of this class.

Inheritance—Object.TypeConverter.TypeListConverter

```
public class System.ComponentModel.TypeListConverter
  ' Methods
  CanConvertFrom(context As ITypeDescriptorContext,
    sourceType As Type) As Boolean
  CanConvertTo(context As ITypeDescriptorContext,
    destinationType As Type) As Boolean
  ConvertFrom(context As ITypeDescriptorContext,
    culture As CultureInfo, value As Object) As Object
  ConvertTo(context As ITypeDescriptorContext,
    culture As CultureInfo, value As Object,
    destinationType As Type) As Object
  GetStandardValues(context As ITypeDescriptorContext)
    As StandardValuesCollection
  GetStandardValuesExclusive(
    context As ITypeDescriptorContext) As Boolean
  GetStandardValuesSupported(
    context As ITypeDescriptorContext) As Boolean
```

UInt16Converter Class

Converts a 16-bit unsigned integer object to and from a String data type. Use the GetConverter() method of the TypeDescriptor object to obtain an instance of this class.

Inheritance—Object.TypeConverter. BaseNumberConverter.UInt16Converter

```
public class System.ComponentModel.UInt16Converter
  ' Constructors
  UInt16Converter()
```


UInt32Converter Class

Converts a 32-bit unsigned integer object to and from a String data type. Use the GetConverter() method of the TypeDescriptor object to obtain an instance of this class.

Inheritance—Object.TypeConverter. BaseNumberConverter.UInt32Converter

```
public class System.ComponentModel.UInt32Converter
  ' Constructors
  UInt32Converter()
```

UInt64Converter Class

Converts a 64-bit unsigned integer object to and from a String data type. Use the GetConverter() method of the TypeDescriptor object to obtain an instance of this class.

Inheritance—Object.TypeConverter. BaseNumberConverter.UInt64Converter

```
public class System.ComponentModel.UInt64Converter
  ' Constructors
  UInt64Converter()
```

Chapter 7
Threading

Threading capabilities are an important facet of the resource management abilities of the .NET framework. A thread is an independent process or operation that can be used to effectively segregate divisions of execution. For example, while a program such as Microsoft Excel has a core event loop, a thread might be created to handle printing in the background while the user can continue working with the program. Additionally, a calculation thread might be used to provide background tabulation so the user doesn't have to wait until formula recalculation is complete.

Threading becomes even more important in a multiprocessor system. By having processes split into several threads, they can be distributed across multiple processors for the most effective use of resources. Threads require the OS to devote special resources to the management of each separate process, so for greatest performance, remain frugal in your use of threads.

Threads should be used primarily for background processes, unattended communication such as network server interaction, and operations that can benefit from multiprocessor execution. Operations between threads can also be synchronized for most effective use of limited resources including communication ports, file handles, and global/shared variables.

In the .NET system, threads execute in the application domain (represented by the AppDomain class) where they were created. Each application domain is an isolated environment that keeps the applications separate from one another while executing on the runtime system.

To create a simple application that spawns an additional execution thread, start a new Windows application project in Visual Basic. Add a new class file to the project and call it myThreadClass. Then enter the following code into that class:

```
Public Class myThreadClass
    Public Sub myThreadSub()
        Dim i, j As Integer
        Console.WriteLine( _
          "This line is written from myThread.")
```

```
        For i = 0 To 100000
            j = j + 1
        Next
        Console.WriteLine("Completed myThread process.")
    End Sub
End Class
```

On the main form of this project, place a command button and name it *cmdStartThread*. At the top of the source code for the form, add the following statement:

```
Imports System.Threading
```

Insert this code into the Click event of the command button:

```
Sub cmdStartThread_Click()
  Dim myObject As New myThreadClass()
  Dim myThread As _
    New Thread(AddressOf myObject.myThreadSub)

  MyThread.Start()
End Sub
```

Run the application and click on the button to cause a new thread to be created and executed. Console messages will be written into the Output window by the thread.

AutoResetEvent Class

Holds the state of "signaled" until a single waiting thread is released. Then the state is changed to "unsignaled." See the "WaitHandle Class" section later in this chapter for more information on the parent of this class. This class is not inheritable.

Inheritance—Object.MarshalByRefObject. WaitHandle.AutoResetEvent

```
public class System.Threading.AutoResetEvent
  ' Constructors
  AutoResetEvent(initialState As Boolean)
  ' Methods
  Reset() As Boolean
  Set() As Boolean
```

Interlocked Class

Provides a way to manage variables that are shared between different threads. This class can synchronize access for incrementing, decrementing, exchanging, and comparing data between two threads. Shared variables can have an Int32, Int64, Single, or Object data type.

Inheritance—Object.Interlocked

```
public class System.Threading.Interlocked
  ' Methods
  CompareExchange(location1 As Int32&, value As Int32,
    comparand As Int32) As Int32
  CompareExchange(location1 As Single&, value As Single,
    comparand As Single) As Single
  CompareExchange(location1 As Object&, value As Object,
    comparand As Object) As Object
  Decrement(location As Int64&) As Int64
  Decrement(location As Int32&) As Int32
  Exchange(location1 As Object&, value As Object) As Object
  Exchange(location1 As Single&, value As Single) As Single
  Exchange(location1 As Int32&, value As Int32) As Int32
  Increment(location As Int32&) As Int32
  Increment(location As Int64&) As Int64
```


Monitor Class

Provides synchronization among threads through lock, unlock, and wait signal mechanisms. Using the functions Enter, TryEnter, and Exit that are included in all .NET languages, this class provides the ability to manipulate the sync lock block of an object. Sync locking is recommended only on private objects, because a lock on a public object could cause a deadlock with another unrelated thread or process.

Inheritance—Object.Monitor

```
public class System.Threading.Monitor
  ' Methods
  Enter(obj As Object)
```

```
Exit(obj As Object)
Pulse(obj As Object)
PulseAll(obj As Object)
TryEnter(obj As Object, timeout As TimeSpan) As Boolean
TryEnter(obj As Object) As Boolean
TryEnter(obj As Object, millisecondsTimeout As Int32)
  As Boolean
Wait(obj As Object) As Boolean
Wait(obj As Object, timeout As TimeSpan) As Boolean
Wait(obj As Object, millisecondsTimeout As Int32,
  exitContext As Boolean) As Boolean
Wait(obj As Object, timeout As TimeSpan,
  exitContext As Boolean) As Boolean
Wait(obj As Object, millisecondsTimeout As Int32)
  As Boolean
```

Mutex Class

Provides a primitive mechanism for interprocess synchronization by allowing a thread to place an exclusive lock on a shared resource. When a thread acquires a mutex lock on a resource, other threads attempting to access that resource will be suspended until the lock is removed. The Wait language function can be used to query a resource for the current lock condition.

Inheritance—Object.MarshalByRefObject.WaitHandle.Mutex

```
public class System.Threading.Mutex
  ' Constructors
  Mutex(initiallyOwned As Boolean)
  Mutex()
  Mutex(initiallyOwned As Boolean, name As String)
  Mutex(initiallyOwned As Boolean, name As String,
    gotOwnership As Boolean&)
  ' Methods
  ReleaseMutex()
```

Overlapped Class

Converts a class between the two types of overlapped classes: the managed overlapped class and the native overlapped class.

Overlapped classes are classes that have working editions in both the managed environment (the .NET Common Language Runtime) and unmanaged environment (such as a traditional COM object or DLL). Objects of this class can also pack and unpack objects of either type of class. Unlike managed overlapped classes, objects created as native overlapped classes are not CLS compliant. Note that some of the methods for classes that handle overlapped structures are not available from Visual Basic.NET (check the Visual Studio documentation for exact specifications).

Inheritance—Object.Overlapped

```
public class System.Threading.Overlapped
  ' Constructors
  Overlapped()
  Overlapped(offsetLo As Int32, offsetHi As Int32,
    hEvent As Int32, ar As IAsyncResult)
  ' Properties
  AsyncResult As System.IAsyncResult
  EventHandle As System.Int32
  OffsetHigh As System.Int32
  OffsetLow As System.Int32
  ' Methods
  Free(nativeOverlappedPtr As NativeOverlapped*)
  Pack(iocb As IOCompletionCallback) As NativeOverlapped*
  Unpack(nativeOverlappedPtr As NativeOverlapped*)
    As Overlapped
  UnsafePack(iocb As IOCompletionCallback)
    As NativeOverlapped*
```


ReaderWriterLock Class

Indicates what reader and writer locks exist on a thread. This class can be used to define the rules of a single-reader/multiple-writer configuration.

Inheritance—Object.ReaderWriterLock

```
public class System.Threading.ReaderWriterLock
  ' Constructors
  ReaderWriterLock()
  ' Properties
  IsReaderLockHeld As System.Boolean (read only)
  IsWriterLockHeld As System.Boolean (read only)
  WriterSeqNum As System.Int32 (read only)
  ' Methods
```

```
  AcquireReaderLock(millisecondsTimeout As Int32)
  AcquireReaderLock(timeout As TimeSpan)
  AcquireWriterLock(timeout As TimeSpan)
  AcquireWriterLock(millisecondsTimeout As Int32)
  AnyWritersSince(seqNum As Int32) As Boolean
  DowngradeFromWriterLock(lockCookie As LockCookie&)
  ReleaseLock() As LockCookie
  ReleaseReaderLock()
  ReleaseWriterLock()
  RestoreLock(lockCookie As LockCookie&)
  UpgradeToWriterLock(millisecondsTimeout As Int32)
    As LockCookie
  UpgradeToWriterLock(timeout As TimeSpan) As LockCookie
```

RegisteredWaitHandle Class

Holds a handle to a registered wait operation that may have been initialized through the ThreadPool class. The Unregister() method cancels the wait operation.

Inheritance—Object.RegisteredWaitHandle

```
public class System.Threading.RegisteredWaitHandle
  ' Methods
  Unregister(waitObject As WaitHandle) As Boolean
```

Thread Class

Foundation class that represents each execution thread on the current system. This class manages the characteristics of each thread, including the thread execution, priority, and current status.

Inheritance—Object.Thread

```
public class System.Threading.Thread
  ' Constructors
  Thread(start As ThreadStart)
  ' Properties
  ApartmentState As System.Threading.ApartmentState
  CurrentContext As
    System.Runtime.Remoting.Contexts.Context (read only)
```

```
CurrentCulture As System.Globalization.CultureInfo
CurrentPrincipal As System.Security.Principal.IPrincipal
CurrentThread As System.Threading.Thread (read only)
CurrentUICulture As System.Globalization.CultureInfo
IsAlive As System.Boolean (read only)
IsBackground As System.Boolean
Name As System.String
Priority As System.Threading.ThreadPriority
ThreadState As System.Threading.ThreadState (read only)
' Methods
Abort()
Abort(stateInfo As Object)
AllocateDataSlot() As LocalDataStoreSlot
AllocateNamedDataSlot(name As String)
  As LocalDataStoreSlot
FreeNamedDataSlot(name As String)
GetData(slot As LocalDataStoreSlot) As Object
GetDomain() As AppDomain
GetDomainID() As Int32
GetNamedDataSlot(name As String) As LocalDataStoreSlot
Interrupt()
Join()
Join(millisecondsTimeout As Int32) As Boolean
Join(timeout As TimeSpan) As Boolean
ResetAbort()
Resume()
SetData(slot As LocalDataStoreSlot, data As Object)
Sleep(timeout As TimeSpan)
Sleep(millisecondsTimeout As Int32)
Start()
Suspend()
```

7

ThreadPool Class

Used to manage a thread pool, including queuing and requesting wait designations for items. This class is not inheritable.

Inheritance—Object.ThreadPool

```
public class System.Threading.ThreadPool
  ' Methods
  BindHandle(osHandle As IntPtr) As Boolean
  QueueUserWorkItem(callBack As WaitCallback,
    state As Object) As Boolean
  QueueUserWorkItem(callBack As WaitCallback) As Boolean
  RegisterWaitForSingleObject(waitObject As WaitHandle,
    callBack As WaitOrTimerCallback, state As Object,
```

```
  millisecondsTimeOutInterval As UInt32, executeOnlyOnce
  As Boolean) As RegisteredWaitHandle
RegisterWaitForSingleObject(waitObject As WaitHandle,
  callBack As WaitOrTimerCallback, state As Object,
  timeout As TimeSpan, executeOnlyOnce As Boolean)
  As RegisteredWaitHandle
RegisterWaitForSingleObject(waitObject As WaitHandle,
  callBack As WaitOrTimerCallback, state As Object,
  millisecondsTimeOutInterval As Int32, executeOnlyOnce
  As Boolean) As RegisteredWaitHandle
RegisterWaitForSingleObject(waitObject As WaitHandle,
  callBack As WaitOrTimerCallback, state As Object,
  millisecondsTimeOutInterval As Int64, executeOnlyOnce
  As Boolean) As RegisteredWaitHandle
UnsafeQueueUserWorkItem(callBack As WaitCallback, state
  As Object) As Boolean
UnsafeRegisterWaitForSingleObject(waitObject As
  WaitHandle, callBack As WaitOrTimerCallback, state As
  Object, millisecondsTimeOutInterval As Int32,
  executeOnlyOnce As Boolean) As RegisteredWaitHandle
UnsafeRegisterWaitForSingleObject(waitObject As
  WaitHandle, callBack As WaitOrTimerCallback, state As
  Object, millisecondsTimeOutInterval As UInt32,
  executeOnlyOnce As Boolean) As RegisteredWaitHandle
UnsafeRegisterWaitForSingleObject(waitObject As
  WaitHandle, callBack As WaitOrTimerCallback, state As
  Object, timeout As TimeSpan, executeOnlyOnce As
  Boolean) As RegisteredWaitHandle
UnsafeRegisterWaitForSingleObject(waitObject As
  WaitHandle, callBack As WaitOrTimerCallback, state As
  Object, millisecondsTimeOutInterval As Int64,
  executeOnlyOnce As Boolean) As RegisteredWaitHandle
```

Timeout Class

Contains the constant timeout value for thread interruption. This class is not inheritable. Found as System.Threading.**Timeout**.

Timer Class

Activates a delegate when signaled by expiration of the specified time. When the time (specified in absolute or relative terms) expires, the timer is set in a signaled state. The Timer class can only be used on Windows 2000, Windows XP, and later OS editions. On other OS versions, activating this class will throw an exception. This class is not inheritable.

Inheritance—Object.Timer

```
public class System.Threading.Timer
  ' Constructors
  Timer(callback As TimerCallback, state As Object,
    dueTime As TimeSpan, period As TimeSpan)
  Timer(callback As TimerCallback, state As Object,
    dueTime As Int32, period As Int32)
  Timer(callback As TimerCallback, state As Object,
    dueTime As Int64, period As Int64)
  Timer(callback As TimerCallback, state As Object,
    dueTime As UInt32, period As UInt32)
  ' Methods
  Change(dueTime As Int64, period As Int64) As Boolean
  Change(dueTime As TimeSpan, period As TimeSpan)
    As Boolean
  Change(dueTime As Int32, period As Int32) As Boolean
  Change(dueTime As UInt32, period As UInt32) As Boolean
  Dispose()
  Dispose(notifyObject As WaitHandle) As Boolean
```


WaitHandle Class

Provides a foundation class for all synchronization objects that execute at runtime. Child classes AutoResetEvent, ManualResetEvent, and Mutex all inherit from this class. The IOStream, Thread, Mutex, Event, Process, AppDomain, and other Win32 synchronization objects are also derived from this class.

Inheritance—Object.MarshalByRefObject.WaitHandle

```
public class System.Threading.WaitHandle
  ' Constructors
  WaitHandle()
  ' Properties
  Handle As System.IntPtr
  ' Methods
  Close()
  WaitAll(waitHandles As WaitHandle[], timeout As TimeSpan,
    exitContext As Boolean) As Boolean
```

```
WaitAll(waitHandles As WaitHandle[]) As Boolean
WaitAll(waitHandles As WaitHandle[],
 millisecondsTimeout As Int32, exitContext As Boolean)
 As Boolean
WaitAny(waitHandles As WaitHandle[], timeout As TimeSpan,
  exitContext As Boolean) As Int32
WaitAny(waitHandles As WaitHandle[]) As Int32
WaitAny(waitHandles As WaitHandle[],
  millisecondsTimeout As Int32, exitContext As Boolean)
  As Int32
WaitOne() As Boolean
WaitOne(timeout As TimeSpan, exitContext As Boolean)
  As Boolean
WaitOne(millisecondsTimeout As Int32,
  exitContext As Boolean) As Boolean
```

Chapter 8
System

The System namespace contains many classes for data conversion, argument modification, mathematics, control of the execution environment, remote and local program invocation, and administration of all execution processes (managed and unmanaged). The System classes offer common functionality and enumeration of values that are needed by most applications, regardless of type.

Some of the most useful classes in the System namespace are used for the management and modification of system data types. The Array class, for example, represents the data type that is used for array structures. The Copy() method of the Array object can be used to quickly and easily duplicate values between two arrays like this:

```
Dim myIntArray() As Integer = {10, 20, 30, 40, 50, 60}
Dim myObjArray() As Object = {"A", "B", "C", "D", "E", "F"}

' Copy the first three numbers into the object array
Array.Copy(myIntArray, myObjArray, 3)
```

This code demonstrates one simple example of the utility methods available in the System classes.

8

Activator Class

Provides a method to create local or remote objects and to retrieve references of existing objects.

Inheritance—Object.Activator

```
public class System.Activator
  ' Methods
  CreateComInstanceFrom(assemblyName As String,
    typeName As String) As ObjectHandle
  CreateInstance(assemblyName As String, typeName As String
    [,activationAttributes As Object() ]) As ObjectHandle
  CreateInstance(type As Type [, args As Object()
    [, activationAttributes As Object() ]]) As Object
  CreateInstance(assemblyName As String, typeName As
    String, ignoreCase As Boolean, bindingAttr As
    BindingFlags, binder As Binder, args As Object(),
```

```
    culture As CultureInfo, activationAttributes As
    Object(), securityInfo As Evidence) As ObjectHandle
  CreateInstance(type As Type, bindingAttr As BindingFlags,
    binder As Binder, args As Object(), culture As
    CultureInfo [, activationAttributes As Object()])
    As Object
  CreateInstanceFrom(assemblyFile As String, typeName
    As String, ignoreCase As Boolean, bindingAttr As
    BindingFlags, binder As Binder, args As Object(),
    culture As CultureInfo, activationAttributes As
    Object(), securityInfo As Evidence) As ObjectHandle
  CreateInstanceFrom(assemblyFile As String, typeName As
    String [,activationAttributes As Object() ])
    As ObjectHandle
  GetObject(type As Type, url As String
    [, state As Object]) As Object
```

AppDomain Class

Holds the execution environment for each application. Each AppDomain instance contains an enumeration of assemblies and threads executing in that domain. Each application domain also holds routines for creating dynamic assemblies, loading assemblies, handling domain termination events, and managing manual loading of assemblies and types. This class is not inheritable. Found as System.**AppDomain.**

AppDomainSetup Class

Holds the foundation information used to set up a new AppDomain class.

Inheritance—Object.AppDomainSetup

```
public class System.AppDomainSetup
  ' Constructors
  AppDomainSetup()
  ' Properties
  ApplicationBase As System.String
  ApplicationName As System.String
  CachePath As System.String
```

```
ConfigurationFile As System.String
DynamicBase As System.String
LicenseFile As System.String
LoaderOptimization As System.LoaderOptimization
PrivateBinPath As System.String
PrivateBinPathProbe As System.String
ShadowCopyDirectories As System.String
ShadowCopyFiles As System.String
```

Array Class

Provides the foundation class for all array use and management. This class includes routines to create, sort, merge, and modify arrays.

Inheritance—Object.Array

```
public class System.Array
  ' Properties
  IsFixedSize As System.Boolean (read only)
  IsReadOnly As System.Boolean (read only)
  IsSynchronized As System.Boolean (read only)
  Length As System.Int32 (read only)
  Rank As System.Int32 (read only)
  SyncRoot As System.Object (read only)
  ' Methods
  BinarySearch(array As Array, value As Object
    [, comparer As IComparer]) As Int32
  BinarySearch(array As Array, index As Int32,
    length As Int32, value As Object
    [, comparer As IComparer] ) As Int32
  Clear(array As Array, index As Int32, length As Int32)
  Clone() As Object
  Copy(sourceArray As Array, destinationArray As Array,
    length As Int32)
  Copy(sourceArray As Array, sourceIndex As Int32,
    destinationArray As Array, destinationIndex As Int32,
    length As Int32)
  CopyTo(array As Array, index As Int32)
  CreateInstance(elementType As Type, lengths As Int32(),
    lowerBounds As Int32()) As Array
  CreateInstance(elementType As Type, lengths As Int32())
    As Array
  CreateInstance(elementType As Type, length As Int32)
    As Array
  CreateInstance(elementType As Type, length1 As Int32,
    length2 As Int32 [, length3 As Int32] ) As Array
```

8

```
GetEnumerator() As IEnumerator
GetLength(dimension As Int32) As Int32
GetLowerBound(dimension As Int32) As Int32
GetUpperBound(dimension As Int32) As Int32
GetValue(index As Int32) As Object
GetValue(indices As Int32()) As Object
GetValue(index1 As Int32, index2 As Int32
  [, index3 As Int32 ]) As Object
IndexOf(array As Array, value As Object
  [, startIndex As Int32 [, count As Int32 ]]) As Int32
Initialize()
LastIndexOf(array As Array, value As Object
  [, startIndex As Int32 [, count As Int32 ]]) As Int32
Reverse(array As Array [, index As Int32,
  length As Int32])
SetValue(value As Object, index As Int32)
SetValue(value As Object, indices As Int32())
SetValue(value As Object, index1 As Int32,
  index2 As Int32 [, index3 As Int32])
Sort(array As Array [, index As Int32, length As Int32])
Sort(keys As Array, items As Array [, index As Int32
  [, length As Int32, comparer As IComparer ]] )
Sort(keys As Array, items As Array, comparer
  As IComparer)
Sort(array As Array, index As Int32, length As Int32,
  comparer As IComparer)
Sort(array As Array, comparer As IComparer)
```

Attribute Class

Provides the foundation class for system and custom attributes. Attributes may be attached to a single target element, as multiple instances for a single element, or as a child element derived from the target element. A custom attribute may be stored with any element in the metadata.

Inheritance—Object.Attribute

```
public class System.Attribute
  ' Properties
  TypeId As System.Object (read only)
  ' Methods
  Equals(obj As Object) As Boolean
  GetCustomAttribute(element As
    [Assembly | MemberInfo | Module | ParameterInfo],
```

```
    attributeType As Type [, inherit As Boolean])
    As Attribute
  GetCustomAttributes(element As
    [Assembly | MemberInfo | Module | ParameterInfo]
    [,inherit As Boolean]) As Attribute()
  GetCustomAttributes(element As
    [Assembly | MemberInfo | Module | ParameterInfo],
    attributeType As Type [, inherit As Boolean])
    As Attribute()
  GetHashCode() As Int32
  IsDefaultAttribute() As Boolean
  IsDefined(element As
    [Assembly | MemberInfo | Module | ParameterInfo],
    attributeType As Type [,inherit As Boolean]) As Boolean
  Match(obj As Object) As Boolean
```

BitConverter Class

Provides routines to convert base data types to and from an array of bytes. Each byte is defined as an 8-bit unsigned integer.

Inheritance—Object.BitConverter

```
public class System.BitConverter
  ' Methods
  DoubleToInt64Bits(value As Double) As Int64
*  GetBytes(value) As Byte()
  Int64BitsToDouble(value As Int64) As Double
  ToBoolean(value As Byte(), startIndex As Int32) As Boolean
  ToChar(value As Byte(), startIndex As Int32) As Char
  ToDouble(value As Byte(), startIndex As Int32) As Double
  ToInt16(value As Byte(), startIndex As Int32) As Int16
  ToInt32(value As Byte(), startIndex As Int32) As Int32
  ToInt64(value As Byte(), startIndex As Int32) As Int64
  ToSingle(value As Byte(), startIndex As Int32) As Single
  ToString(value As Byte(), startIndex As Int32) As String
  ToString(value As Byte()) As String
  ToString(value As Byte(), startIndex As Int32,
    length As Int32) As String
  ToUInt16(value As Byte(), startIndex As Int32) As UInt16
  ToUInt32(value As Byte(), startIndex As Int32) As UInt32
  ToUInt64(value As Byte(), startIndex As Int32) As UInt64
```

* The ***value*** could be UInt16, UInt32, UInt64, Double, Single, Char, Boolean, Int16, Int32, or Int64.

Buffer Class

Holds an unmanaged block of memory and represents it as an array of bytes. This class can be used to retrieve byte saves, store byte values, determine the length of the byte array, and copy bytes from one primitive array to another while avoiding data typing.

Inheritance—Object.Buffer

```
public class System.Buffer
  ' Methods
  BlockCopy(src As Array, srcOffset As Int32, dst As Array,
    dstOffset As Int32, count As Int32)
  ByteLength(array As Array) As Int32
  GetByte(array As Array, index As Int32) As Byte
  SetByte(array As Array, index As Int32, value As Byte)
```

CharEnumerator Class

Provides read-only iterative access to individual characters stored in a String type variable.

Inheritance—Object.CharEnumerator

```
public class System.CharEnumerator
  ' Properties
  Current As System.Char (read only)
  ' Methods
  Clone() As Object
  MoveNext() As Boolean
  Reset()
```

Console Class

Provides a representation of the input, output, and error streams for console applications. This class is used for commands such as Console.WriteLine("Hello World"). This class is not inheritable.

Inheritance—Object.Console

```
public class System.Console
  ' Properties
  Error As System.IO.TextWriter (read only)
  In As System.IO.TextReader (read only)
  Out As System.IO.TextWriter (read only)
  ' Methods
  OpenStandardError( [bufferSize As Int32] ) As Stream
  OpenStandardInput( [bufferSize As Int32] ) As Stream
  OpenStandardOutput( [bufferSize As Int32] ) As Stream
  Read() As Int32
  ReadLine() As String
  SetError(newError As TextWriter)
  SetIn(newIn As TextReader)
  SetOut(newOut As TextWriter)
*  Write(value As Char)
  Write(buffer As Char() [, index As Int32,
    count As Int32] )
  Write(format As String, arg As Object())
  Write(format As String, arg0 As Object [,arg1 As Object
    [,arg2 As Object [,arg3 As Object ]]])
  WriteLine()
*  WriteLine(value)
  WriteLine(buffer As Char() [, index As Int32,
    count As Int32] )
  WriteLine(format As String, arg As Object())
  WriteLine(format As String, arg0 As Object [,arg1 As
    Object [,arg2 As Object [,arg3 As Object ]]])
```

* The parameter ***value*** can be passed as a data type of Boolean, Byte, Char, DateTime, Decimal, Double, Int16, Int32, Int64, Object, SByte, Single, String, UInt16, UInt32, or UInt64.

ContextBoundObject Class

Provides an abstract foundation class for all context-bound classes such as ServicedComponent. Found as System.**ContextBoundObject.**

Convert Class

Provides routines to convert between base data types.

8

Inheritance—Object.Convert

```
public class System.Convert
  ' Methods
  ChangeType(value As Object, typeCode As TypeCode
    [, provider As IFormatProvider] ) As Object
  ChangeType(value As Object, conversionType As Type
    [, provider As IFormatProvider ]) As Object
  FromBase64CharArray(inArray As Char(), offset As Int32,
    length As Int32) As Byte()
  FromBase64String(s As String) As Byte()
  GetTypeCode(value As Object) As TypeCode
  IsDBNull(value As Object) As Boolean
  ToBase64CharArray(inArray As Byte(), offsetIn As Int32,
    length As Int32, outArray As Char(), offsetOut As
    Int32) As Int32
  ToBase64String(inArray As Byte() [, offset As Int32,
    length As Int32]) As String
*  ToBoolean(value) As Boolean
  ToBoolean(value As String, provider As IFormatProvider)
    As Boolean
  ToBoolean(value As Object, provider As IFormatProvider)
    As Boolean
*  ToByte(value) As Byte
  ToByte(value As Object, provider As IFormatProvider)
    As Byte
  ToByte(value As String, fromBase As Int32) As Byte
  ToByte(value As String, provider As IFormatProvider)
    As Byte
*  ToChar(value) As Char
  ToChar(value As Object, provider As IFormatProvider)
    As Char
  ToChar(value As String, provider As IFormatProvider)
    As Char
*  ToDateTime(value) As DateTime
  ToDateTime(value As Object, provider As IFormatProvider)
    As DateTime
  ToDateTime(value As String, provider As IFormatProvider)
    As DateTime
*  ToDecimal(value) As Decimal
  ToDecimal(value As Object, provider As IFormatProvider)
    As Decimal
  ToDecimal(value As String, provider As IFormatProvider)
    As Decimal
*  ToDouble(value) As Double
  ToDouble(value As Object, provider As IFormatProvider)
    As Double
  ToDouble(value As String, provider As IFormatProvider)
    As Double
*  ToInt16(value) As Int16
  ToInt16(value As String, provider As IFormatProvider)
    As Int16
```

```
  ToInt16(value As Object, provider As IFormatProvider)
    As Int16
*  ToInt32(value) As Int32
  ToInt32(value As String, fromBase As Int32) As Int32
  ToInt32(value As Object, provider As IFormatProvider)
    As Int32
  ToInt32(value As String, provider As IFormatProvider)
    As Int32
*  ToInt64(value) As Int64
  ToInt64(value As String, provider As IFormatProvider)
    As Int64
  ToInt64(value As String, fromBase As Int32) As Int64
  ToInt64(value As Object, provider As IFormatProvider)
    As Int64
*  ToSByte(value) As SByte
  ToSByte(value As Object, provider As IFormatProvider)
    As SByte
  ToSByte(value As String, provider As IFormatProvider)
    As SByte
  ToSByte(value As String, fromBase As Int32) As SByte
*  ToSingle(value) As Single
  ToSingle(value As String, provider As IFormatProvider)
    As Single
*  ToString(value) As String
*  ToString(value, provider As IFormatProvider) As String
  ToString(value As [Byte | Int16 | Int32 | Int64],
    toBase As Int32) As String
*  ToUInt16(value) As UInt16
  ToUInt16(value As String, fromBase As Int32) As UInt16
  ToUInt16(value As String, provider As IFormatProvider)
    As UInt16
  ToUInt16(value As Object, provider As IFormatProvider)
    As UInt16
*  ToUInt32(value) As UInt32
  ToUInt32(value As String, fromBase As Int32) As UInt32
  ToUInt32(value As String, provider As IFormatProvider)
    As UInt32
  ToUInt32(value As Object, provider As IFormatProvider)
    As UInt32
*  ToUInt64(value) As UInt64
  ToUInt64(value As Object, provider As IFormatProvider)
    As UInt64
  ToUInt64(value As String, fromBase As Int32) As UInt64
  ToUInt64(value As String, provider As IFormatProvider)
    As UInt64
```

* The parameter ***value*** can be passed as a data type of Boolean, Byte, Char, DateTime, Decimal, Double, Int16, Int32, Int64, Object, SByte, Single, String, UInt16, UInt32, or UInt64.

8

DBNull Class

Holds a null value, which is typically used with database types. A DBNull reference indicates that the field contains no data. Use of nulls is very effective at saving space, particularly with string fields or columns. For example, if a LastName field is set to occupy 80 characters, a DBNull can indicate that no value is held within the field without taking up the 80 characters of memory or disk space that an empty string ("") would still require.

Inheritance—Object.DBNull

```
public class System.DBNull
  ' Methods
  GetObjectData(info As SerializationInfo,
    context As StreamingContext)
  GetTypeCode() As TypeCode
  ToString() As String
  ToString(provider As IFormatProvider) As String
```

Delegate Class

Provides the foundation class for delegate classes.

Inheritance—Object.Delegate

```
public class System.Delegate
  ' Properties
  Method As System.Reflection.MethodInfo (read only)
  Target As System.Object (read only)
  ' Methods
  Clone() As Object
  Combine(a As Delegate, b As Delegate) As Delegate
  Combine(delegates As Delegate()) As Delegate
  CreateDelegate(type As Type, target As Object,
    method As String) As Delegate
  CreateDelegate(type As Type, target As Type,
    method As String) As Delegate
  CreateDelegate(type As Type, method As MethodInfo)
    As Delegate
  DynamicInvoke(args As Object()) As Object
  Equals(obj As Object) As Boolean
  GetHashCode() As Int32
```

```
GetInvocationList() As Delegate()
GetObjectData(info As SerializationInfo,
  context As StreamingContext)
Remove(source As Delegate, value As Delegate) As Delegate
```

Environment Class

Holds information related to the current state of the environment and platform. Some of the properties (for example, the CurrentDirectory property) are available for modifications that change the state of the current environment.

Inheritance—Object.Environment

```
public class System.Environment
  ' Properties
  CommandLine As System.String (read only)
  CurrentDirectory As System.String
  ExitCode As System.Int32
  MachineName As System.String (read only)
  NewLine As System.String (read only)
  OSVersion As System.OperatingSystem (read only)
  StackTrace As System.String (read only)
  SystemDirectory As System.String (read only)
  TickCount As System.Int32 (read only)
  UserDomainName As System.String (read only)
  UserInteractive As System.Boolean (read only)
  UserName As System.String (read only)
  Version As System.Version (read only)
  WorkingSet As System.Int64 (read only)
  ' Methods
  Exit(exitCode As Int32)
  ExpandEnvironmentVariables(name As String) As String
  GetCommandLineArgs() As String()
  GetEnvironmentVariable(variable As String) As String
  GetEnvironmentVariables() As IDictionary
  GetFolderPath(folder As SpecialFolder) As String
  GetLogicalDrives() As String()
```


Exception Class

Provides the base class for all exception classes. Classes derived from this parent include ApplicationException,

CodeDomSerializerException, InvalidPrinterException, IOException, IsolatedStorageException, PathTooLongException, CookieException, ProtocolViolationException, WebException, MissingManifestResourceException, SUDSGeneratorException, SUDSParserException, SystemException, UriFormatException, and SoapException.

Inheritance—Object.Exception

```
public class System.Exception
  ' Constructors
  Exception( [message As String [, innerException As
    Exception ]])
  ' Properties
  HelpLink As System.String
  InnerException As System.Exception (read only)
  Message As System.String (read only)
  Source As System.String
  StackTrace As System.String (read only)
  TargetSite As System.Reflection.MethodBase (read only)
  ' Methods
  GetBaseException() As Exception
  GetObjectData(info As SerializationInfo,
    context As StreamingContext)
  ToString() As String
```

GC Class

Provides the garbage collection facilities that are critical to .NET memory management. This class allows independent manual control of the elimination settings of specific objects. See also the WeakReference class.

Inheritance—Object.GC

```
public class System.GC
  ' Properties
  MaxGeneration As System.Int32 (read only)
  ' Methods
  Collect( [generation As Int32] )
  GetGeneration(obj As Object) As Int32
  GetGeneration(wo As WeakReference) As Int32
  GetTotalMemory(forceFullCollection As Boolean) As Int64
  KeepAlive(obj As Object)
  ReRegisterForFinalize(obj As Object)
```

```
SuppressFinalize(obj As Object)
WaitForPendingFinalizers()
```

LoaderOptimizationAttribute Class

Provides the settings to optimize loading (for SingleDomain, MultiDomain, or MultiDomainHost loader optimization types) handled by the system. Settings may be adjusted when passing arguments to the constructor, but changes elsewhere will be ignored.

Inheritance—Object.Attribute. LoaderOptimizationAttribute

```
public class System.LoaderOptimizationAttribute
  ' Constructors
  LoaderOptimizationAttribute(value As
LoaderOptimization)
  LoaderOptimizationAttribute(value As Byte)
  ' Properties
  Value As System.LoaderOptimization (read only)
```

8

LocalDataStoreSlot Class

Provides a memory slot that can be used to store local data. Local data slots are used by the thread and context processes to store data local to the related object. This class is not inheritable. Found as System.**LocalDataStoreSlot.**

MarshalByRefObject Class

Provides the foundation class used for remoting objects, particularly to other parts of the .NET object framework. Classes derived from this class have a distributed identity and may appear in disparate parts of the namespace.

Inheritance—Object.MarshalByRefObject

```
public class System.MarshalByRefObject
  ' Methods
  CreateObjRef(requestedType As Type) As ObjRef
  GetLifetimeService() As Object
  InitializeLifetimeService() As Object
```

Math Class

Provides the constants and methods needed to perform most math operations, including logarithmic, trigonometric, and other functions.

Inheritance—Object.Math

```
public class System.Math
  ' Methods
  Abs(value As [Decimal | Double | Int16 | Int32 | Int64 |
    SByte | Single]) As Int32
  Acos(d As Double) As Double
  Asin(d As Double) As Double
  Atan(d As Double) As Double
  Atan2(y As Double, x As Double) As Double
  Ceiling(a As Double) As Double
  Cos(d As Double) As Double
  Cosh(value As Double) As Double
  Exp(d As Double) As Double
  Floor(d As Double) As Double
  IEEERemainder(x As Double, y As Double) As Double
  Log(a As Double [, newBase As Double]) As Double
  Log10(d As Double) As Double
*  Max(value1, value2) As value3
*  Min(value1, value2) As value3
  Pow(x As Double, y As Double) As Double
  Round(d As Decimal [, decimals As Int32]) As Decimal
  Round(value As Double, digits As Int32) As Double
  Round(a As Double) As Double
  Sign(value As [Decimal | Double | Int16 | Int32 | Int64 |
    SByte | Single]) As Int32
  Sin(a As Double) As Double
  Sinh(value As Double) As Double
  Sqrt(d As Double) As Double
  Tan(a As Double) As Double
  Tanh(value As Double) As Double
```

* The parameter ***valueX*** can be passed as a data type of Byte, Decimal, Double, Int16, Int32, Int64, SByte, Single, UInt16, UInt32, or UInt64. Note that in the functions Min and Max, the parameters passed and the values received must all be the same type.

MulticastDelegate Class

Provides a representation of a multicast delegate. This type of delegate, a child of the Delegate class, can have more than one element in its invocation list that are called sequentially when the delegate is invoked.

Inheritance—Object.Delegate.MulticastDelegate

```
public class System.MulticastDelegate
  ' Methods
  Equals(obj As Object) As Boolean
  GetHashCode() As Int32
  GetInvocationList() As Delegate()
```

Object Class

Provides the foundation class for the generic Object data type. This class is the root of the entire .NET framework object hierarchy.

8

Inheritance—Object

```
public class System.Object
  ' Constructors
  Object()
  ' Methods
  Equals(obj As Object) As Boolean
  Equals(objA As Object, objB As Object) As Boolean
  GetHashCode() As Int32
  GetType() As Type
  ReferenceEquals(objA As Object, objB As Object)
    As Boolean
  ToString() As String
```

ObsoleteAttribute Class

Indicates that a program element (such as a method or property) is deprecated and will be eliminated in future versions. This attribute may not be applied to assemblies, modules, parameters, or return values. This class is not inheritable.

Inheritance—Object.Attribute.ObsoleteAttribute

```
public class System.ObsoleteAttribute
  ' Constructors
  ObsoleteAttribute([message As String
    [, error As Boolean]])
  ' Properties
  IsError As System.Boolean (read only)
  Message As System.String (read only)
```

OperatingSystem Class

Holds information about the operating system that can be cloned or returned as a String object.

Inheritance—Object.OperatingSystem

```
public class System.OperatingSystem
  ' Constructors
  OperatingSystem(platform As PlatformID,
    version As Version)
  ' Properties
  Platform As System.PlatformID (read only)
  Version As System.Version (read only)
  ' Methods
  Clone() As Object
  ToString() As String
```

Random Class

Provides the foundation class that generates statistically valid random values. The numbers returned by this class are chosen with equal probability and are sufficiently random for most applications.

Inheritance—Object.Random

```
public class System.Random
  ' Constructors
```

```
Random( [Seed As Int32] )
' Methods
Next() As Int32
Next(minValue As Int32, maxValue As Int32) As Int32
Next(maxValue As Int32) As Int32
NextBytes(buffer As Byte())
NextDouble() As Double
```

String Class

Provides the foundation class for the String data type. The index of the string indicates a position within the string and is counted from the first character, which has an index of 0. Unless explicitly specified, search and compare operations are case-sensitive and use the cultural standards settings of the execution thread.

Inheritance—Object.String

```
public class System.String
  ' Constructors
  String(value As Char())
  String(value As Char* [, startIndex As Int32,
    length As Int32])
  String(value As SByte* [, startIndex As Int32,
    length As Int32, enc As Encoding])
  String(value As SByte*, startIndex As Int32,
    length As Int32)
  String(value As Char(), startIndex As Int32,
    length As Int32)
  String(c As Char, count As Int32)
  ' Properties
  Chars As System.Char (read only)
  Length As System.Int32 (read only)
  ' Methods
  Clone() As Object
  Compare(strA As String, indexA As Int32, strB As String,
    indexB As Int32, length As Int32 [,ignoreCase As
    Boolean [,culture As CultureInfo]]) As Int32
  Compare(strA As String, strB As String [, ignoreCase As
    Boolean [, culture As CultureInfo ]]) As Int32
  CompareOrdinal(strA As String, strB As String) As Int32
  CompareOrdinal(strA As String, indexA As Int32, strB As
    String, indexB As Int32, length As Int32) As Int32
  CompareTo(strB As String) As Int32
  CompareTo(value As Object) As Int32
```

8

Concat(arg0 As Object) As String
Concat(str0 As String, str1 As String, str2 As String, str3 As String) As String
Concat(args As Object()) As String
Concat(str0 As String, str1 As String [, str2 As String]) As String
Concat(arg0 As Object, arg1 As Object [,arg2 As Object [,arg3 As Object]]) As String
Concat(values As String()) As String
Copy(str As String) As String
CopyTo(sourceIndex As Int32, destination As Char(), destinationIndex As Int32, count As Int32)
EndsWith(value As String) As Boolean
Equals(obj As Object) As Boolean
Equals(a As String, b As String) As Boolean
Equals(value As String) As Boolean
Format(format As String, arg0 As Object [,arg1 As Object [,arg2 As Object]]) As String
Format(format As String, args As Object()) As String
Format(provider As IFormatProvider, format As String, args As Object()) As String
GetEnumerator() As CharEnumerator
GetHashCode() As Int32
GetTypeCode() As TypeCode
IndexOf(value As [Char | String]) As Int32
IndexOf(value As [Char | String], startIndex As Int32 [,count As Int32]) As Int32
IndexOfAny(anyOf As Char() [, startIndex As Int32]) As Int32
IndexOfAny(anyOf As Char(), startIndex As Int32, count As Int32) As Int32
Insert(startIndex As Int32, value As String) As String
Intern(str As String) As String
IsInterned(str As String) As String
Join(separator As String, value As String() [, startIndex As Int32, count As Int32]) As String
LastIndexOf(value As [Char | String] [,startIndex As Int32 [,count As Int32]]) As Int32
LastIndexOfAny(anyOf As Char() [,startIndex As Int32 [,count As Int32]]) As Int32
PadLeft(totalWidth As Int32 [,paddingChar As Char]) As String
PadRight(totalWidth As Int32 [,paddingChar As Char]) As String
Remove(startIndex As Int32, count As Int32) As String
Replace(oldValue As String, newValue As String) As String
Replace(oldChar As Char, newChar As Char) As String
Split(separator As Char() [, count As Int32]) As String()
StartsWith(value As String) As Boolean
Substring(startIndex As Int32 [, length As Int32]) As String

```
ToCharArray( [startIndex As Int32, length As Int32] )
  As Char()
ToLower( [culture As CultureInfo] ) As String
ToString( [provider As IFormatProvider] ) As String
ToUpper( [culture As CultureInfo] ) As String
Trim( [trimChars As Char() ]) As String
TrimEnd(trimChars As Char()) As String
TrimStart(trimChars As Char()) As String
```

TimeZone Class

Provides a representation of a time zone, including daylight savings and other time offset settings.

Inheritance—Object.TimeZone

```
public class System.TimeZone
  ' Properties
  CurrentTimeZone As System.TimeZone (read only)
  DaylightName As System.String (read only)
  StandardName As System.String (read only)
  ' Methods
  GetDaylightChanges(year As Int32) As DaylightTime
  GetUtcOffset(time As DateTime) As TimeSpan
  IsDaylightSavingTime(time As DateTime, daylightTimes
    As DaylightTime) As Boolean
  IsDaylightSavingTime(time As DateTime) As Boolean
  ToLocalTime(time As DateTime) As DateTime
  ToUniversalTime(time As DateTime) As DateTime
```


Type Class

Provides the abstract foundation class used for reflection with: array types, enumeration types, class types, interface types, and value types.

Inheritance—Object.MemberInfo.Type

```
public class System.Type
  ' Properties
  Assembly As System.Reflection.Assembly (read only)
  AssemblyQualifiedName As System.String (read only)
  Attributes As System.Reflection.TypeAttributes (read only)
```

```
BaseType As System.Type (read only)
DeclaringType As System.Type (read only)
DefaultBinder As System.Reflection.Binder (read only)
FullName As System.String (read only)
GUID As System.Guid (read only)
HasElementType As System.Boolean (read only)
IsAbstract As System.Boolean (read only)
IsAnsiClass As System.Boolean (read only)
IsArray As System.Boolean (read only)
IsAutoClass As System.Boolean (read only)
IsAutoLayout As System.Boolean (read only)
IsByRef As System.Boolean (read only)
IsClass As System.Boolean (read only)
IsCOMObject As System.Boolean (read only)
IsContextful As System.Boolean (read only)
IsEnum As System.Boolean (read only)
IsExplicitLayout As System.Boolean (read only)
IsImport As System.Boolean (read only)
IsInterface As System.Boolean (read only)
IsLayoutSequential As System.Boolean (read only)
IsMarshalByRef As System.Boolean (read only)
IsNestedAssembly As System.Boolean (read only)
IsNestedFamANDAssem As System.Boolean (read only)
IsNestedFamily As System.Boolean (read only)
IsNestedFamORAssem As System.Boolean (read only)
IsNestedPrivate As System.Boolean (read only)
IsNestedPublic As System.Boolean (read only)
IsNotPublic As System.Boolean (read only)
IsPointer As System.Boolean (read only)
IsPrimitive As System.Boolean (read only)
IsPublic As System.Boolean (read only)
IsSealed As System.Boolean (read only)
IsSerializable As System.Boolean (read only)
IsSpecialName As System.Boolean (read only)
IsUnicodeClass As System.Boolean (read only)
IsValueType As System.Boolean (read only)
MemberType As System.Reflection.MemberTypes (read only)
Module As System.Reflection.Module (read only)
Namespace As System.String (read only)
ReflectedType As System.Type (read only)
TypeHandle As System.RuntimeTypeHandle (read only)
TypeInitializer As System.Reflection.ConstructorInfo
  (read only)
UnderlyingSystemType As System.Type (read only)
' Methods
Equals(o As Object) As Boolean
Equals(o As Type) As Boolean
FindInterfaces(filter As TypeFilter, filterCriteria As
  Object) As Type()
```

FindMembers(memberType As MemberTypes, bindingAttr As BindingFlags, filter As MemberFilter, filterCriteria As Object) As MemberInfo()
GetArrayRank() As Int32
GetConstructor(bindingAttr As BindingFlags, binder As Binder, callConvention As CallingConventions, types As Type(), modifiers As ParameterModifier()) As ConstructorInfo
GetConstructor(bindingAttr As BindingFlags, binder As Binder, types As Type(), modifiers As ParameterModifier()) As ConstructorInfo
GetConstructor(types As Type()) As ConstructorInfo
GetConstructors() As ConstructorInfo()
GetConstructors(bindingAttr As BindingFlags) As ConstructorInfo()
GetDefaultMembers() As MemberInfo()
GetElementType() As Type
GetEvent(name As String [,bindingAttr As BindingFlags]) As EventInfo
GetEvents([bindingAttr As BindingFlags]) As EventInfo()
GetField(name As String [,bindingAttr As BindingFlags]) As FieldInfo
GetFields([bindingAttr As BindingFlags]) As FieldInfo()
GetHashCode() As Int32
GetInterface(name As String [, ignoreCase As Boolean]) As Type
GetInterfaceMap(interfaceType As Type) As InterfaceMapping
GetInterfaces() As Type()
GetMember(name As String [, bindingAttr As BindingFlags]) As MemberInfo()
GetMember(name As String, type As MemberTypes, bindingAttr As BindingFlags) As MemberInfo()
GetMembers() As MemberInfo()
GetMembers(bindingAttr As BindingFlags) As MemberInfo()
GetMethod(name As String [,types As Type() [,modifiers As ParameterModifier()]]) As MethodInfo
GetMethod(name As String, bindingAttr As BindingFlags [,binder As Binder, types As Type(), modifiers As ParameterModifier()]) As MethodInfo
GetMethod(name As String, bindingAttr As BindingFlags, binder As Binder, callConvention As CallingConventions, types As Type(), modifiers As ParameterModifier()) As MethodInfo
GetMethods([bindingAttr As BindingFlags]) As MethodInfo()
GetNestedType(name As String [, bindingAttr As BindingFlags]) As Type
GetNestedTypes([bindingAttr As BindingFlags]) As Type()
GetProperties([bindingAttr As BindingFlags]) As PropertyInfo()

```
GetProperty(name As String
  [,returnType As Type [,types As Type()
  [,modifiers As ParameterModifier()]]]])As PropertyInfo
GetProperty(name As String, bindingAttr As BindingFlags
  [,binder As Binder, returnType As Type, types As Type()
  ,modifiers As ParameterModifier()]) As PropertyInfo
GetProperty(name As String, types As Type())
  As PropertyInfo
GetType(typeName As String [,throwOnError As Boolean
  [,ignoreCase As Boolean]]) As Type
GetTypeArray(args As Object()) As Type()
GetTypeCode(type As Type) As TypeCode
GetTypeFromCLSID(clsid As Guid [,server As String
  [,throwOnError As Boolean ]]) As Type
GetTypeFromCLSID(clsid As Guid, throwOnError As Boolean)
  As Type
GetTypeFromHandle(handle As RuntimeTypeHandle) As Type
GetTypeFromProgID(progID As String [,throwOnError
  As Boolean] ) As Type
GetTypeFromProgID(progID As String, server As String
  [,throwOnError As Boolean]) As Type
GetTypeHandle(o As Object) As RuntimeTypeHandle
InvokeMember(name As String, invokeAttr As BindingFlags,
  binder As Binder, target As Object, args As Object(),
  culture As CultureInfo) As Object
InvokeMember(name As String, invokeAttr As BindingFlags,
  binder As Binder, target As Object, args As Object()
  [,modifiers As ParameterModifier(), culture As
  CultureInfo, namedParameters As String()] ) As Object
IsAssignableFrom(c As Type) As Boolean
IsInstanceOfType(o As Object) As Boolean
IsSubclassOf(c As Type) As Boolean
ToString() As String
```

Uri Class

Provides a representation of a Uniform Resource Identifier (URI) for resources available on the Internet. The URI is an object implementation of the capabilities presented by a standard URL. All references held in a Uri object are absolute (that is, http://www.microsoft.com/msdn) although the MakeRelative() method can return the URI as a relative string (that is, /msdn). An object created with this class is read-only and may only be modified using the UriBuilder class.

Inheritance—Object.MarshalByRefObject.Uri

```
public class System.Uri
  ' Constructors
  Uri(baseUri As Uri, relativeUri As String)
  Uri(uriString As String [, dontEscape As Boolean] )
  Uri(baseUri As Uri, relativeUri As String,
    dontEscape As Boolean)
  ' Properties
  AbsolutePath As System.String (read only)
  AbsoluteUri As System.String (read only)
  Authority As System.String (read only)
  Fragment As System.String (read only)
  Host As System.String (read only)
  HostNameType As System.UriHostNameType (read only)
  IsDefaultPort As System.Boolean (read only)
  IsFile As System.Boolean (read only)
  IsLoopback As System.Boolean (read only)
  IsUnc As System.Boolean (read only)
  LocalPath As System.String (read only)
  PathAndQuery As System.String (read only)
  Port As System.Int32 (read only)
  Query As System.String (read only)
  Scheme As System.String (read only)
  Segments As System.String() (read only)
  UserEscaped As System.Boolean (read only)
  UserInfo As System.String (read only)
  ' Methods
  CheckHostName(name As String) As UriHostNameType
  CheckSchemeName(schemeName As String) As Boolean
  Equals(comparand As Object) As Boolean
  FromHex(digit As Char) As Int32
  GetHashCode() As Int32
  GetLeftPart(part As UriPartial) As String
  HexEscape(character As Char) As String
  HexUnescape(pattern As String, index As Int32&) As Char
  IsHexDigit(character As Char) As Boolean
  IsHexEncoding(pattern As String, index As Int32)
    As Boolean
  MakeRelative(toUri As Uri) As String
  ToString() As String
```

8

UriBuilder Class

Provides the ability to create a new Uniform Resource Identifier (URI) object or modify existing ones. Through this class, the read-only properties of the Uri class may be modified.

Inheritance—Object.UriBuilder

```
public class System.UriBuilder
  ' Constructors
  UriBuilder(schemeName As String, hostName As String)
  UriBuilder(scheme As String, host As String,
    portNumber As Int32)
  UriBuilder( [uri As Uri] )
  UriBuilder(uri As String)
  UriBuilder(scheme As String, host As String, port As
    Int32, path As String, extraValue As String)
  UriBuilder(scheme As String, host As String, port As
    Int32, pathValue As String)
  ' Properties
  Fragment As System.String
  Host As System.String
  Password As System.String
  Path As System.String
  Port As System.Int32
  Query As System.String
  Scheme As System.String
  Uri As System.Uri (read only)
  UserName As System.String
  ' Methods
  Equals(rparam As Object) As Boolean
  GetHashCode() As Int32
  ToString() As String
```

ValueType Class

Provides a foundation class for value data types. Most of the numeric data types are derived from this class. The ValueType class inherits for its parent (the Object class) and overrides the virtual members with ones that are more appropriate for use with values.

Inheritance—Object.ValueType

```
public class System.ValueType
  ' Methods
  Equals(obj As Object) As Boolean
  GetHashCode() As Int32
  ToString() As String
```

Version Class

Holds the version number of the Common Language Runtime (CLR) assembly. The version is represented in four parts: major version, minor version, build number, and revision.

Inheritance—Object.Version

```
public class System.Version
  ' Constructors
  Version(major As Int32, minor As Int32, build As Int32)
  Version(version As String)
  Version(major As Int32, minor As Int32, build As Int32,
    revision As Int32)
  Version(major As Int32, minor As Int32)
  ' Properties
  Build As System.Int32 (read only)
  Major As System.Int32 (read only)
  Minor As System.Int32 (read only)
  Revision As System.Int32 (read only)
  ' Methods
  Clone() As Object
  CompareTo(version As Object) As Int32
  Equals(obj As Object) As Boolean
  GetHashCode() As Int32
  ToString() As String
  ToString(fieldCount As Int32) As String
```


WeakReference Class

Provides a "weak reference," which is a reference to an object that is marked for garbage collection but has not yet been eliminated. Using a weak reference, an object assigned for deletion may be resurrected, although it is not a recommended procedure because unpredictable results may occur.

Inheritance—Object.WeakReference

```
public class System.WeakReference
  ' Constructors
```

```
WeakReference(target As Object)
WeakReference(target As Object, trackResurrection
  As Boolean)
' Properties
IsAlive As System.Boolean (read only)
Target As System.Object
TrackResurrection As System.Boolean (read only)
' Methods
GetObjectData(info As SerializationInfo, context
  As StreamingContext)
```

Chapter 9
Database Access

Providing the best desktop-based database access has always been a priority at Microsoft. From the industry standard Microsoft Access database to the full-powered SQL Server, Microsoft is the leader of nonmainframe database solutions. Visual Studio has played a key role in making Microsoft solutions so effective. Beginning with the creation of ODBC to the evolution of OLE DB and ADO, the development products in Visual Studio have led the way in creating PC-based database applications. ADO.NET further expands the power available through the Visual Studio development system.

The ADO.NET capabilities included with the .NET framework refine and simplify earlier implementations of ADO. Much has been done to standardize the way data sources of all types are addressed, from file-based sources to database servers to object data stores. To allow Microsoft to optimize ADO.NET for SQL Server, the primary database access objects have been split into two database source types: OLE DB and SQL Server. This division is directly visible in the classes of the .NET Framework.

The Organization of the System.Data Namespace

All of the objects that provide database access are located in the System.Data namespace. There are four primary namespace children of System.Data that provide most of the data features available through .NET:

System.Data — The root level that contains all of the core functionality for database access including definitions for data columns, rows, constraints, datasets, dataviews, and extended properties.

System.Data.Common	Holds the foundation DataAdapter objects and provides the primary access bridge to the actual data stores.
System.Data.OleDb	For solutions based on the OLE DB technology, the classes found in this namespace allow queries, data inserts, deletions, and execution of SQL code and stored procedures against an OLE DB data source.
System.Data.SqlClient	For solutions based on Microsoft SQL Server technology, the classes found in this namespace allow queries, data inserts, deletions, and execution of Transact-SQL code and stored procedures against an SQL Server data source.
System.Data.SqlTypes	Provides classes for the native data types used by SQL Server. Functions in these classes allow for conversion between .NET Framework data types and native SQL Server data types.

Within these four primary classes are all of the functions of ADO.NET. Note that the System.Data.OleDb and the System.Data.SqlClient classes mirror each other and contain parallel functions, although the SqlClient has more robust classes to handle the specialized functionality of SQL Server.

Reading OLE DB Data

Employing the OleDb classes is very similar to using earlier versions of ADO. In the following example, ADO.Net is used to address the Microsoft Access sample database known as Northwind. The example will read the contact name entries from the Northwind database and place them in an array.

The name of the Northwind database will vary depending on the applications you have installed. In this example, the database included with FrontPage (FPNWIND.MDB) is used. If you don't know where your Northwind database is located or what it is called (usually NWind.mdb), try searching for *NWIND.MDB to locate it:

1. Create a new Windows application project in Visual Basic.
2. In the header of the default form, enter the following:

```
Imports System.Data.OleDb
```

3. Add a command button and set the Name property of the button to **cmdReadOLEDB**.
4. Enter the following code into the Click event of the button:

```
Sub cmdReadOLEDB_Click()
  Dim myConn As OleDbConnection
  Dim myCmd As OleDbCommand
  Dim myReader As OleDbDataReader
  Dim myConnStr As String
  Dim myArray(0) As String
  Dim i As Integer


  myConnStr = "Provider=" & _
    "Microsoft.Jet.OLEDB.4.0;Password=;" & _
    "User ID=Admin;Data Source=" & _
    "C:\myData\FPNWIND.MDB;" & _
    "Mode=Share Deny None;"
  myConn = New OleDbConnection(myConnStr)
  myCmd = New OleDbCommand()
  myCmd.CommandType = CommandType.Text
  myCmd.CommandText = "Select * from Customers"

  myCmd.Connection = myConn
  myConn.Open()
  myReader = myCmd.ExecuteReader()
  Do While myReader.Read()
    myArray(i) = myReader!ContactName
    ReDim Preserve myArray(UBound(myArray) + 1)
    i += 1
  Loop
  MsgBox("Found " & i & " records")
  myConn.Close()
End Sub
```

5. Execute the application.

Reading SQL Server Data

Accessing an SQL Server mirrors the functionality provided for OLE DB data sources. This example uses an SQL Server installed on the local machine to read orders from the Northwind database and display each OrderID and customer name in the Console window. Place another button onto the form, name it **cmdReadSQL**, and add the following code to the Click event:

```
Sub cmdReadOLEDB_Click()
  Dim myConnStr, queryStr As String
  Dim myOrderID, myCustomer As String
  myConnStr = "Provider=SQLOLEDB;Data Source=" & _
    "localhost;Initial Catalog=Northwind;" & _
    "Integrated Security=SSPI;"
  queryStr = "Select OrderID, Customer From Orders"
  Dim myReader As SqlDataReader
  ' Create a connection and a command object
  Dim myConn As New SqlConnection(myConnStr)
  Dim myCmd As New SqlCommand(queryStr, myConn)

  myConn.Open()
  myReader = myCommand.ExecuteReader()
  While myReader.Read()
    myOrderID = myReader.GetInt32(0).ToString
    myCustomer = myReader.GetString(1)
    Console.WriteLine(myOrderID & ", " & myCustomer)
  End While
  ' Close the reader and liberate the connection
  myReader.Close()
  myConn.Close()
End Sub
```

When you click the button to execute this code, a command object will be created to access the local SQL Server. From the command object, a data reader provides simple forward-only access to a data source. While the data reader is in use, it monopolizes the attached SqlConnection until the Close method of the data reader is called. Once the connection is closed, only the properties IsClosed and RecordsAffected of the data reader object remain valid.

Constraint Class

Provides a constraint that may be applied to one or more columns represented by DataColumn objects. Constraints are rules used to maintain data integrity and force compliance of the associated columns. For example, a UniqueConstraint guarantees that all values within the specified column will be unique.

Inheritance—Object.Constraint

```
public class System.Data.Constraint
  ' Properties
  ConstraintName As System.String
  Table As System.Data.DataTable (read only)
  ' Methods
  ToString() As String
```

ConstraintCollection Class

Holds a collection of Constraint objects and is accessed through the Constraints property of a DataTable object. Found as System.Data.**ConstraintCollection**.

9

DataAdapter Class

Provides the connection used to fill a DataSet object with information from a data producer and send changes made to a DataSet object back to the data source. For SQL Server-based applications, use the SqlDataAdapter object instead.

Inheritance—Object.MarshalByRefObject. Component.DataAdapter

```
public class System.Data.Common.DataAdapter
  ' Properties
```

```
AcceptChangesDuringFill As System.Boolean
MissingMappingAction As System.Data.MissingMappingAction
MissingSchemaAction As System.Data.MissingSchemaAction
TableMappings As System.Data.Common.
  DataTableMappingCollection (read only)
' Methods
Fill(dataSet As DataSet) As Int32
FillSchema(dataSet As DataSet, schemaType As SchemaType)
  As DataTable()
GetFillParameters() As IDataParameter()
Update(dataSet As DataSet) As Int32
```

DataColumn Class

Holds the schema of a column in a DataTable object. The DataType property determines the type of data stored in the column (Boolean, Byte, Char, String, etc.). This object and the DataRow object are the primary items used by a DataTable object.

Inheritance—Object.MarshalByValueComponent.DataColumn

```
public class System.Data.DataColumn
  ' Constructors
  DataColumn( [columnName As String [,dataType As Type
    [,expr As String [,type As MappingType]]]] )
  ' Properties
  AllowDBNull As System.Boolean
  AutoIncrement As System.Boolean
  AutoIncrementSeed As System.Int64
  AutoIncrementStep As System.Int64
  Caption As System.String
  ColumnMapping As System.Data.MappingType
  ColumnName As System.String
  DataType As System.Type
  DefaultValue As System.Object
  Expression As System.String
  ExtendedProperties As
    System.Data.PropertyCollection (read only)
  MaxLength As System.Int32
  Namespace As System.String
  Ordinal As System.Int32 (read only)
  Prefix As System.String
  ReadOnly As System.Boolean
```

```
Table As System.Data.DataTable (read only)
Unique As System.Boolean
' Methods
ToString() As String
```

DataColumnCollection Class

Holds a collection of DataColumn objects for a DataTable object. Found as System.Data.**DataColumnCollection**.

DataColumnMapping Class

Provides column mapping between what a column is named in a DataTable object and the column's actual name in the data source. New column names may be created for use like an alias to simplify or differentiate the name in the programming code. Found as System.Data.Common.**DataColumnMapping**.

DataColumnMappingCollection Class

Holds a collection of DataColumnMapping objects. This class is not inheritable. Found as System.Data.Common.**DataColumnMappingCollection**.

DataRelation Class

Provides a join relationship between two DataTable objects through primary key/foreign key data columns. Note that the data types of the key columns must be identical. The DataRelation does not take effect until it is added to the DataRelationCollection. This collection is available through the Relations property of a DataSet object or the ChildRelations and ParentRelations properties of a DataTable. Until the relation is added to the collection, schema changes may be made to the source columns. Afterwards, the relation must be deleted before any changes may be made.

Inheritance—Object.DataRelation

```
public class System.Data.DataRelation
  ' Constructors
  DataRelation(relationName As String, parentColumn As
    DataColumn, childColumn As DataColumn
    [,createConstraints As Boolean] )
  DataRelation(relationName As String, parentColumns As
    DataColumn(), childColumns As DataColumn()
    [,createConstraints As Boolean] )
  DataRelation(relationName As String,
    parentTableName As String, childTableName As String,
    parentColumnNames As String(), childColumnNames As
    String(), nested As Boolean)
  ' Properties
  ChildColumns As System.Data.DataColumn() (read only)
  ChildKeyConstraint As
    System.Data.ForeignKeyConstraint (read only)
  ChildTable As System.Data.DataTable (read only)
  DataSet As System.Data.DataSet (read only)
  ExtendedProperties As
    System.Data.PropertyCollection (read only)
  Nested As System.Boolean
  ParentColumns As System.Data.DataColumn() (read only)
  ParentKeyConstraint As
    System.Data.UniqueConstraint (read only)
  ParentTable As System.Data.DataTable (read only)
  RelationName As System.String
  ' Methods
  ToString() As String
```

DataRelationCollection Class

Holds a collection of DataRelation objects. This collection is available through the Relations property of a DataSet object or the ChildRelations and ParentRelations properties of a DataTable. Found as System.Data.**DataRelationCollection**.

DataRow Class

Provides a representation of a data row or record in a DataTable object. This object and the DataColumn object are the primary items used within a DataTable object. To add a new row to a table, you must: use the NewRow method of the DataTable object to create a row, execute the Add method to add the row to the DataRowCollection, and execute the AcceptChanges method of the DataTable object to actually place it in the table.

Inheritance—Object.DataRow

```
public class System.Data.DataRow
  ' Properties
  HasErrors As System.Boolean (read only)
  Item As System.Object
  ItemArray As System.Object()
  RowError As System.String
  RowState As System.Data.DataRowState (read only)
  Table As System.Data.DataTable (read only)
  ' Methods
  AcceptChanges()
  BeginEdit()
  CancelEdit()
  ClearErrors()
  Delete()
  EndEdit()
  GetChildRows(relation As DataRelation,
    version As DataRowVersion) As DataRow()
  GetChildRows(relationName As String
    [,version As DataRowVersion] ) As DataRow()
  GetChildRows(relation As DataRelation) As DataRow()
  GetColumnError(columnName As String) As String
  GetColumnError(column As DataColumn) As String
  GetColumnError(columnIndex As Int32) As String
  GetColumnsInError() As DataColumn()
  GetParentRow(relation As DataRelation
    [,version As DataRowVersion]) As DataRow
  GetParentRow(relationName As String
    [,version As DataRowVersion]) As DataRow
  GetParentRows(relation As DataRelation
    [,version As DataRowVersion]) As DataRow()
  GetParentRows(relationName As String
    [,version As DataRowVersion] ) As DataRow()
```

9

```
HasVersion(version As DataRowVersion) As Boolean
IsNull(columnIndex As Int32) As Boolean
IsNull(columnName As String) As Boolean
IsNull(column As DataColumn
  [,version As DataRowVersion] ) As Boolean
RejectChanges()
SetColumnError(columnIndex As Int32, error As String)
SetColumnError(columnName As String, error As String)
SetColumnError(column As DataColumn, error As String)
SetParentRow(parentRow As DataRow,
  relation As DataRelation)
SetParentRow(parentRow As DataRow)
SetUnspecified(column As DataColumn)
```

DataRowCollection Class

Holds a collection of DataRow objects in a DataTable object. Found as System.Data.**DataRowCollection**.

DataRowView Class

Provides a Windows Forms control, which can display a custom view of data contained in a DataRow object. This object is used by the DataGrid control for individual row display. The DataRowView has four separate modes: Default, Original (data matches its original value), Current (changes have been made to the data, but not marked for updating the original source), and Proposed (when changes have been made to the data but not yet saved).

Inheritance—Object.DataRowView

```
public class System.Data.DataRowView
  ' Properties
  DataView As System.Data.DataView (read only)
  IsEdit As System.Boolean (read only)
  IsNew As System.Boolean (read only)
  Item As System.Object
  Item As System.Object
```

```
Row As System.Data.DataRow (read only)
RowVersion As System.Data.DataRowVersion (read only)
' Methods
BeginEdit()
CancelEdit()
CreateChildView(relation As DataRelation) As DataView
CreateChildView(relationName As String) As DataView
Delete()
EndEdit()
Equals(other As Object) As Boolean
GetHashCode() As Int32
```

DataSet Class

Provides the cornerstone object for holding in-memory data. Data is typically received by a DataSet object from an instance of the DataAdapter class. It holds a collection of DataTable objects to represent that data. A DataSet can import and export all data and schema information in XML format.

Inheritance—Object.MarshalByValueComponent. DataSet

```
public class System.Data.DataSet
  ' Constructors
  DataSet( [dataSetName As String] )
  ' Properties
  CaseSensitive As System.Boolean
  DataSetName As System.String
  DefaultViewManager As
    System.Data.DataViewManager (read only)
  EnforceConstraints As System.Boolean
  ExtendedProperties As
    System.Data.PropertyCollection (read only)
  HasErrors As System.Boolean (read only)
  Locale As System.Globalization.CultureInfo
  Namespace As System.String
  Prefix As System.String
  Relations As
    System.Data.DataRelationCollection (read only)
  Site As System.ComponentModel.ISite
  Tables As System.Data.DataTableCollection (read only)
  ' Methods
```

```
AcceptChanges()
BeginInit()
Clear()
Clone() As DataSet
Copy() As DataSet
EndInit()
GetChanges() As DataSet
GetChanges(rowStates As DataRowState) As DataSet
GetXml() As String
GetXmlSchema() As String
HasChanges(rowStates As DataRowState) As Boolean
HasChanges() As Boolean
InferXmlSchema(stream As Stream, nsArray As String())
InferXmlSchema(reader As TextReader, nsArray As String())
InferXmlSchema(fileName As String, nsArray As String())
InferXmlSchema(reader As XmlReader, nsArray As String())
Merge(table As DataTable [,preserveChanges As Boolean,
  missingSchemaAction As MissingSchemaAction] )
Merge(dataSet As DataSet [,preserveChanges As Boolean
  [,missingSchemaAction As MissingSchemaAction] )
Merge(rows As DataRow() [,preserveChanges As Boolean,
  missingSchemaAction As MissingSchemaAction] )
ReadXml(stream As Stream [,mode As XmlReadMode] )
  As XmlReadMode
ReadXml(reader As TextReader [,mode As XmlReadMode] )
  As XmlReadMode
ReadXml(reader As XmlReader [,mode As XmlReadMode] )
  As XmlReadMode
ReadXml(fileName As String [,mode As XmlReadMode] )
  As XmlReadMode
ReadXmlSchema(reader As TextReader)
ReadXmlSchema(fileName As String)
ReadXmlSchema(reader As XmlReader)
ReadXmlSchema(stream As Stream)
RejectChanges()
Reset()
WriteXml(writer As TextWriter [,mode As XmlWriteMode] )
WriteXml(writer As XmlWriter [,mode As XmlWriteMode] )
WriteXml(stream As Stream [,mode As XmlWriteMode] )
WriteXml(fileName As String [,mode As XmlWriteMode] )
WriteXmlSchema(writer As TextWriter)
WriteXmlSchema(stream As Stream)
WriteXmlSchema(fileName As String)
WriteXmlSchema(writer As XmlWriter)
' Events
MergeFailed As System.Data.MergeFailedEventHandler
```

DataSysDescriptionAttribute Class

Holds a description for display in the visual designers (of the Visual Studio development environment) of a property, event, or extender. Found as System.Data.**DataSysDescriptionAttribute**.

DataTable Class

Provides an in-memory representation of a table. DataTable objects are held in a collection in an instance of a DataSet object. A DataTable object may represent a table in a data source or may be constructed manually with program code as a disconnected table. Use the NewRow() method to add rows to the table. If there is more than one table with the same name, table names are case-sensitive. Otherwise, table naming is case-insensitive.

Inheritance—Object.MarshalByValueComponent.DataTable

```
public class System.Data.DataTable
  ' Constructors
  DataTable( [tableName As String] )
  ' Properties
  CaseSensitive As System.Boolean
  ChildRelations As
    System.Data.DataRelationCollection (read only)
  Columns As System.Data.DataColumnCollection (read only)
  Constraints As
    System.Data.ConstraintCollection (read only)
  DataSet As System.Data.DataSet (read only)
  DefaultView As System.Data.DataView (read only)
  DisplayExpression As System.String
  ExtendedProperties As
    System.Data.PropertyCollection (read only)
  HasErrors As System.Boolean (read only)
  Locale As System.Globalization.CultureInfo
  MinimumCapacity As System.Int32
  Namespace As System.String
```

```
ParentRelations As
  System.Data.DataRelationCollection (read only)
Prefix As System.String
PrimaryKey As System.Data.DataColumn()
Rows As System.Data.DataRowCollection (read only)
Site As System.ComponentModel.ISite
TableName As System.String
' Methods
AcceptChanges()
BeginInit()
BeginLoadData()
Clear()
Clone() As DataTable
Compute(expression As String, filter As String) As Object
Copy() As DataTable
EndInit()
EndLoadData()
GetChanges(rowStates As DataRowState) As DataTable
GetChanges() As DataTable
GetErrors() As DataRow()
ImportRow(row As DataRow)
LoadDataRow(values As Object(),
  fAcceptChanges As Boolean) As DataRow
NewRow() As DataRow
RejectChanges()
Reset()
Select( [filterExpression As String [,sort As String
  [,recordStates As DataViewRowState]]] ) As DataRow()
ToString() As String
' Events
ColumnChanged As System.Data.DataColumnChangeEventHandler
ColumnChanging As
  System.Data.DataColumnChangeEventHandler
RowChanged As System.Data.DataRowChangeEventHandler
RowChanging As System.Data.DataRowChangeEventHandler
RowDeleted As System.Data.DataRowChangeEventHandler
RowDeleting As System.Data.DataRowChangeEventHandler
```

DataTableCollection Class

Holds a collection of DataTable objects for use by a dataset object. Found as System.Data.**DataTableCollection**.

DataTableMapping Class

Provides a mapping relationship between the actual table on the data source and the DataTable object that represents it. This class is not inheritable. Found as System.Data.Common.**DataTableMapping**.

DataTableMappingCollection Class

Holds a collection of DataTableMapping objects. This class is not inheritable. Found as System.Data.Common.**DataTableMappingCollection**.

DataView Class

Provides a Windows Forms control to display a DataTable object. The DataView object includes features for sorting, filtering, searching, editing, and navigation of the represented data.

Inheritance—Object.MarshalByValueComponent. DataView

```
public class System.Data.DataView
  ' Constructors
  DataView( [table As DataTable] )
  ' Properties
  AllowDelete As System.Boolean
  AllowEdit As System.Boolean
  AllowNew As System.Boolean
  ApplyDefaultSort As System.Boolean
  Count As System.Int32 (read only)
  DataViewManager As
    System.Data.DataViewManager (read only)
  Item As System.Data.DataRowView (read only)
```

```
RowFilter As System.String
RowStateFilter As System.Data.DataViewRowState
Sort As System.String
Table As System.Data.DataTable
' Methods
AddNew() As DataRowView
BeginInit()
CopyTo(array As Array, index As Int32)
Delete(index As Int32)
Dispose()
EndInit()
Find(key As Object) As Int32
Find(key As Object()) As Int32
GetEnumerator() As IEnumerator
' Events
ListChanged As
  System.ComponentModel.ListChangedEventHandler
```

DataViewManager Class

Provides a default DataViewSetting collection for each DataTable object contained in the collection of dataset objects. Found as System.Data.**DataViewManager**.

DataViewSetting Class

Holds the default settings for the following DataView properties: ApplyDefaultSort, DataViewManager, RowFilter, RowStateFilter, Sort, and Table. Objects of this class are created by the DataViewManager. *See also* the DataViewManager class. Found as System.Data.**DataViewSetting**.

DataViewSettingCollection Class

Holds a read-only collection of DataViewSetting objects for the DataViewManager of each DataTable object held in a DataSet. Found as System.Data.**DataViewSettingCollection**.

DbDataAdapter Class

Provides an abstract foundation implementation for DataAdapter classes. This class is not used for direct instantiation, but as a parent class for a new implementation of a data adapter class. The OleDbDataAdapter and SqlDataAdapter classes are both children of this class.

Inheritance—Object.MarshalByRefObject.Component.DataAdapter.DbDataAdapter

```
public class System.Data.Common.DbDataAdapter
  ' Methods
  Fill(dataTable As DataTable) As Int32
  Fill(dataSet As DataSet [,srcTable As String] ) As Int32
  Fill(dataSet As DataSet, startRecord As Int32,
    maxRecords As Int32, srcTable As String) As Int32
  FillSchema(dataSet As DataSet, schemaType As SchemaType
    [,srcTable As String] ) As DataTable()
  FillSchema(dataTable As DataTable,
    schemaType As SchemaType) As DataTable
  GetFillParameters() As IDataParameter()
  Update(dataSet As DataSet [,srcTable As String] )
    As Int32
  Update(dataRows As DataRow()) As Int32
  Update(dataTable As DataTable) As Int32
  ' Events
  FillError As System.Data.FillErrorEventHandler
```

DBDataPermission Class

Provides an abstract foundation implementation for classes that supply user-level security for data access. This class is not used for direct instantiation, but as a parent class for a new implementation of a security class. The OleDbPermission and SqlClientPermission classes are both children of this class.

Inheritance—Object.CodeAccessPermission.DBDataPermission

```
public class System.Data.Common.DBDataPermission
  ' Properties
  AllowBlankPassword As System.Boolean
  ' Methods
  Copy() As IPermission
  FromXml(securityElement As SecurityElement)
  Intersect(target As IPermission) As IPermission
  IsSubsetOf(target As IPermission) As Boolean
  IsUnrestricted() As Boolean
  ToXml() As SecurityElement
  Union(target As IPermission) As IPermission
```

DBDataPermissionAttribute Class

Provides an abstract foundation implementation for classes that supply a custom security attribute. The OleDbPermissionAttribute and SqlClientPermissionAttribute classes are both children of this class. Found as System.Data.Common.**DBDataPermissionAttribute**.

ForeignKeyConstraint Class

Provides a constraint action that activates when a primary key column is changed or deleted. In such a situation, a number of processes may occur such as cascading updates, cascading deletes, or column value replacement with null or default values—or an exception may be generated. ForeignKeyConstraint objects are stored in the ConstraintCollection of a DataTable object. Found as System.Data.**ForeignKeyConstraint**.

InternalDataCollectionBase Class

Provides a foundation implementation for creating data structure collections. Children of this class include ConstraintCollection, DataColumnCollection, DataRelationCollection, DataRowCollection, and DataTableCollection. This class is not meant for direct instantiation, but as a parent class for a new implementation of a collection class. Found as System.Data.**InternalDataCollectionBase**.

OleDbCommand Class

Provides a representation of a Transact-SQL statement or stored procedure that may be sent to an OLE DB data source. Use the ExecuteReader() method to execute a command that returns data rows, the ExecuteScalar() method for commands that return a single value, or the ExecuteNonQuery() method for commands that return no data.

9

Inheritance—Object.MarshalByRefObject. Component.OleDbCommand

```
public class System.Data.OleDb.OleDbCommand
  ' Constructors
  OleDbCommand( [cmdText As String [,connection As
    OleDbConnection [,transaction As OleDbTransaction]]] )
  ' Properties
  CommandText As System.String
  CommandTimeout As System.Int32
  CommandType As System.Data.CommandType
  Connection As System.Data.OleDb.OleDbConnection
  DesignTimeVisible As System.Boolean
  Parameters As
    System.Data.OleDb.OleDbParameterCollection (read only)
  Transaction As System.Data.OleDb.OleDbTransaction
  UpdatedRowSource As System.Data.UpdateRowSource
  ' Methods
```

```
Cancel()
CreateParameter() As OleDbParameter
ExecuteNonQuery() As Int32
ExecuteReader(behavior As CommandBehavior)
  As OleDbDataReader
ExecuteReader() As OleDbDataReader
ExecuteScalar() As Object
Prepare()
ResetCommandTimeout()
```

OleDbCommandBuilder Class

Provides a process for generating commands that execute a single-table update. An OleDbDataAdapter doesn't automatically generate the SQL needed to provide synchronization between changes to a DataSet object and the data source itself. This class allows the proper SQL update statements to be created and modified. This class is not inheritable.

Inheritance—Object.MarshalByRefObject. Component.OleDbCommandBuilder

```
public class System.Data.OleDb.OleDbCommandBuilder
  ' Constructors
  OleDbCommandBuilder( [adapter As OleDbDataAdapter] )
  ' Properties
  DataAdapter As System.Data.OleDb.OleDbDataAdapter
  QuotePrefix As System.String
  QuoteSuffix As System.String
  ' Methods
  GetDeleteCommand() As OleDbCommand
  GetInsertCommand() As OleDbCommand
  GetUpdateCommand() As OleDbCommand
  RefreshSchema()
```

OleDbConnection Class

Provides a representation of an open connection for an OLE DB data source. The capabilities available through this object will vary depending on the implementation of the OLE DB driver used to interface with the data source. Connections must be explicitly closed with the Close() or Dispose() methods. Eliminating this object explicitly or implicitly (through garbage collection) will not close the connection.

Inheritance—Object.MarshalByRefObject. Component.OleDbConnection

```
public class System.Data.OleDb.OleDbConnection
  ' Constructors
  OleDbConnection( [connectionString As String] )
  ' Properties
  ConnectionString As System.String
  ConnectionTimeout As System.Int32 (read only)
  Database As System.String (read only)
  DataSource As System.String (read only)
  Provider As System.String (read only)
  ServerVersion As System.String (read only)
  State As System.Data.ConnectionState (read only)
  ' Methods
  BeginTransaction( [isolationLevel As IsolationLevel] )
    As OleDbTransaction
  ChangeDatabase(value As String)
  Close()
  CreateCommand() As OleDbCommand
  GetOleDbSchemaTable(schema As Guid,
    restrictions As Object()) As DataTable
  Open()
  ReleaseObjectPool()
  ' Events
  InfoMessage As
    System.Data.OleDb.OleDbInfoMessageEventHandler
  StateChange As System.Data.StateChangeEventHandler
```


OleDbDataAdapter Class

Provides the connection used to fill a DataSet object with information from a data producer and send changes made to a DataSet object back to the data source. This class is not inheritable.

Inheritance—Object.MarshalByRefObject. Component.DataAdapter.DbDataAdapter. OleDbDataAdapter

```
public class System.Data.OleDb.OleDbDataAdapter
  ' Constructors
```

```
OleDbDataAdapter( [selectCommand As OleDbCommand] )
OleDbDataAdapter(selectCommandText As String,
  selectConnectionString As String)
OleDbDataAdapter(selectCommandText As String,
  selectConnection As OleDbConnection)
' Properties
DeleteCommand As System.Data.OleDb.OleDbCommand
InsertCommand As System.Data.OleDb.OleDbCommand
SelectCommand As System.Data.OleDb.OleDbCommand
UpdateCommand As System.Data.OleDb.OleDbCommand
' Methods
Fill(dataTable As DataTable, adodb As Object) As Int32
Fill(dataSet As DataSet, adodb As Object,
  srcTable As String) As Int32
' Events
RowUpdated As
  System.Data.OleDb.OleDbRowUpdatedEventHandler
RowUpdating As
  System.Data.OleDb.OleDbRowUpdatingEventHandler
```

OleDbDataReader Class

Provides a data reader that simplifies forward-only access to a data source. This object should not be created directly, but is returned by the ExecuteReader method of the OleDbCommand object. While in use, objects of this class monopolize the attached OleDbConnection until the Close method of the OleDbDataReader is called. After the connection is closed, only the properties IsClosed and RecordsAffected of the OleDbDataReader object remain valid.

Inheritance—Object.MarshalByRefObject.OleDbDataReader

```
public class System.Data.OleDb.OleDbDataReader
  ' Properties
  Depth As System.Int32 (read only)
  FieldCount As System.Int32 (read only)
  IsClosed As System.Boolean (read only)
  Item As System.Object (read only)
  RecordsAffected As System.Int32 (read only)
  ' Methods
  Close()
  GetBoolean(ordinal As Int32) As Boolean
  GetByte(ordinal As Int32) As Byte
```

```
GetBytes(ordinal As Int32, dataIndex As Int64, buffer As
  Byte(), bufferIndex As Int32, length As Int32) As Int64
GetChar(ordinal As Int32) As Char
GetChars(ordinal As Int32, dataIndex As Int64, buffer As
  Char(), bufferIndex As Int32, length As Int32) As Int64
GetData(ordinal As Int32) As OleDbDataReader
GetDataTypeName(index As Int32) As String
GetDateTime(ordinal As Int32) As DateTime
GetDecimal(ordinal As Int32) As Decimal
GetDouble(ordinal As Int32) As Double
GetFieldType(index As Int32) As Type
GetFloat(ordinal As Int32) As Single
GetGuid(ordinal As Int32) As Guid
GetInt16(ordinal As Int32) As Int16
GetInt32(ordinal As Int32) As Int32
GetInt64(ordinal As Int32) As Int64
GetName(index As Int32) As String
GetOrdinal(name As String) As Int32
GetSchemaTable() As DataTable
GetString(ordinal As Int32) As String
GetTimeSpan(ordinal As Int32) As TimeSpan
GetValue(ordinal As Int32) As Object
GetValues(values As Object()) As Int32
IsDBNull(ordinal As Int32) As Boolean
NextResult() As Boolean
Read() As Boolean
```

OleDbError Class

Holds information on any warnings or errors that have occurred on the data source. Instances of this class are created automatically by the OLE DB adapter when an error occurs. This class is not inheritable.

Inheritance—Object.OleDbError

```
public class System.Data.OleDb.OleDbError
  ' Properties
  Message As System.String (read only)
  NativeError As System.Int32 (read only)
  Source As System.String (read only)
  SQLState As System.String (read only)
  ' Methods
  ToString() As String
```

OleDbErrorCollection Class

Holds a collection of OleDbError objects generated by the OLE DB data adapter. This class is not inheritable. Found as System.Data.OleDb.**OleDbErrorCollection**.

OleDbParameter Class

Holds a parameter that will be used when executing SQL code in an OleDbCommand object. This class may also hold a mapping of the parameter to its associated DataSet column. This class is not inheritable.

Inheritance—Object.MarshalByRefObject.OleDbParameter

```
public class System.Data.OleDb.OleDbParameter
  ' Constructors
  OleDbParameter( [name As String, value As Object] )
  OleDbParameter(name As String, dataType As OleDbType
    [,size As Int32 [,srcColumn As String]] )
  OleDbParameter(parameterName As String, dbType As
    OleDbType, size As Int32, direction As
    ParameterDirection, isNullable As Boolean, precision
    As Byte, scale As Byte, srcColumn As String,
    srcVersion As DataRowVersion, value As Object)
  ' Properties
  DbType As System.Data.DbType
  Direction As System.Data.ParameterDirection
  IsNullable As System.Boolean
  OleDbType As System.Data.OleDb.OleDbType
  ParameterName As System.String
  Precision As System.Byte
  Scale As System.Byte
  Size As System.Int32
  SourceColumn As System.String
  SourceVersion As System.Data.DataRowVersion
  Value As System.Object
  ' Methods
  ToString() As String
```

OleDbParameterCollection Class

Holds a collection of OleDbParameter objects for an OleDbCommand object. The number of parameters in the collection must exactly match the number of placeholders in the code of the OleDbCommand object. The names of parameters are not case-sensitive. This class is not inheritable. Found as System.Data.OleDb.**OleDbParameterCollection**.

OleDbPermission Class

Provides user-level security for data access. The DBDataPermission class is the parent of this class. This class is not inheritable.

Inheritance—Object.CodeAccessPermission. DBDataPermission.OleDbPermission

```
public class System.Data.OleDb.OleDbPermission
  ' Constructors
  OleDbPermission( [state As PermissionState
    [,allowBlankPassword As Boolean]] )
  OleDbPermission(connectionStringProperties As Hashtable,
    allowBlankPassword As Boolean)
  ' Properties
  Provider As System.String
  ' Methods
  Copy() As IPermission
  FromXml(securityElement As SecurityElement)
  Intersect(target As IPermission) As IPermission
  IsSubsetOf(target As IPermission) As Boolean
  ToXml() As SecurityElement
  Union(target As IPermission) As IPermission
```

9

OleDbPermissionAttribute Class

Holds a custom security attribute for the OleDbPermission object. This class is not inheritable. Found as System.Data.OleDb.**OleDbPermissionAttribute**.

OleDbSchemaGuid Class

Holds the type of schema table specified with the GetOleDbSchemaTable method. Objects of this class have fields that exactly relate to each row in an OLE DB schema rowset. This class is not inheritable. Found as System.Data.OleDb.**OleDbSchemaGuid**.

OleDbTransaction Class

Provides a representation of a transaction on a data source. This object is not created directly, but instead is generated when calling the BeginTransaction method on the OleDbConnection object. This class is not inheritable.

Inheritance—Object.MarshalByRefObject. OleDbTransaction

```
public class System.Data.OleDb.OleDbTransaction
  ' Properties
  IsolationLevel As System.Data.IsolationLevel (read only)
  ' Methods
  Begin( [isolevel As IsolationLevel] ) As OleDbTransaction
  Commit()
  Rollback()
```

PropertyCollection Class

Holds a collection of properties available through the ExtendedProperties property in the DataColumn, DataSet, and DataTable objects. Found as System.Data.**PropertyCollection**.

SqlClientPermission Class

Provides user-level security for data access. The DBDataPermission class is the parent of this class. This class is not inheritable.

Inheritance—Object.CodeAccessPermission. DBDataPermission.SqlClientPermission

```
public class System.Data.SqlClient.SqlClientPermission
  ' Constructors
  SqlClientPermission( [state As PermissionState
    [,allowBlankPassword As Boolean]] )
  SqlClientPermission(connectionStringProperties As
    Hashtable, allowBlankPassword As Boolean)
  ' Methods
  IsSubsetOf(target As IPermission) As Boolean
```

SqlClientPermissionAttribute Class

Holds a custom security attribute for the SqlClientPermission object. This class is not inheritable. Found as System.Data.SqlClient.**SqlClientPermissionAttribute**.

SqlCommand Class

Provides execution for an SQL, Transact-SQL, or stored procedure command against SQL Server. Use the ExecuteReader() method to execute a command that returns data rows, the ExecuteScalar() method for commands that return a single value, or the ExecuteNonQuery() method for commands that return no data. Use the ExecuteXmlReader() method to execute the command and receive the returned data rows in an XmlReader object. This class is not inheritable.

Inheritance—Object.MarshalByRefObject. Component.SqlCommand

```
public class System.Data.SqlClient.SqlCommand
  ' Constructors
  SqlCommand( [cmdText As String [,connection As
    SqlConnection [,transaction As SqlTransaction]]] )
  ' Properties
  CommandText As System.String
  CommandTimeout As System.Int32
  CommandType As System.Data.CommandType
  Connection As System.Data.SqlClient.SqlConnection
  DesignTimeVisible As System.Boolean
  Parameters As System.Data.SqlClient.
    SqlParameterCollection (read only)
  Transaction As System.Data.SqlClient.SqlTransaction
  UpdatedRowSource As System.Data.UpdateRowSource
  ' Methods
  Cancel()
  CreateParameter() As SqlParameter
  ExecuteNonQuery() As Int32
  ExecuteReader(behavior As CommandBehavior)
    As SqlDataReader
  ExecuteReader() As SqlDataReader
  ExecuteScalar() As Object
  ExecuteXmlReader() As XmlReader
  Prepare()
  ResetCommandTimeout()
```

SqlCommandBuilder Class

Provides a process for generating commands that execute a single-table update. SqlDataAdapter doesn't automatically generate the SQL needed to provide synchronization between changes to a DataSet object and the data source itself. This class allows the proper SQL update statements to be created and modified. This class is not inheritable.

Inheritance—Object.MarshalByRefObject. Component.SqlCommandBuilder

```
public class System.Data.SqlClient.SqlCommandBuilder
  ' Constructors
  SqlCommandBuilder( [adapter As SqlDataAdapter] )
  ' Properties
```

```
DataAdapter As System.Data.SqlClient.SqlDataAdapter
QuotePrefix As System.String
QuoteSuffix As System.String
' Methods
GetDeleteCommand() As SqlCommand
GetInsertCommand() As SqlCommand
GetUpdateCommand() As SqlCommand
RefreshSchema()
```

SqlConnection Class

Provides a representation of an open connection for an SQL Server data source. Connections must be explicitly closed with the Close or Dispose methods. Eliminating this object explicitly or implicitly (through garbage collection) will not close the connection.

Inheritance—Object.MarshalByRefObject.Component.SqlConnection

```
public class System.Data.SqlClient.SqlConnection
  ' Constructors
  SqlConnection( [connectionString As String] )
  ' Properties
  ConnectionString As System.String
  ConnectionTimeout As System.Int32 (read only)
  Database As System.String (read only)
  DataSource As System.String (read only)
  PacketSize As System.Int32 (read only)
  ServerVersion As System.String (read only)
  State As System.Data.ConnectionState (read only)
  WorkstationId As System.String (read only)
  ' Methods
  BeginTransaction( [transactionName As String] )
    As SqlTransaction
  BeginTransaction(iso As IsolationLevel
    [,transactionName As String] ) As SqlTransaction
  ChangeDatabase(database As String)
  Close()
  CreateCommand() As SqlCommand
  Open()
  ' Events
  InfoMessage As
```

```
    System.Data.SqlClient.SqlInfoMessageEventHandler
  StateChange As System.Data.StateChangeEventHandler
```

SqlDataAdapter Class

Provides the connection used to fill a DataSet object with information from a data producer and send changes made to a DataSet object back to the data source.

Inheritance—Object.MarshalByRefObject. Component.DataAdapter.DbDataAdapter. SqlDataAdapter

```
public class System.Data.SqlClient.SqlDataAdapter
  ' Constructors
  SqlDataAdapter( [selectCommand As SqlCommand] )
  SqlDataAdapter(selectCommandText As String,
    selectConnection As SqlConnection)
  SqlDataAdapter(selectCommandText As String,
    selectConnectionString As String)
  ' Properties
  DeleteCommand As System.Data.SqlClient.SqlCommand
  InsertCommand As System.Data.SqlClient.SqlCommand
  SelectCommand As System.Data.SqlClient.SqlCommand
  UpdateCommand As System.Data.SqlClient.SqlCommand
  ' Events
  RowUpdated As
    System.Data.SqlClient.SqlRowUpdatedEventHandler
  RowUpdating As
    System.Data.SqlClient.SqlRowUpdatingEventHandler
```

SqlDataReader Class

Provides a data reader that simplifies forward-only access to a data source. This object should not be created directly, but is returned by the ExecuteReader() method of the SqlCommand object. While in use, objects of this class monopolize the attached SqlConnection until the Close() method of the SqlDataReader is called. After the connection is closed, only the properties IsClosed and RecordsAffected of the SqlDataReader object remain valid.

Inheritance—Object.MarshalByRefObject.SqlDataReader

```
public class System.Data.SqlClient.SqlDataReader
  ' Properties
  Depth As System.Int32 (read only)
  FieldCount As System.Int32 (read only)
  IsClosed As System.Boolean (read only)
  Item As System.Object (read only)
  RecordsAffected As System.Int32 (read only)
  ' Methods
  Close()
  GetBoolean(i As Int32) As Boolean
  GetByte(i As Int32) As Byte
  GetBytes(i As Int32, dataIndex As Int64, buffer As
    Byte(), bufferIndex As Int32, length As Int32) As Int64
  GetChar(i As Int32) As Char
  GetChars(i As Int32, dataIndex As Int64, buffer As
    Char(), bufferIndex As Int32, length As Int32) As Int64
  GetData(i As Int32) As IDataReader
  GetDataTypeName(i As Int32) As String
  GetDateTime(i As Int32) As DateTime
  GetDecimal(i As Int32) As Decimal
  GetDouble(i As Int32) As Double
  GetFieldType(i As Int32) As Type
  GetFloat(i As Int32) As Single
  GetGuid(i As Int32) As Guid
  GetInt16(i As Int32) As Int16
  GetInt32(i As Int32) As Int32
  GetInt64(i As Int32) As Int64
  GetName(i As Int32) As String
  GetOrdinal(name As String) As Int32
  GetSchemaTable() As DataTable
  GetSqlBinary(i As Int32) As SqlBinary
  GetSqlBoolean(i As Int32) As SqlBoolean
  GetSqlByte(i As Int32) As SqlByte
  GetSqlDateTime(i As Int32) As SqlDateTime
  GetSqlDecimal(i As Int32) As SqlDecimal
  GetSqlDouble(i As Int32) As SqlDouble
  GetSqlGuid(i As Int32) As SqlGuid
  GetSqlInt16(i As Int32) As SqlInt16
  GetSqlInt32(i As Int32) As SqlInt32
  GetSqlInt64(i As Int32) As SqlInt64
  GetSqlMoney(i As Int32) As SqlMoney
  GetSqlSingle(i As Int32) As SqlSingle
  GetSqlString(i As Int32) As SqlString
  GetSqlValue(i As Int32) As Object
  GetSqlValues(values As Object()) As Int32
  GetString(i As Int32) As String
  GetValue(i As Int32) As Object
  GetValues(values As Object()) As Int32
```

```
IsDBNull(i As Int32) As Boolean
NextResult() As Boolean
Read() As Boolean
```

SqlError Class

Holds information on any warnings or errors that have occurred on the data source. Instances of this class are created automatically by the SQL Server adapter when an error occurs. This class mirrors the OleDbError class. This class is not inheritable. Found as System.Data.SqlClient.**SqlError**.

SqlErrorCollection Class

Holds a collection of SqlError objects. This class is not inheritable. Found as System.Data.SqlClient.**SqlErrorCollection**.

SqlParameter Class

Holds a parameter that will be used when executing the code in a SqlCommand object. The names of parameters are not case-sensitive. This class may also hold a mapping of the parameter to its DataSet column. This class is not inheritable.

Inheritance—Object.MarshalByRefObject. SqlParameter

```
public class System.Data.SqlClient.SqlParameter
  ' Constructors
  SqlParameter( [parameterName As String,
    value As Object] )
  SqlParameter(parameterName As String, dbType As SqlDbType
    [,size As Int32 [,sourceColumn As String]] )
  SqlParameter(parameterName As String, dbType As
    SqlDbType, size As Int32, direction As
    ParameterDirection, isNullable As Boolean, precision
    As Byte, scale As Byte, sourceColumn As String,
    sourceVersion As DataRowVersion, value As Object)
  ' Properties
```

```
DbType As System.Data.DbType
Direction As System.Data.ParameterDirection
IsNullable As System.Boolean
Offset As System.Int32
ParameterName As System.String
Precision As System.Byte
Scale As System.Byte
Size As System.Int32
SourceColumn As System.String
SourceVersion As System.Data.DataRowVersion
SqlDbType As System.Data.SqlDbType
Value As System.Object
' Methods
ToString() As String
```

SqlParameterCollection Class

Holds a collection of SqlParameter objects for an SqlCommand object. The number of parameters in the collection must exactly match the number of placeholders in the code of the SqlCommand object. This class is not inheritable. Found as System.Data.SqlClient.**SqlParameterCollection**.

SqlTransaction Class

Provides a representation of a Transact-SQL transaction for a data source. This object is not created directly, but instead is generated when calling the BeginTransaction method on the SqlConnection object. This class is not inheritable.

Inheritance—Object.MarshalByRefObject. SqlTransaction

```
public class System.Data.SqlClient.SqlTransaction
  ' Properties
  IsolationLevel As System.Data.IsolationLevel (read only)
  ' Methods
  Commit()
  Dispose()
  Rollback(transactionName As String)
  Rollback()
  Save(savePointName As String)
```

TypedDataSetGenerator Class

Provides an abstract foundation class for creating a strongly typed DataSet object.

Inheritance—Object.TypedDataSetGenerator

```
public class System.Data.TypedDataSetGenerator
  ' Constructors
  TypedDataSetGenerator()
  ' Methods
  Generate(dataSet As DataSet, codeNamespace As
    CodeNamespace, codeGen As ICodeGenerator)
  GenerateIdName(name As String, codeGen As ICodeGenerator)
    As String
```

UniqueConstraint Class

Provides a constraint on one or more database columns that ensures values are unique. Contraints are only enforced when the EnforceConstraints property is set to True. When two DataSets are merged, constraint enforcement is suspended until the merge is complete.

Inheritance—Object.Constraint.UniqueConstraint

```
public class System.Data.UniqueConstraint
  ' Constructors
  UniqueConstraint(column As DataColumn)
  UniqueConstraint(columns As DataColumn())
  UniqueConstraint(name As String, column As DataColumn)
  UniqueConstraint(name As String, columns As DataColumn())
  UniqueConstraint(name As String, columnNames As String(),
    isKey As Boolean)
  ' Properties
  Columns As System.Data.DataColumn() (read only)
  IsPrimaryKey As System.Boolean (read only)
  Table As System.Data.DataTable (read only)
  ' Methods
  Equals(key2 As Object) As Boolean
  GetHashCode() As Int32
```

Chapter 10
Extensible Markup Language (XML)

One of the most important new technologies supported by the .NET framework is the Extensible Markup Language (XML). XML is the data exchange equivalent of HTML. It allows data to be written into a nonproprietary system-independent format. Since XML files are stored as standard ASCII or Unicode text, they are human readable and available for editing by a simple text editor such as Notepad.

The .NET framework embraces XML and provides a number of classes to simplify XML loading, parsing, augmenting, and writing. XML excels at handling hierarchical data formats, but since managing a hierarchical tree is a challenging programming task, Microsoft has included full XML parsing capabilities within the framework.

For a basic level of compatibility, all XML documents should contain only a single root node. For example, if an HTML page was treated as an XML file, the root node would be defined by the <HTML></HTML> encapsulation tags since no text may occur outside of them.

An XML file is said to be *well-formed* if it complies with the standard XML formatting guidelines. The most important of these rules requires that all nodes explicitly have both an opening and a closing tag (i.e., <data></data>). This stands in contrast to several HTML tags that require only an opening tag with the closing tag handled implicitly (i.e., <P>, <HR>, <BR>, etc.). The only exception to this rule in XML is available through the null field operator where the field itself is defined as empty by using a single tag ending in a slash character (i.e., <data/>).

An XML document may be much more explicitly structured than the simple *well-formed* definition. The XML document may specify a Document Type Definition (DTD) by either direct inclusion in the file or a reference to an external DTD. A DTD can contain everything from field data types to logical rules that must be followed by the data. If an XML file complies with a specified DTD, it is called a *validated* document. The XmlValidatingReader class can be used to ensure that the XML file being accessed conforms to its DTD.

Writing a Basic XML File

To write to an XML file using the .NET framework is a simple process. Most of the formatting and file access are handled automatically by the XmlTextWriter class. In this example, an XML file that contains sample football team data is created and written to the disk. The data fields for a single player are written into a well-formed XML data document.

Add this header to the beginning of a new VB Windows application project:

```
Imports System.Xml
```

Now place the following code in the Click event of a button:

```
Sub cmdXMLWrite_Click()
    ' For testing, you can use this line instead:
    ' Dim myTW As New XmlTextWriter(Console.Out)
    Dim myTW As New XmlTextWriter("C:\myTeam.xml", Nothing)
    ' Inset the <?xml > version header
    myTW.WriteStartDocument()
    myTW.Formatting = Formatting.Indented
    ' Open the root node
    myTW.WriteStartElement("Team")
    ' Open a data node
    myTW.WriteStartElement("Player")
    myTW.WriteAttributeString("Name", "George Zip")
    myTW.WriteAttributeString("Position", "QB")
    myTW.WriteElementString("Nickname", "Zippy")
    myTW.WriteElementString("JerseyNumber", _
      XmlConvert.ToString(7))
    ' Close the data node
    myTW.WriteEndElement()
    ' Close the root node
    myTW.WriteEndElement()
    myTW.WriteEndDocument()
    myTW.Close()
End Sub
```

Even the simplest XML file should have the XML header and a single root node that encompasses all of the other data. Executing the application and clicking the button will generate the following well-formed XML data file:

```
<?xml version="1.0"?>
<Team>
  <Player Name="George Zip" Position="QB">
    <Nickname>Zippy</Nickname>
    <JerseyNumber>7</JerseyNumber>
  </Player>
</Team>
```

Reading the XML File

If you place the following code in another button, the XmlTextReader class will read the contents of the myTeam XML file and display each item to the Output window:

```
Sub cmdXMLRead_Click()
    Dim myTR As New XmlTextReader("c:\myTeam.xml")
    Dim myAttr As String
    While myTR.Read()
        If myTR.NodeType = XmlNodeType.Element Then
            Console.Write(myTR.Name & "")
            ' Check for any attributes
            myAttr = "<"
            While myTR.MoveToNextAttribute()
                myAttr = myAttr & " " & myTR.Name & _
                  "='" & myTR.Value & "'"
            End While
            ' If there were attributes, display them
             If myAttr.Length > 1 Then
                Console.WriteLine(myAttr & "> ")
             Else
                Console.WriteLine("")
             End If
             If myTR.IsEmptyElement = True Then
                Console.Write("--- Empty element ---")
             End If
        ElseIf myTR.NodeType = XmlNodeType.Text Then
            Console.WriteLine("    " & myTR.Value)
        End If
```

```
    End While
End Sub
```

NameTable Class

Provides a single threaded implementation of a table of name values (XmlNameTable) that work like tokens for common strings. Rather than providing a new string each time a common name appears in an XML data set (such as Product), an object reference to an item in the NameTable is used by the system. This method aids in speeding string comparison since only the object reference needs to be compared to determine that two strings are identical.

Inheritance—Object.XmlNameTable.NameTable

```
public class System.Xml.NameTable
  ' Constructors
  NameTable()
  ' Methods
  Add(key As Char(), start As Int32, len As Int32)
    As String
  Add(key As String) As String
  Get(key As Char(), start As Int32, len As Int32)
    As String
  Get(value As String) As String
```

XmlAttribute Class

Holds an attribute with default and valid values defined in the XML Document Type Definition (DTD) or schema.

Inheritance—Object.XmlNode.XmlAttribute

```
public class System.Xml.XmlAttribute
  ' Properties
  BaseURI As System.String (read only)
  InnerText As System.String
  InnerXml As System.String
  LocalName As System.String (read only)
  Name As System.String (read only)
  NamespaceURI As System.String (read only)
  NodeType As System.Xml.XmlNodeType (read only)
```

```
OwnerDocument As System.Xml.XmlDocument (read only)
OwnerElement As System.Xml.XmlElement (read only)
ParentNode As System.Xml.XmlNode (read only)
Prefix As System.String
Specified As System.Boolean (read only)
Value As System.String
' Methods
CloneNode(deep As Boolean) As XmlNode
WriteContentTo(w As XmlWriter)
WriteTo(w As XmlWriter)
```

XmlCDataSection Class

Defines a section of character data that will not be interpreted by the XML parser. By avoiding the parser, text in a CData section can contain characters or tags that would be erroneously understood by the parser as markup language. For example, a CData element can contain quotation marks (such as *<![CDATA[<p>This is a test of the "character data" system.]]>*) that would typically cause the XML parser to treat the text in quotes as attribute data.

Inheritance—Object.XmlNode.XmlLinkedNode.XmlCharacterData.XmlCDataSection

```
public class System.Xml.XmlCDataSection
  ' Properties
  LocalName As System.String (read only)
  Name As System.String (read only)
  NodeType As System.Xml.XmlNodeType (read only)
  ' Methods
  CloneNode(deep As Boolean) As XmlNode
  WriteContentTo(w As XmlWriter)
  WriteTo(w As XmlWriter)
```


XmlCharacterData Class

Provides the abstract foundation class for handling character data. This class is used as a parent by the following classes: XmlCDataSection, XmlComment, XmlSignificantWhitespace, XmlText, and XmlWhitespace.

Inheritance—Object.XmlNode.XmlLinkedNode.XmlCharacterData

```
public class System.Xml.XmlCharacterData
  ' Properties
  Data As System.String
  InnerText As System.String
  Length As System.Int32 (read only)
  Value As System.String
  ' Methods
  AppendData(strData As String)
  DeleteData(offset As Int32, count As Int32)
  InsertData(offset As Int32, strData As String)
  ReplaceData(offset As Int32, count As Int32,
    strData As String)
  Substring(offset As Int32, count As Int32) As String
```

XmlComment Class

Holds the contents of a comment field in the XML file.

Inheritance—Object.XmlNode.XmlLinkedNode.XmlCharacterData.XmlComment

```
public class System.Xml.XmlComment
  ' Properties
  LocalName As System.String (read only)
  Name As System.String (read only)
  NodeType As System.Xml.XmlNodeType (read only)
  ' Methods
  CloneNode(deep As Boolean) As XmlNode
  WriteContentTo(w As XmlWriter)
  WriteTo(w As XmlWriter)
```

XmlConvert Class

Provides conversion between standard XML schema types (XSD) and Common Language Runtime (CLR) types. Also encodes and decodes XML names to convert between XML names and the names used by ADO.NET objects, such as those represented in DataColumn and DataTable objects.

Inheritance—Object.XmlConvert

```
public class System.Xml.XmlConvert
  ' Constructors
  XmlConvert()
  ' Methods
  DecodeName(name As String) As String
  EncodeLocalName(name As String) As String
  EncodeName(name As String) As String
  EncodeNmToken(name As String) As String
  ToBoolean(s As String) As Boolean
  ToByte(s As String) As Byte
  ToChar(s As String) As Char
  ToDateTime(s As String) As DateTime
  ToDateTime(s As String, formats As String()) As DateTime
  ToDateTime(s As String, format As String) As DateTime
  ToDecimal(s As String) As Decimal
  ToDouble(s As String) As Double
  ToGuid(s As String) As Guid
  ToInt16(s As String) As Int16
  ToInt32(s As String) As Int32
  ToInt64(s As String) As Int64
  ToSByte(s As String) As SByte
  ToSingle(s As String) As Single
*  ToString(value) As String
  ToString(value As DateTime, format As String) As String
  ToTimeSpan(s As String) As TimeSpan
  ToUInt16(s As String) As UInt16
  ToUInt32(s As String) As UInt32
  ToUInt64(s As String) As UInt64
```

* The ***value*** can be of type Boolean, Byte, Char, Decimal, Guid, Int16, SByte, Int32, Int64, TimeSpan, Double, DateTime, UInt16, UInt32, UInt64, or Single.

XmlDataDocument Class

Holds the bridge between a relational DataSet object and the structured data that can be accessed and modified through it. This class is a child of XMLDocument and allows data manipulation as specified in the W3C standard for the Document Object Model (DOM). Data is presented as a number of hierarchical node objects. Use the ReadXmlSchema() method to create the relational mapping from a DataSet and the Load() or LoadXml() methods to fill the object with XML data. Found as System.Xml.**XmlDataDocument**.

XmlDeclaration Class

Contains the XML declaration node that must occur at the beginning of every XML document in the form of *<?xml version='1.0' ?>* followed by any specified attributes.

Inheritance—Object.XmlNode.XmlLinkedNode.XmlDeclaration

```
public class System.Xml.XmlDeclaration
  ' Properties
  Encoding As System.String
  InnerText As System.String
  LocalName As System.String (read only)
  Name As System.String (read only)
  NodeType As System.Xml.XmlNodeType (read only)
  Standalone As System.String
  Value As System.String
  Version As System.String (read only)
  ' Methods
  CloneNode(deep As Boolean) As XmlNode
  WriteContentTo(w As XmlWriter)
  WriteTo(w As XmlWriter)
```

XmlDocument Class

Provides the foundation for an XML document. The XMLDataDocument class uses this class as a parent.

Inheritance—Object.XmlNode.XmlDocument

```
public class System.Xml.XmlDocument
  ' Constructors
  XmlDocument(nt As XmlNameTable)
  XmlDocument()
  ' Properties
  BaseURI As System.String (read only)
  DocumentElement As System.Xml.XmlElement (read only)
  DocumentType As
    System.Xml.XmlDocumentType (read only)
  Implementation As
    System.Xml.XmlImplementation (read only)
```

```
InnerXml As System.String
IsReadOnly As System.Boolean (read only)
LocalName As System.String (read only)
Name As System.String (read only)
NameTable As System.Xml.XmlNameTable (read only)
NodeType As System.Xml.XmlNodeType (read only)
OwnerDocument As System.Xml.XmlDocument (read only)
PreserveWhitespace As System.Boolean
XmlResolver As System.Xml.XmlResolver (write only)
' Methods
CloneNode(deep As Boolean) As XmlNode
CreateAttribute(prefix As String, localName As String,
  namespaceURI As String) As XmlAttribute
CreateAttribute(name As String) As XmlAttribute
CreateAttribute(qualifiedName As String,
  namespaceURI As String) As XmlAttribute
CreateCDataSection(data As String) As XmlCDataSection
CreateComment(data As String) As XmlComment
CreateDocumentFragment() As XmlDocumentFragment
CreateDocumentType(name As String, publicId As String,
  systemId As String, internalSubset As String)
  As XmlDocumentType
CreateElement(name As String) As XmlElement
CreateElement(prefix As String, localName As String,
  namespaceURI As String) As XmlElement
CreateElement(qualifiedName As String,
  namespaceURI As String) As XmlElement
CreateEntityReference(name As String)
  As XmlEntityReference
CreateNode(nodeTypeString As String, name As String,
  namespaceURI As String) As XmlNode
CreateNode(type As XmlNodeType, name As String,
  namespaceURI As String) As XmlNode
CreateNode(type As XmlNodeType, prefix As String,
  name As String, namespaceURI As String) As XmlNode
CreateProcessingInstruction(target As String,
  data As String) As XmlProcessingInstruction
CreateSignificantWhitespace(text As String)
  As XmlSignificantWhitespace
CreateTextNode(text As String) As XmlText
CreateWhitespace(text As String) As XmlWhitespace
CreateXmlDeclaration(version As String, encoding As
  String, standalone As String) As XmlDeclaration
GetElementById(elementId As String) As XmlElement
GetElementsByTagName(localName As String,
  namespaceURI As String) As XmlNodeList
GetElementsByTagName(name As String) As XmlNodeList
ImportNode(node As XmlNode, deep As Boolean) As XmlNode
Load(inStream As Stream)
```

```
Load(filename As String)
Load(txtReader As TextReader)
Load(reader As XmlReader)
LoadXml(xml As String)
ReadNode(reader As XmlReader) As XmlNode
Save(writer As XmlWriter)
Save(writer As TextWriter)
Save(filename As String)
Save(outStream As Stream)
WriteContentTo(w As XmlWriter)
WriteTo(w As XmlWriter)
' Events
NodeChanged As System.Xml.XmlNodeChangedEventHandler
NodeChanging As System.Xml.XmlNodeChangedEventHandler
NodeInserted As System.Xml.XmlNodeChangedEventHandler
NodeInserting As System.Xml.XmlNodeChangedEventHandler
NodeRemoved As System.Xml.XmlNodeChangedEventHandler
NodeRemoving As System.Xml.XmlNodeChangedEventHandler
```

XmlDocumentFragment Class

Provides a lightweight class appropriate for fast tree insert operations. Found as System.Xml.**XmlDocumentFragment**.

XmlDocumentType Class

Contains the XML node for the document type declaration. Found as System.Xml.**XmlDocumentType**.

XmlElement Class

Provides a representation of an XML element.

Inheritance—Object.XmlNode.XmlLinkedNode. XmlElement

```
public class System.Xml.XmlElement
  ' Properties
```

```
Attributes As
  System.Xml.XmlAttributeCollection (read only)
HasAttributes As System.Boolean (read only)
InnerText As System.String
InnerXml As System.String
IsEmpty As System.Boolean
LocalName As System.String (read only)
Name As System.String (read only)
NamespaceURI As System.String (read only)
NextSibling As System.Xml.XmlNode (read only)
NodeType As System.Xml.XmlNodeType (read only)
OwnerDocument As System.Xml.XmlDocument (read only)
Prefix As System.String
' Methods
CloneNode(deep As Boolean) As XmlNode
GetAttribute(name As String) As String
GetAttribute(localName As String,
  namespaceURI As String) As String
GetAttributeNode(name As String) As XmlAttribute
GetAttributeNode(localName As String,
  namespaceURI As String) As XmlAttribute
GetElementsByTagName(localName As String,
  namespaceURI As String) As XmlNodeList
GetElementsByTagName(name As String) As XmlNodeList
HasAttribute(localName As String, namespaceURI As String)
  As Boolean
HasAttribute(name As String) As Boolean
RemoveAll()
RemoveAllAttributes()
RemoveAttribute(name As String)
RemoveAttribute(localName As String,
  namespaceURI As String)
RemoveAttributeAt(i As Int32) As XmlNode
RemoveAttributeNode(oldAttr As XmlAttribute)
  As XmlAttribute
RemoveAttributeNode(localName As String,
  namespaceURI As String) As XmlAttribute
SetAttribute(name As String, value As String)
SetAttribute(localName As String, namespaceURI As String,
  value As String) As String
SetAttributeNode(localName As String,
  namespaceURI As String) As XmlAttribute
SetAttributeNode(newAttr As XmlAttribute) As XmlAttribute
WriteContentTo(w As XmlWriter)
WriteTo(w As XmlWriter)
```

XmlEntity Class

Provides a representation of an entity created by the XML syntax *<!ENTITY ... >*. An entity may be an image, data file, or other resource used within the XML document.

Inheritance—Object.XmlNode.XmlEntity

```
public class System.Xml.XmlEntity
  ' Properties
  BaseURI As System.String (read only)
  InnerText As System.String
  InnerXml As System.String
  IsReadOnly As System.Boolean (read only)
  LocalName As System.String (read only)
  Name As System.String (read only)
  NodeType As System.Xml.XmlNodeType (read only)
  NotationName As System.String (read only)
  OuterXml As System.String (read only)
  PublicId As System.String (read only)
  SystemId As System.String (read only)
  ' Methods
  CloneNode(deep As Boolean) As XmlNode
  WriteContentTo(w As XmlWriter)
  WriteTo(w As XmlWriter)
```

XmlEntityReference Class

Provides a representation of an entity reference node. Found as System.Xml.**XmlEntityReference**.

XmlImplementation Class

Provides a shared XML context for multiple XML documents. If several documents use the same schema, this class utilizes a shared XmlNameTable to provide the identical fields. Despite the shared schema, the XML documents must still use the ImportNode() method to transfer data between them.

Inheritance—Object.XmlImplementation

```
public class System.Xml.XmlImplementation
  ' Constructors
  XmlImplementation()
  ' Methods
  CreateDocument() As XmlDocument
  HasFeature(strFeature As String, strVersion As String)
    As Boolean
```

XmlLinkedNode Class

Provides a reference to the node preceding or following this node.

Inheritance—Object.XmlNode.XmlLinkedNode

```
public class System.Xml.XmlLinkedNode
  ' Properties
  NextSibling As System.Xml.XmlNode (read only)
  PreviousSibling As System.Xml.XmlNode (read only)
```

XmlNamedNodeMap Class

Holds a collection of node references that can be accessed through a numerical index or the name of the node.

Inheritance—Object.XmlNamedNodeMap

```
public class System.Xml.XmlNamedNodeMap
  ' Properties
  Count As System.Int32 (read only)
  ' Methods
  GetEnumerator() As IEnumerator
  GetNamedItem(name As String) As XmlNode
  GetNamedItem(localName As String, namespaceURI As String)
    As XmlNode
  Item(index As Int32) As XmlNode
  RemoveNamedItem(localName As String,
    namespaceURI As String) As XmlNode
```

```
  RemoveNamedItem(name As String) As XmlNode
  SetNamedItem(node As XmlNode) As XmlNode
```

XmlNamespaceManager Class

Provides management for a collection of objects that allows adding, deleting, and resolving references to each object. This class also provides scope management for the objects and is used by the XmlReader and XsltContext classes.

Inheritance—Object.XmlNamespaceManager

```
public class System.Xml.XmlNamespaceManager
  ' Constructors
  XmlNamespaceManager(nameTable As XmlNameTable)
  ' Properties
  DefaultNamespace As System.String (read only)
  NameTable As System.Xml.XmlNameTable (read only)
  ' Methods
  AddNamespace(prefix As String, uri As String)
  GetEnumerator() As IEnumerator
  HasNamespace(prefix As String) As Boolean
  LookupNamespace(prefix As String) As String
  LookupPrefix(uri As String) As String
  PopScope() As Boolean
  PushScope()
  RemoveNamespace(prefix As String, uri As String)
```

XmlNameTable Class

Provides an abstract class for a table of name values that work like tokens for common strings. Rather than providing a new string each time a common name appears in an XML data set (such as Product), an object reference to an item in the name table is used by the system. This method aids in speeding string comparison since only the object reference needs to be compared to determine if two strings are identical. The XmlNameTable class is the parent of the NameTable class.

Inheritance—Object.XmlNameTable

```
public class System.Xml.XmlNameTable
  ' Methods
  Add(array As Char(), offset As Int32, length As Int32)
    As String
  Add(array As String) As String
  Get(array As Char(), offset As Int32, length As Int32)
    As String
  Get(array As String) As String
```

XmlNode Class

Provides an abstract class representation of an XML node. The following node classes are based on this class: XmlAttribute, XmlDocument, XmlDocumentFragment, XmlEntity, XmlLinkedNode, and XmlNotation.

Inheritance—Object.XmlNode

```
public class System.Xml.XmlNode
  ' Properties
  Attributes As
    System.Xml.XmlAttributeCollection (read only)
  BaseURI As System.String (read only)
  ChildNodes As System.Xml.XmlNodeList (read only)
  FirstChild As System.Xml.XmlNode (read only)
  HasChildNodes As System.Boolean (read only)
  InnerText As System.String
  InnerXml As System.String
  IsReadOnly As System.Boolean (read only)
  Item As System.Xml.XmlElement (read only)
  Item As System.Xml.XmlElement (read only)
  LastChild As System.Xml.XmlNode (read only)
  LocalName As System.String (read only)
  Name As System.String (read only)
  NamespaceURI As System.String (read only)
  NextSibling As System.Xml.XmlNode (read only)
  NodeType As System.Xml.XmlNodeType (read only)
  OuterXml As System.String (read only)
  OwnerDocument As System.Xml.XmlDocument (read only)
  ParentNode As System.Xml.XmlNode (read only)
  Prefix As System.String
  PreviousSibling As System.Xml.XmlNode (read only)
  Value As System.String
  ' Methods
```

```
AppendChild(newChild As XmlNode) As XmlNode
Clone() As XmlNode
CloneNode(deep As Boolean) As XmlNode
CreateNavigator() As XPathNavigator
GetEnumerator() As IEnumerator
GetNamespaceOfPrefix(prefix As String) As String
GetPrefixOfNamespace(namespaceURI As String) As String
InsertAfter(newChild As XmlNode, refChild As XmlNode)
  As XmlNode
InsertBefore(newChild As XmlNode, refChild As XmlNode)
  As XmlNode
Normalize()
PrependChild(newChild As XmlNode) As XmlNode
RemoveAll()
RemoveChild(oldChild As XmlNode) As XmlNode
ReplaceChild(newChild As XmlNode, oldChild As XmlNode)
  As XmlNode
SelectNodes(xpath As String,
  nsmgr As XmlNamespaceManager) As XmlNodeList
SelectNodes(xpath As String) As XmlNodeList
SelectSingleNode(xpath As String) As XmlNode
SelectSingleNode(xpath As String,
  nsmgr As XmlNamespaceManager) As XmlNode
Supports(feature As String, version As String) As Boolean
WriteContentTo(w As XmlWriter)
WriteTo(w As XmlWriter)
```

XmlNodeList Class

Holds an ordered collection of XML nodes. This class is dynamic such that any changes to any of the nodes in the collection will be immediately reflected in the XmlNodeList object.

Inheritance—Object.XmlNodeList

```
public class System.Xml.XmlNodeList
  ' Properties
  Count As System.Int32 (read only)
  ItemOf As System.Xml.XmlNode (read only)
  ' Methods
  GetEnumerator() As IEnumerator
  Item(index As Int32) As XmlNode
```

XmlNodeReader Class

Provides fast, forward-only read-only access to node data stored in an object from an XmlNode-derived class. This class reads data from the Document Object Model (DOM) subtree without any validation from the DTD or schema. For validated data access, use the XmlValidatingReader class. To provide strong typing, use this class in conjunction with the XmlConverter class.

Inheritance—Object.XmlReader.XmlNodeReader

```
public class System.Xml.XmlNodeReader
  ' Constructors
  XmlNodeReader(node As XmlNode)
  ' Properties
  AttributeCount As System.Int32 (read only)
  BaseURI As System.String (read only)
  CanResolveEntity As System.Boolean (read only)
  Depth As System.Int32 (read only)
  EOF As System.Boolean (read only)
  HasAttributes As System.Boolean (read only)
  HasValue As System.Boolean (read only)
  IsDefault As System.Boolean (read only)
  IsEmptyElement As System.Boolean (read only)
  Item As System.String (read only)
  Item As System.String (read only)
  Item As System.String (read only)
  LocalName As System.String (read only)
  Name As System.String (read only)
  NamespaceURI As System.String (read only)
  NameTable As System.Xml.XmlNameTable (read only)
  NodeType As System.Xml.XmlNodeType (read only)
  Prefix As System.String (read only)
  QuoteChar As System.Char (read only)
  ReadState As System.Xml.ReadState (read only)
  Value As System.String (read only)
  XmlLang As System.String (read only)
  XmlSpace As System.Xml.XmlSpace (read only)
  ' Methods
  Close()
  GetAttribute(i As Int32) As String
  GetAttribute(name As String) As String
```

10

```
GetAttribute(name As String, namespaceURI As String)
  As String
LookupNamespace(prefix As String) As String
MoveToAttribute(i As Int32)
MoveToAttribute(name As String) As Boolean
MoveToAttribute(name As String, namespaceURI As String)
  As Boolean
MoveToElement() As Boolean
MoveToFirstAttribute() As Boolean
MoveToNextAttribute() As Boolean
Read() As Boolean
ReadAttributeValue() As Boolean
ReadInnerXml() As String
ReadOuterXml() As String
ReadString() As String
ResolveEntity()
Skip()
```

XmlNotation Class

Provides a representation of a notation created by the XML syntax *<!NOTATION ... >*.

Inheritance—Object.XmlNode.XmlNotation

```
public class System.Xml.XmlNotation
  ' Properties
  InnerXml As System.String
  IsReadOnly As System.Boolean (read only)
  LocalName As System.String (read only)
  Name As System.String (read only)
  NodeType As System.Xml.XmlNodeType (read only)
  OuterXml As System.String (read only)
  PublicId As System.String (read only)
  SystemId As System.String (read only)
  ' Methods
  CloneNode(deep As Boolean) As XmlNode
  WriteContentTo(w As XmlWriter)
  WriteTo(w As XmlWriter)
```

XmlParserContext Class

Provides the context parsing information to the XmlTextReader and XmlValidatingReader classes. Found as System.Xml.**XmlParserContext**.

XmlProcessingInstruction Class

Provides a representation of an XML processing instruction that holds processor-specific information.

Inheritance—Object.XmlNode.XmlLinkedNode.XmlProcessingInstruction

```
public class System.Xml.XmlProcessingInstruction
  ' Properties
  Data As System.String
  InnerText As System.String
  LocalName As System.String (read only)
  Name As System.String (read only)
  NodeType As System.Xml.XmlNodeType (read only)
  Target As System.String (read only)
  Value As System.String
  ' Methods
  CloneNode(deep As Boolean) As XmlNode
  WriteContentTo(w As XmlWriter)
  WriteTo(w As XmlWriter)
```


XmlQualifiedName Class

Holds the qualified name of an XML object. The "namespace:localname" format is the style used for an XML qualified name.

Inheritance—Object.XmlQualifiedName

```
public class System.Xml.XmlQualifiedName
  ' Constructors
  XmlQualifiedName(name As String, ns As String)
  XmlQualifiedName()
  XmlQualifiedName(name As String)
  ' Properties
  IsEmpty As System.Boolean (read only)
  Name As System.String (read only)
  Namespace As System.String (read only)
  ' Methods
  Equals(other As Object) As Boolean
  GetHashCode() As Int32
  ToString() As String
  ToString(name As String, ns As String) As String
```

XmlReader Class

Provides an abstract foundation class for fast, forward-only read-only access to XML data. This class is the parent of the following classes: XmlNodeReader, XmlTextReader, and XmlValidatingReader. Found as System.Xml.**XmlReader**.

XmlResolver Class

Provides an abstract class that has the ability to resolve, from a Uniform Resource Identifier (URI), any external XML resources. This class can resolve DTD/schema URIs and import elements of XSL style sheets or XSD schemas. This class is the parent of the XmlUrlResolver class.

Inheritance—Object.XmlResolver

```
public class System.Xml.XmlResolver
  ' Properties
  Credentials As System.Net.ICredentials (write only)
  ' Methods
  GetEntity(absoluteUri As Uri, role As String,
    ofObjectToReturn As Type) As Object
  ResolveUri(baseUri As Uri, relativeUri As String) As Uri
```

XmlSignificantWhitespace Class

Provides a representation of significant whitespace in an XML document. Significant whitespace is text whitespace specified explicitly through markup code. Nodes of this class are created automatically by the Load() method of the XmlDocument class if the PreserveWhitespace flag is set to True (the default is False). Found as System.Xml.**XmlSignificantWhitespace**.

XmlText Class

Provides a representation of the text held in an element or an attribute.

Inheritance—Object.XmlNode.XmlLinkedNode.XmlCharacterData.XmlText

```
public class System.Xml.XmlText
  ' Properties
  LocalName As System.String (read only)
  Name As System.String (read only)
  NodeType As System.Xml.XmlNodeType (read only)
  Value As System.String
  ' Methods
  CloneNode(deep As Boolean) As XmlNode
  SplitText(offset As Int32) As XmlText
  WriteContentTo(w As XmlWriter)
  WriteTo(w As XmlWriter)
```


XmlTextReader Class

Provides a class for fast, forward-only read-only access to XML data. This class enforces XML well-formed rules (i.e., matching open and close tags, etc.) for the document, DocumentType nodes, and entity declarations. This class does not provide data validation and also does not expand default attributes. For full data validation, use the XmlValidatingReader class.

Inheritance—Object.XmlReader.XmlTextReader

```
public class System.Xml.XmlTextReader
  ' Constructors
  XmlTextReader(input As TextReader [,nt As XmlNameTable])
  XmlTextReader(url As String, input As TextReader
    [,nt As XmlNameTable])
  XmlTextReader(url As String, input As Stream
    [,nt As XmlNameTable])
  XmlTextReader(input As Stream [,nt As XmlNameTable])
  XmlTextReader(url As String [,nt As XmlNameTable])
  XmlTextReader(xmlFragment As String,
    fragType As XmlNodeType, context As XmlParserContext)
  XmlTextReader(xmlFragment As Stream,
    fragType As XmlNodeType, context As XmlParserContext)
  ' Properties
  AttributeCount As System.Int32 (read only)
  BaseURI As System.String (read only)
  Depth As System.Int32 (read only)
  Encoding As System.Text.Encoding (read only)
  EOF As System.Boolean (read only)
  HasValue As System.Boolean (read only)
  IsDefault As System.Boolean (read only)
  IsEmptyElement As System.Boolean (read only)
  Item As System.String (read only)
  Item As System.String (read only)
  Item As System.String (read only)
  LineNumber As System.Int32 (read only)
  LinePosition As System.Int32 (read only)
  LocalName As System.String (read only)
  Name As System.String (read only)
  Namespaces As System.Boolean
  NamespaceURI As System.String (read only)
  NameTable As System.Xml.XmlNameTable (read only)
  NodeType As System.Xml.XmlNodeType (read only)
  Normalization As System.Boolean
  Prefix As System.String (read only)
  QuoteChar As System.Char (read only)
  ReadState As System.Xml.ReadState (read only)
  Value As System.String (read only)
  WhitespaceHandling As System.Xml.WhitespaceHandling
  XmlLang As System.String (read only)
  XmlResolver As System.Xml.XmlResolver (write only)
  XmlSpace As System.Xml.XmlSpace (read only)
  ' Methods
  Close()
  GetAttribute(i As Int32) As String
  GetAttribute(localName As String,
    namespaceURI As String) As String
  GetAttribute(name As String) As String
  GetRemainder() As TextReader
```

```
LookupNamespace(prefix As String) As String
MoveToAttribute(name As String) As Boolean
MoveToAttribute(i As Int32)
MoveToAttribute(localName As String,
  namespaceURI As String) As Boolean
MoveToElement() As Boolean
MoveToFirstAttribute() As Boolean
MoveToNextAttribute() As Boolean
Read() As Boolean
ReadAttributeValue() As Boolean
ReadBase64(array As Byte(), offset As Int32,
  len As Int32) As Int32
ReadBinHex(array As Byte(), offset As Int32,
  len As Int32) As Int32
ReadChars(buffer As Char(), index As Int32,
  count As Int32) As Int32
ReadInnerXml() As String
ReadOuterXml() As String
ReadString() As String
ResolveEntity()
```

XmlTextWriter Class

Provides a class for fast, forward-only write access to an XML file that conforms to the W3C XML specification. This class is a child of the XmlWriter class. Note, if the *encoding* argument in the constructor is passed as a null reference (Nothing in VB), the file will be written in ASCII UTF-8 format.

Inheritance—Object.XmlWriter.XmlTextWriter

```
public class System.Xml.XmlTextWriter
  ' Constructors
  XmlTextWriter(w As TextWriter)
  XmlTextWriter(filename As String, encoding As Encoding)
  XmlTextWriter(w As Stream, encoding As Encoding)
  ' Properties
  Formatting As System.Xml.Formatting
  Indentation As System.Int32
  IndentChar As System.Char
  Namespaces As System.Boolean
  QuoteChar As System.Char
  WriteState As System.Xml.WriteState (read only)
  XmlLang As System.String (read only)
  XmlSpace As System.Xml.XmlSpace (read only)
  ' Methods
```

```
Close()
Flush()
LookupPrefix(ns As String) As String
WriteBase64(buffer As Byte(), index As Int32,
  count As Int32)
WriteBinHex(buffer As Byte(), index As Int32,
  count As Int32)
WriteCData(text As String)
WriteCharEntity(ch As Char)
WriteChars(buffer As Char(), index As Int32,
  count As Int32)
WriteComment(text As String)
WriteDocType(name As String, pubid As String,
  sysid As String, subset As String)
WriteEndAttribute()
WriteEndDocument()
WriteEndElement()
WriteEntityRef(name As String)
WriteFullEndElement()
WriteName(name As String)
WriteNmToken(name As String)
WriteProcessingInstruction(name As String,
  text As String)
WriteQualifiedName(localName As String, ns As String)
WriteRaw(buffer As Char(), index As Int32,
  count As Int32)
WriteRaw(data As String)
WriteStartAttribute(prefix As String,
  localName As String, ns As String)
WriteStartDocument()
WriteStartDocument(standalone As Boolean)
WriteStartElement(prefix As String, localName As String,
  ns As String)
WriteString(text As String)
WriteSurrogateCharEntity(lowChar As Char,
  highChar As Char)
WriteWhitespace(ws As String)
```

XmlUrlResolver Class

Provides a class that has the ability to resolve, from a Uniform Resource Identifier (URI), any external XML resources. This class can resolve DTD/schema URIs and import elements of XSL stylesheets or XSD schemas. This class is the child of the XmlResolver class.

Inheritance—Object.XmlResolver.XmlUrlResolver

```
public class System.Xml.XmlUrlResolver
  ' Constructors
  XmlUrlResolver()
  ' Properties
  Credentials As System.Net.ICredentials (write only)
  ' Methods
  GetEntity(absoluteUri As Uri, role As String,
    ofObjectToReturn As Type) As Object
  ResolveUri(baseUri As Uri, relativeUri As String) As Uri
```

XmlValidatingReader Class

Provides a class for reading XML data while validating that it conforms to the DTD, XDR, XSD schema, and well-formed conventions of an XML document. This class enforces XML well-formed rules (i.e., matching open and close tags, etc.) for the document, DocumentType nodes, and entity declarations. Schema files from an XmlSchemaCollection can be specified in the Schemas property to be used for verification. Specify the validation type with the ValidationType property.

Inheritance—Object.XmlReader. XmlValidatingReader

```
public class System.Xml.XmlValidatingReader
  ' Constructors
  XmlValidatingReader(xmlFragment As Stream,
    fragType As XmlNodeType, context As XmlParserContext)
  XmlValidatingReader(xmlFragment As String,
    fragType As XmlNodeType, context As XmlParserContext)
  XmlValidatingReader(reader As XmlReader)
  ' Properties
  AttributeCount As System.Int32 (read only)
  BaseURI As System.String (read only)
  CanResolveEntity As System.Boolean (read only)
  Depth As System.Int32 (read only)
  Encoding As System.Text.Encoding (read only)
  EntityHandling As System.Xml.EntityHandling
  EOF As System.Boolean (read only)
  HasValue As System.Boolean (read only)
  IsDefault As System.Boolean (read only)
  IsEmptyElement As System.Boolean (read only)
  Item As System.String (read only)
```

```
Item As System.String (read only)
Item As System.String (read only)
LocalName As System.String (read only)
Name As System.String (read only)
Namespaces As System.Boolean
NamespaceURI As System.String (read only)
NameTable As System.Xml.XmlNameTable (read only)
NodeType As System.Xml.XmlNodeType (read only)
Prefix As System.String (read only)
QuoteChar As System.Char (read only)
Reader As System.Xml.XmlReader (read only)
ReadState As System.Xml.ReadState (read only)
Schemas As
  System.Xml.Schema.XmlSchemaCollection (read only)
SchemaType As System.Object (read only)
ValidationType As System.Xml.ValidationType
Value As System.String (read only)
XmlLang As System.String (read only)
XmlResolver As System.Xml.XmlResolver (write only)
XmlSpace As System.Xml.XmlSpace (read only)
' Methods
Close()
GetAttribute(name As String) As String
GetAttribute(i As Int32) As String
GetAttribute(localName As String, namespaceURI As String)
  As String
LookupNamespace(prefix As String) As String
MoveToAttribute(name As String) As Boolean
MoveToAttribute(localName As String,
  namespaceURI As String) As Boolean
MoveToAttribute(i As Int32)
MoveToElement() As Boolean
MoveToFirstAttribute() As Boolean
MoveToNextAttribute() As Boolean
Read() As Boolean
ReadAttributeValue() As Boolean
ReadInnerXml() As String
ReadOuterXml() As String
ReadString() As String
ReadTypedValue() As Object
ResolveEntity()
' Events
ValidationEventHandler As
  System.Xml.Schema.ValidationEventHandler
```

XmlWhitespace Class

Provides a representation of whitespace (usually represented by space characters in a text stream) in the element content of an XML document. Nodes of this class are created automatically by the Load() method of the XmlDocument class if the PreserveWhitespace flag is set to True (the default is False).

Inheritance—Object.XmlNode.XmlLinkedNode.XmlCharacterData.XmlWhitespace

```
public class System.Xml.XmlWhitespace
  ' Properties
  LocalName As System.String (read only)
  Name As System.String (read only)
  NodeType As System.Xml.XmlNodeType (read only)
  Value As System.String
  ' Methods
  CloneNode(deep As Boolean) As XmlNode
  WriteContentTo(w As XmlWriter)
  WriteTo(w As XmlWriter)
```

XmlWriter Class

Provides an abstract foundation class for fast, forward-only write access to an XML file that conforms to the W3C XML specification. This class is the parent of the XmlTextWriter class. Found as System.Xml.**XmlWriter**.

Chapter 11
Runtime Classes

The System.Runtime classes contain routines that can modify the runtime execution environment. These classes can modify the compilation process, handle object activation, and offer serialization and deserialization of objects. The execution environment is supplied by the new Common Language Runtime (CLR) that provides the foundation for all of the Visual Studio.NET languages.

The execution capabilities of the CLR can be controlled through many of the Runtime classes. Note that since the System.Runtime.CompilerServices namespace contains classes that are for compiler use only, they have not been included in this chapter. The Visual Studio.Net documentation contains a complete description of the compiler services.

Serialize an Object

Serialization is the process of taking an executing object, with all of its properties and current settings, and writing it to nonvolatile storage (such as a hard disk). Once an object is serialized, it may be reloaded later and reactivated in the same condition as when written. This process is called *deserialization*. Serialization is useful for everything from making object backups to providing emergency storage options (in the event of power failure or system fault) to cloning the exact state of existing objects.

11

The Formatter class performs the actual process of serialization. A serialized object can be stored in XML, SOAP, compact binary format, or a custom format that may be created for use by the formatter objects. It can then be reloaded using the same Formatter class with the Deserialize() method.

The following example demonstrates serializing an object and allowing an instance of that same object to be retrieved and activated. In the code, a class is created using the <Serializable()> attribute, which designates that any instances of this class can be serialized. The project allows the creation of an instance of this serializable class and then stores the instance in a compact binary file. Clicking the Deserialize button will resurrect the object into an object reference variable of the correct object type.

To create this serialization example project, execute Visual Studio.NET. Create a new VB Windows application and add a new class called *mySerialClass* to the project. Open the class in the development IDE and add the following code to define the class:

```
<Serializable()> Public Class mySerialClass
  Public myInt As Integer
  Public myStr As String

  Public Sub initVars()
    myInt = 1999
    myStr = "Hello Serialized World"
  End Sub
  Public Sub displayVars()
    MessageBox.Show("myInt: " & myInt & " myStr: " _
      & myStr)
  End Sub
End Class
```

Open the form window and add three buttons (name them *cmdInit*, *cmdSerialize*, and *cmdDeSerialize*). From the code window of this form, add the following code:

```
Imports System.IO
Imports System.Runtime.Serialization.Formatters.Binary

Public Class Form1
  Inherits System.Windows.Forms.Form

  Dim myInstance As mySerialClass

  Private Sub cmdInit_Click()
    myInstance = New mySerialClass()
    myInstance.initVars()
    myInstance.displayVars()
  End Sub

  Private Sub cmdSerialize_Click()
    Dim myFileStream As Stream = File.Create( _
      "c:\mySerialFile.txt")
    Dim serializer As New BinaryFormatter()
```

```
    serializer.Serialize(myFileStream, myInstance)
    myFileStream.Close()
  End Sub

  Private Sub cmdDeserialize_Click()
    Dim myRestoredInstance As mySerialClass

    Dim myStream As Stream = File.OpenRead( _
      "c:\mySerialFile.txt")
    Dim deserializer As New BinaryFormatter()
    ' Convert type of first object to 2nd type specified
    myRestoredInstance = CType( _
      deserializer.Deserialize(myStream), mySerialClass)
    myStream.Close()
    myRestoredInstance.displayVars()
  End Sub
End Class
```

When you execute the application, clicking the cmdInit button will initialize an instance of the serializable class, store values in it, and display those values. Clicking the cmdSerialize button will write the object to a file named mySerialFile.txt. The cmdDeserialize button will load the object stored in the mySerialFile.txt into a new object reference and display the values initially set by the cmdInit button.

ActivatedClientTypeEntry Class

Holds the type value of the object registered on the client so that the same object type can be activated on the server. Found as System.Runtime.Remoting.**ActivatedClientTypeEntry.**

ActivatedServiceTypeEntry Class

Holds the type value of the object registered on the server so that the same object type can be activated on the client. Found as System.Runtime.Remoting.**ActivatedServiceTypeEntry.**

BinaryFormatter Class

Provides serialization and deserialization of an object graph (the central objects and all objects directly related to it) into a binary format.

Inheritance—Object.BinaryFormatter

```
public class System.Runtime.Serialization.
  Formatters.Binary.BinaryFormatter
  ' Constructors
  BinaryFormatter( [selector As ISurrogateSelector,
    context As StreamingContext] )
  ' Properties
  AssemblyFormat As System.Runtime.Serialization.
    Formatters.FormatterAssemblyStyle
  Binder As
    System.Runtime.Serialization.SerializationBinder
  Context As System.Runtime.Serialization.StreamingContext
  SurrogateSelector As
    System.Runtime.Serialization.ISurrogateSelector
  TypeFormat As System.Runtime.Serialization.
    Formatters.FormatterTypeStyle
  ' Methods
  Deserialize(serializationStream As Stream
    [,handler As HeaderHandler] ) As Object
  DeserializeMethodResponse(serializationStream As Stream,
    handler As HeaderHandler, methodCallMessage As
    IMethodCallMessage) As Object
  Serialize(serializationStream As Stream,
    graph As Object [,headers As Header()])
```

Formatter Class

Provides an abstract foundation class for serialization formatting on the Common Language Runtime (CLR). Note that the machine-specific nature of the serialization implementation makes the Formatter class itself not Common Language Specification (CLS) compliant. This class can also generate unique IDs for objects and provide queuing for serialization of a series of objects.

Inheritance—Object.Formatter

```
public class System.Runtime.Serialization.Formatter
  ' Properties
  Binder As
    System.Runtime.Serialization.SerializationBinder
  Context As System.Runtime.Serialization.StreamingContext
  SurrogateSelector As
    System.Runtime.Serialization.ISurrogateSelector
  ' Methods
  Deserialize(serializationStream As Stream) As Object
  Serialize(serializationStream As Stream, graph As Object)
```

FormatterConverter Class

Provides a foundation implementation of the Convert class unified with the IConvertible interface.

Inheritance—Object.FormatterConverter

```
public class
  System.Runtime.Serialization.FormatterConverter
  ' Constructors
  FormatterConverter()
  ' Methods
  Convert(value As Object, type As Type) As Object
  Convert(value As Object, typeCode As TypeCode) As Object
*  ToNNN(value As Object) As NNN
```

* **NNN** may be of type: Boolean, Byte, Char, DateTime, Decimal, Double, Int16, Int32, Int64, Object, SByte, Single, UInt16, UInt32, or UInt64. For example, a method would appear as: GetInt64(name As String) As Int64.

FormatterServices Class

Provides a static class that implements key methods used for serialization through a serialization Formatter object. This class is not inheritable.

Inheritance—Object.FormatterServices

```
public class System.Runtime.Serialization.FormatterServices
  ' Methods
  GetObjectData(obj As Object, members As MemberInfo())
    As Object()
  GetSerializableMembers(type As Type,
    context As StreamingContext) As MemberInfo()
  GetSerializableMembers(type As Type) As MemberInfo()
  GetTypeFromAssembly(assem As Assembly, name As String)
    As Type
  GetUninitializedObject(type As Type) As Object
  PopulateObjectMembers(obj As Object,
    members As MemberInfo(), data As Object()) As Object
```

ObjectHandle Class

Holds a wrapped object reference that may be passed between AppDomains. This class allows the object reference passing to occur without loading the object metadata into each object through which the ObjectHandle is moved. This allows the caller to determine when the remote Type will be loaded.

Inheritance—Object.MarshalByRefObject. ObjectHandle

```
public class System.Runtime.Remoting.ObjectHandle
  ' Constructors
  ObjectHandle(o As Object)
  ' Methods
  InitializeLifetimeService() As Object
  Unwrap() As Object
```

ObjectIDGenerator Class

Returns the 64-bit ObjectID number of an object. If that object already has an assigned ID, the existing ID is returned. Otherwise, the class generates a new ID. ObjectIDs are only valid within the context of the serialization that is executing and generally only have a lifetime to match the existence of the serialization Formatter object.

Inheritance—Object.ObjectIDGenerator

```
public class System.Runtime.Serialization.ObjectIDGenerator
  ' Constructors
  ObjectIDGenerator()
  ' Methods
  GetId(obj As Object, firstTime As Boolean&) As Int64
  HasId(obj As Object, firstTime As Boolean&) As Int64
```

ObjectManager Class

Provides a manager of all deserialized objects (objects that have been taken from a serialized store and converted to live objects). If the object in the indicated deserialization stream is already live (a backward reference), the correct reference is inserted into the object definition that is being constructed. If not (a forward reference), the ObjectManager class places a marker that is replaced in the fix-up process once the referenced object becomes live.

Inheritance—Object.ObjectManager

```
public class System.Runtime.Serialization.ObjectManager
  ' Constructors
  ObjectManager(selector As ISurrogateSelector,
    context As StreamingContext)
  ' Methods
  DoFixups()
  GetObject(objectID As Int64) As Object
```

```
  RaiseDeserializationEvent()
  RecordArrayElementFixup(arrayToBeFixed As Int64,
    indices As Int32(), objectRequired As Int64)
  RecordArrayElementFixup(arrayToBeFixed As Int64,
    index As Int32, objectRequired As Int64)
  RecordDelayedFixup(objectToBeFixed As Int64,
    memberName As String, objectRequired As Int64)
  RecordFixup(objectToBeFixed As Int64,
    member As MemberInfo, objectRequired As Int64)
  RegisterObject(obj As Object, objectID As Int64
    [,info As SerializationInfo [,idOfContainingObj As
    Int64, member As MemberInfo [,arrayIndex As Int32()]]])
```

ObjRef Class

Holds the information necessary to generate a proxy to access a remote object. This class is an extended serializable child of the MarshallByRefObject class. An ObjRef instance can be passed across AppDomains.

Inheritance—Object.ObjRef

```
public class System.Runtime.Remoting.ObjRef
  ' Constructors
  ObjRef( [o As MarshalByRefObject,
    requestedType As Type] )
  ' Properties
  ChannelInfo As System.Runtime.Remoting.IChannelInfo
  EnvoyInfo As System.Runtime.Remoting.IEnvoyInfo
  TypeInfo As System.Runtime.Remoting.IRemotingTypeInfo
  URI As System.String
  ' Methods
  GetObjectData(info As SerializationInfo,
    context As StreamingContext)
  GetRealObject(context As StreamingContext) As Object
  IsFromThisAppDomain() As Boolean
  IsFromThisProcess() As Boolean
```

RemotingConfiguration Class

Provides a static class that may be used to configure the Remoting object system.

Inheritance—Object.RemotingConfiguration

```
public class System.Runtime.Remoting.RemotingConfiguration
  ' Properties
  ApplicationName As System.String
  ' Methods
  Configure(filename As String)
  GetRegisteredActivatedClientTypes()
    As ActivatedClientTypeEntry()
  GetRegisteredActivatedServiceTypes()
    As ActivatedServiceTypeEntry()
  GetRegisteredWellKnownClientTypes()
    As WellKnownClientTypeEntry()
  GetRegisteredWellKnownServiceTypes()
    As WellKnownServiceTypeEntry()
  IsActivationAllowed(svrType As Type) As Boolean
  IsRemotelyActivatedClientType(typeName As String,
    assemblyName As String) As ActivatedClientTypeEntry
  IsRemotelyActivatedClientType(svrType As Type)
    As ActivatedClientTypeEntry
  IsWellKnownClientType(typeName As String,
    assemblyName As String) As WellKnownClientTypeEntry
  IsWellKnownClientType(svrType As Type)
    As WellKnownClientTypeEntry
  RegisterActivatedClientType(type As Type,
    appUrl As String)
  RegisterActivatedClientType(entry
    As ActivatedClientTypeEntry)
  RegisterActivatedServiceType(type As Type)
  RegisterActivatedServiceType(entry
    As ActivatedServiceTypeEntry)
  RegisterWellKnownClientType(type As Type,
    objectUrl As String)
```

```
  RegisterWellKnownClientType(entry
    As WellKnownClientTypeEntry)
  RegisterWellKnownServiceType(type As Type, objectUri
    As String, mode As WellKnownObjectMode)
  RegisterWellKnownServiceType(entry As
    WellKnownServiceTypeEntry)
```

RemotingServices Class

Provides a class to publish and access remote objects and proxies. Unless special object operations such as lifetime specification, transaction analysis, etc., are necessary, proxies (which appear as local objects and make calls to their remote associations) and remote objects may be treated identically. This class is not inheritable.

Inheritance—Object.RemotingServices

```
public class System.Runtime.Remoting.RemotingServices
  ' Methods
  Connect(classToProxy As Type, url As String
    [,data As Object]) As Object
  Disconnect(obj As MarshalByRefObject) As Boolean
  ExecuteMessage(target As MarshalByRefObject, reqMsg
    As IMethodCallMessage) As IMethodReturnMessage
  GetEnvoyChainForProxy(obj As MarshalByRefObject)
    As IMessageSink
  GetLifetimeService(obj As MarshalByRefObject) As Object
  GetMethodBaseFromMethodMessage(msg As IMethodMessage)
    As MethodBase
  GetObjectData(obj As Object, info As SerializationInfo,
    context As StreamingContext)
  GetObjectUri(obj As MarshalByRefObject) As String
  GetObjRefForProxy(obj As MarshalByRefObject) As ObjRef
  GetRealProxy(proxy As Object) As RealProxy
  GetServerTypeForUri(URI As String) As Type
  GetSessionIdForMethodMessage(msg As IMethodMessage)
    As String
  IsMethodOverloaded(msg As IMethodMessage) As Boolean
  IsObjectOutOfAppDomain(tp As Object) As Boolean
  IsObjectOutOfContext(tp As Object) As Boolean
  IsOneWay(method As MethodBase) As Boolean
  IsTransparentProxy(proxy As Object) As Boolean
```

```
LogRemotingStage(stage As Int32)
Marshal(Obj As MarshalByRefObject [, URI As String])
  As ObjRef
Marshal(Obj As MarshalByRefObject, ObjURI As String,
  RequestedType As Type) As ObjRef
SetObjectUriForMarshal(obj As MarshalByRefObject,
  uri As String)
Unmarshal(objectRef As ObjRef [, fRefine As Boolean])
  As Object
```

SerializationBinder Class

Provides an abstract foundation class with the ability to control class loading. An object, when serialized, is stored with its full type name and assembly information (namespace location, version, strong name, etc.). This class allows control of the loading process so that the class version, the assembly location, or other characteristics may be modified as the object is deserialized. Found as System.Runtime.Serialization.**SerializationBinder.**

SerializationInfo Class

Holds information such as the assembly name and the full type name of the object for serialization or deserialization. This class is not inheritable.

11

Inheritance—Object.SerializationInfo

```
public class System.Runtime.Serialization.SerializationInfo
  ' Constructors
  SerializationInfo(type As Type,
    converter As IFormatterConverter)
  ' Properties
  AssemblyName As System.String
  FullTypeName As System.String
  MemberCount As System.Int32 (read only)
  ' Methods
*  AddValue(name As String, value )
  AddValue(name As String, value As Object, type As Type)
```

```
  GetEnumerator() As SerializationInfoEnumerator
**  GetNNN(name As String) As NNN
  GetValue(name As String, type As Type) As Object
  SetType(type As Type)
```

```
* Value may be of type Boolean, Byte, Char, DateTime, Decimal,
Double, Int16, Int32, Int64, Object, SByte, Single, UInt16, UInt32,
or UInt64.

** NNN may be of type Boolean, Byte, Char, DateTime, Decimal,
Double, Int16, Int32, Int64, Object, SByte, Single, UInt16, UInt32,
or UInt64. For example, an NNN method would appear as GetInt64(name
As String) As Int64.
```

SerializationInfoEnumerator Class

Provides a parser for information held in a SerializationInfo instance. This class is not inheritable.

Inheritance—Object.SerializationInfoEnumerator

```
public class
  System.Runtime.Serialization.SerializationInfoEnumerator
  ' Properties
  Current As
    System.Runtime.Serialization.SerializationEntry
    (read only)
  Name As System.String (read only)
  ObjectType As System.Type (read only)
  Value As System.Object (read only)
  ' Methods
  MoveNext() As Boolean
  Reset()
```

SoapServices Class

Provides a class that can publish and access remote objects through the Simple Object Access Protocol (SOAP). SOAP is an XML-based distributed object access standard for exchanging object information, messages, and instructions over a network using the HTTP protocol.

Inheritance—Object.SoapServices

```
public class System.Runtime.Remoting.SoapServices
  ' Properties
  XmlNsForClrType As System.String (read only)
  XmlNsForClrTypeWithAssembly As System.String (read only)
  XmlNsForClrTypeWithNs As System.String (read only)
  XmlNsForClrTypeWithNsAndAssembly
    As System.String (read only)
  ' Methods
  CodeXmlNamespaceForClrTypeNamespace(typeNamespace
    As String, assemblyName As String) As String
  DecodeXmlNamespaceForClrTypeNamespace(inNamespace
    As String, typeNamespace As String&, assemblyName
    As String&) As Boolean
  GetInteropFieldTypeAndNameFromXmlAttribute(containingType
    As Type, xmlAttribute As String, xmlNamespace
    As String, type As Type&, name As String&)
  GetInteropFieldTypeAndNameFromXmlElement(containingType
    As Type, xmlElement As String, xmlNamespace As String,
    type As Type&, name As String&)
  GetInteropTypeFromXmlElement(xmlElement As String,
    xmlNamespace As String) As Type
  GetInteropTypeFromXmlType(xmlType As String,
    xmlTypeNamespace As String) As Type
  GetSoapActionFromMethodBase(mb As MethodBase) As String
  GetTypeAndMethodNameFromSoapAction(soapAction As String,
    typeName As String&, methodName As String&) As Boolean
  GetXmlElementForInteropType(type As Type, xmlElement
    As String&, xmlNamespace As String&) As Boolean
  GetXmlNamespaceForMethodCall(mb As MethodBase) As String
  GetXmlNamespaceForMethodResponse(mb As MethodBase)
    As String
  GetXmlTypeForInteropType(type As Type, xmlType As
    String&, xmlTypeNamespace As String&) As Boolean
  IsClrTypeNamespace(namespaceString As String) As Boolean
  IsSoapActionValidForMethodBase(soapAction As String,
    mb As MethodBase) As Boolean
  PreLoad(type As Type)
  PreLoad(assembly As Assembly)
  RegisterInteropXmlElement(xmlElement As String,
    xmlNamespace As String, type As Type)
  RegisterInteropXmlType(xmlType As String,
    xmlTypeNamespace As String, type As Type)
```

```
RegisterSoapActionForMethodBase(mb As MethodBase)
RegisterSoapActionForMethodBase(mb As MethodBase,
  soapAction As String)
```

SurrogateSelector Class

Provides Formatter class-based objects with information indicating which surrogates to use for serialization. A surrogate is an object that provides a custom process of serialization for a particular object type.

Inheritance—Object.SurrogateSelector

```
public class System.Runtime.Serialization.SurrogateSelector
  ' Constructors
  SurrogateSelector()
  ' Methods
  AddSurrogate(type As Type, context As StreamingContext,
    surrogate As ISerializationSurrogate)
  ChainSelector(selector As ISurrogateSelector)
  GetNextSelector() As ISurrogateSelector
  GetSurrogate(type As Type, context As StreamingContext,
    selector As ISurrogateSelector&)
    As ISerializationSurrogate
  RemoveSurrogate(type As Type, context As
    StreamingContext)
```

TypeEntry Class

Provides a foundation class that holds information used to activate an instance of a remote object type. Children of this class include ActivatedClientTypeEntry, ActivatedServiceTypeEntry, WellKnownClientTypeEntry, and WellKnownServiceTypeEntry.

Inheritance—Object.TypeEntry

```
public class System.Runtime.Remoting.TypeEntry
  ' Properties
  AssemblyName As System.String
  TypeName As System.String
```

WellKnownClientTypeEntry Class

Holds values for well-known client types registered for instantiation on a remote system. Object type management may be either single call (a new instance is created each time a call is made) or singleton (all calls are handled by one instance).

Inheritance—Object.TypeEntry. WellKnownClientTypeEntry

```
public class
  System.Runtime.Remoting.WellKnownClientTypeEntry
  ' Constructors
  WellKnownClientTypeEntry(typeName As String,
    assemblyName As String, objectUrl As String)
  WellKnownClientTypeEntry(type As Type,
    objectUrl As String)
  ' Properties
  ApplicationUrl As System.String
  ObjectType As System.Type (read only)
  ObjectUrl As System.String (read only)
  ' Methods
  ToString() As String
```

WellKnownServiceTypeEntry Class

Holds values for well-known service types registered for instantiation on the server system. Object type management may be either single call (a new instance is created each time a call is made) or singleton (all calls are handled by one instance).

Inheritance—Object.TypeEntry. WellKnownServiceTypeEntry

```
public class
    System.Runtime.Remoting.WellKnownServiceTypeEntry
  ' Constructors
  WellKnownServiceTypeEntry(typeName As String,
    assemblyName As String, objectUri As String,
    mode As WellKnownObjectMode)
```

```
WellKnownServiceTypeEntry(type As Type,
  objectUri As String, mode As WellKnownObjectMode)
' Properties
ContextAttributes As
  System.Runtime.Remoting.Contexts.IContextAttribute()
Mode As
  System.Runtime.Remoting.WellKnownObjectMode (read only)
ObjectType As System.Type (read only)
ObjectUri As System.String (read only)
' Methods
ToString() As String
```

Chapter 12
Globalization

Accommodating international standards is becoming an increasingly important problem to address in modern software. The Internet has been a primary catalyst in the adoption of technology to embrace the global marketplace. Unicode is a standard that has helped to allow computer software to adapt to various non-Roman languages. Further standards solve problems such as mapping date/calendar differences or handling the character display direction (such as left-to-right or right-to-left text). Most of the solutions to these cultural translation issues have been add-ons in previous development systems. In the .NET Framework, they have been included at the foundation level.

The Globalization classes that are part of the .NET Framework provide technology to handle cultural and monetary conversion problems. These classes help minimize the difficulty and expense of amending existing applications or creating new applications with a broader global reach.

Information on numerous cultures can be retrieved and manipulated simply by using the proper classes and specifying the desired society. The following example code retrieves information on both the United States and China and writes the DisplayName property of the data to the Output window:

```
' Get cultural info on the U.S.
Dim myCI As New System.Globalization.CultureInfo("en-US")
Console.WriteLine(myCI.DisplayName)
' Get cultural info on China
Dim myCI2 As New System.Globalization.CultureInfo("zh-CHS")
Console.WriteLine(myCI2.DisplayName)
```

12

Calendar Class

Holds a logical representation of a calendar to provide time divisions such as weeks, months, and years. When used in conjunction with a DateTime object, a Calendar implementation can map dates and times from nearly any type to any other. This class provides the foundation for the following child classes: GregorianCalendar, HebrewCalendar, HijriCalendar, JapaneseCalendar, JulianCalendar, KoreanCalendar, TaiwanCalendar, and ThaiBuddhistCalendar.

Inheritance—Object.Calendar

```
public class System.Globalization.Calendar
  ' Properties
  Eras As System.Int32() (read only)
  TwoDigitYearMax As System.Int32
  ' Methods
  AddDays(time As DateTime, days As Int32) As DateTime
  AddHours(time As DateTime, hours As Int32) As DateTime
  AddMilliseconds(time As DateTime, milliseconds As Double)
    As DateTime
  AddMinutes(time As DateTime, minutes As Int32)
    As DateTime
  AddMonths(time As DateTime, months As Int32) As DateTime
  AddSeconds(time As DateTime, seconds As Int32)
    As DateTime
  AddWeeks(time As DateTime, weeks As Int32) As DateTime
  AddYears(time As DateTime, years As Int32) As DateTime
  GetDayOfMonth(time As DateTime) As Int32
  GetDayOfWeek(time As DateTime) As DayOfWeek
  GetDayOfYear(time As DateTime) As Int32
  GetDaysInMonth(year As Int32, month As Int32,
    era As Int32) As Int32
  GetDaysInMonth(year As Int32, month As Int32) As Int32
  GetDaysInYear(year As Int32, era As Int32) As Int32
  GetDaysInYear(year As Int32) As Int32
  GetEra(time As DateTime) As Int32
  GetHour(time As DateTime) As Int32
  GetMilliseconds(time As DateTime) As Double
  GetMinute(time As DateTime) As Int32
  GetMonth(time As DateTime) As Int32
  GetMonthsInYear(year As Int32, era As Int32) As Int32
  GetMonthsInYear(year As Int32) As Int32
  GetSecond(time As DateTime) As Int32
  GetWeekOfYear(time As DateTime, rule As CalendarWeekRule,
    firstDayOfWeek As DayOfWeek) As Int32
  GetYear(time As DateTime) As Int32
  IsLeapDay(year As Int32, month As Int32, day As Int32
    [,era As Int32]) As Boolean
  IsLeapMonth(year As Int32, month As Int32
    [,era As Int32]) As Boolean
  IsLeapYear(year As Int32 [,era As Int32]) As Boolean
  ToDateTime(year As Int32, month As Int32, day As Int32,
    hour As Int32, minute As Int32, second As Int32,
    millisecond As Int32 [,era As Int32]) As DateTime
  ToFourDigitYear(year As Int32) As Int32
```

CompareInfo Class

Compares strings based on culturally sensitive settings such as case-sensitivity rules, kana types, nonspace characters (i.e., diacritics, etc.), symbols, and character width. This class can also use ordinal comparison (when Unicode values are evaluated) and string-sorted comparison. Note that instead of a constructor, the GetCompareInfo() method has been supplied to obtain an object instance so that this class may be used with late binding.

Inheritance—Object.CompareInfo

```
public class System.Globalization.CompareInfo
  ' Properties
  LCID As System.Int32 (read only)
  ' Methods
  Compare(string1 As String, offset1 As Int32,
    length1 As Int32, string2 As String, offset2 As Int32,
    length2 As Int32) As Int32
  Compare(string1 As String, string2 As String,
    options As CompareOptions) As Int32
  Compare(string1 As String, string2 As String) As Int32
  Compare(string1 As String, offset1 As Int32,
    length1 As Int32, string2 As String, offset2 As Int32,
    length2 As Int32, options As CompareOptions) As Int32
  Compare(string1 As String, offset1 As Int32,
    string2 As String, offset2 As Int32) As Int32
  Compare(string1 As String, offset1 As Int32,
    string2 As String, offset2 As Int32, options As
    CompareOptions) As Int32
  Equals(value As Object) As Boolean
  GetCompareInfo(culture As Int32 [,assembly As Assembly])
    As CompareInfo
  GetCompareInfo(name As String [,assembly As Assembly])
    As CompareInfo
  GetHashCode() As Int32
  GetSortKey(source As String) As SortKey
  GetSortKey(source As String, options As CompareOptions)
    As SortKey
  IndexOf(source As String, value As String
    [,options As CompareOptions]) As Int32
  IndexOf(source As String, value As Char,
    startIndex As Int32) As Int32
  IndexOf(source As String, value As Char
    [,options As CompareOptions]) As Int32
  IndexOf(source As String, value As Char, startIndex As
    Int32, options As CompareOptions) As Int32
```

```
IndexOf(source As String, value As String, startIndex As
  Int32, count As Int32) As Int32
IndexOf(source As String, value As Char, startIndex As
  Int32, count As Int32, options As CompareOptions)
  As Int32
IndexOf(source As String, value As String, startIndex As
  Int32, count As Int32, options As CompareOptions)
  As Int32
IndexOf(source As String, value As Char, startIndex As
  Int32, count As Int32) As Int32
IndexOf(source As String, value As String,
  startIndex As Int32) As Int32
IndexOf(source As String, value As String, startIndex As
  Int32, options As CompareOptions) As Int32
IsPrefix(source As String, prefix As String,
  options As CompareOptions) As Boolean
IsPrefix(source As String, prefix As String) As Boolean
IsSuffix(source As String, suffix As String) As Boolean
IsSuffix(source As String, suffix As String,
  options As CompareOptions) As Boolean
LastIndexOf(source As String, value As String, startIndex
  As Int32, options As CompareOptions) As Int32
LastIndexOf(source As String, value As String,
  startIndex As Int32) As Int32
LastIndexOf(source As String, value As Char, startIndex
  As Int32, count As Int32) As Int32
LastIndexOf(source As String, value As String, startIndex
  As Int32, count As Int32, options As CompareOptions)
  As Int32
LastIndexOf(source As String, value As Char, startIndex
  As Int32, count As Int32, options As CompareOptions)
  As Int32
LastIndexOf(source As String, value As String,
  startIndex As Int32, count As Int32) As Int32
LastIndexOf(source As String, value As Char,
  options As CompareOptions) As Int32
LastIndexOf(source As String, value As String
  [,options As CompareOptions]) As Int32
LastIndexOf(source As String, value As Char [,startIndex
  As Int32 [,options As CompareOptions]]) As Int32
ToString() As String
```

CultureInfo Class

Holds information about a culture including language, sublanguage, writing system, calendar, and other cultural conventions. This class is used indirectly by the foundation data type String and also by other classes in the System.Globalization namespace. When instantiating an object from this class, the name of the culture may be specified using the RFC 1766 standard in the format "*<languagecode2>-<country/regioncode2>*" such as "en-US." The *<languagecode2>* argument is a lowercase two-letter code derived from ISO 639-1. The *<country/regioncode2>* argument is an uppercase two-letter code derived from ISO 3166.

Inheritance—Object.CultureInfo

```
public class System.Globalization.CultureInfo
  ' Constructors
  CultureInfo(culture As Int32, useUserOverride As Boolean)
  CultureInfo(name As String)
  CultureInfo(culture As Int32)
  CultureInfo(name As String, useUserOverride As Boolean)
  ' Properties
  Calendar As System.Globalization.Calendar (read only)
  CompareInfo As
    System.Globalization.CompareInfo (read only)
  CurrentCulture As
    System.Globalization.CultureInfo (read only)
  CurrentUICulture As
    System.Globalization.CultureInfo (read only)
  DateTimeFormat As System.Globalization.DateTimeFormatInfo
  DisplayName As System.String (read only)
  EnglishName As System.String (read only)
  InstalledUICulture As
    System.Globalization.CultureInfo (read only)
  InvariantCulture As
    System.Globalization.CultureInfo (read only)
  IsNeutralCulture As System.Boolean (read only)
  IsReadOnly As System.Boolean (read only)
  LCID As System.Int32 (read only)
  Name As System.String (read only)
  NativeName As System.String (read only)
  NumberFormat As System.Globalization.NumberFormatInfo
  OptionalCalendars As
    System.Globalization.Calendar() (read only)
  Parent As System.Globalization.CultureInfo (read only)
  TextInfo As System.Globalization.TextInfo (read only)
  ThreeLetterISOLanguageName As System.String (read only)
  ThreeLetterWindowsLanguageName As
    System.String (read only)
  TwoLetterISOLanguageName As System.String (read only)
  UseUserOverride As System.Boolean (read only)
  ' Methods
  ClearCachedData()
  Clone() As Object
```

12

```
CreateSpecificCulture(name As String) As CultureInfo
Equals(value As Object) As Boolean
GetCultures(types As CultureTypes) As CultureInfo()
GetFormat(formatType As Type) As Object
GetHashCode() As Int32
ReadOnly(ci As CultureInfo) As CultureInfo
ToString() As String
```

DateTimeFormatInfo Class

Holds formatting settings that specify how date and time values are displayed. Values stored in a DateTime object type use the DateTimeFormatInfo class to determine how they will be presented. Custom patterns can be created with the primary case-sensitive modifiers: d (mm/dd/yy), D (mm/DD/yy), f (dddd, dd MMMM yyyy HH:mm), F (dddd, dd mmmm yyyy hh:mm:ss), g (mm/dd/yyyy hh:mm), G (mm/dd/yyyy HH:mm:ss), m (mm/dd/yy), M (MM/dd/yy), r (ddd, dd mmm yyyy hh':'mm':'ss 'GMT'), R (ddd, dd mmm yyyy hh':'mm':'ss 'GMT'), s (yyyy'-'mm'-'dd'T'hh':'mm':'ss), t (hh:mm), T (hh:mm:ss), u (yyyy'-'mm'-'dd hh':'mm':'ss'Z'), U (dddd, dd mmmm yyyy hh:mm:ss), y (mm/dd/yy), and Y (mm/dd/YY). The ToString() method can be used to retrieve the formatted value like this: *DateTime.ToString("mm/dd/yy").*

Inheritance—Object.DateTimeFormatInfo

```
public class System.Globalization.DateTimeFormatInfo
  ' Constructors
  DateTimeFormatInfo()
  ' Properties
  AbbreviatedDayNames As System.String()
  AbbreviatedMonthNames As System.String()
  AMDesignator As System.String
  Calendar As System.Globalization.Calendar
  CalendarWeekRule As System.Globalization.CalendarWeekRule
  CurrentInfo As
    System.Globalization.DateTimeFormatInfo (read only)
  DateSeparator As System.String
  DayNames As System.String()
  FirstDayOfWeek As System.DayOfWeek
  FullDateTimePattern As System.String
  InvariantInfo As
    System.Globalization.DateTimeFormatInfo (read only)
  IsReadOnly As System.Boolean (read only)
```

```
LongDatePattern As System.String
LongTimePattern As System.String
MonthDayPattern As System.String
MonthNames As System.String()
PMDesignator As System.String
RFC1123Pattern As System.String (read only)
ShortDatePattern As System.String
ShortTimePattern As System.String
SortableDateTimePattern As System.String (read only)
TimeSeparator As System.String
UniversalSortableDateTimePattern As
  System.String (read only)
YearMonthPattern As System.String
' Methods
Clone() As Object
GetAbbreviatedDayName(dayofweek As DayOfWeek) As String
GetAbbreviatedEraName(era As Int32) As String
GetAbbreviatedMonthName(month As Int32) As String
GetAllDateTimePatterns(format As Char) As String()
GetAllDateTimePatterns() As String()
GetDayName(dayofweek As DayOfWeek) As String
GetEra(eraName As String) As Int32
GetEraName(era As Int32) As String
GetFormat(formatType As Type) As Object
GetInstance(provider As IFormatProvider)
  As DateTimeFormatInfo
GetMonthName(month As Int32) As String
ReadOnly(dtfi As DateTimeFormatInfo)
  As DateTimeFormatInfo
```

DaylightTime Class

Holds the time period that is used for daylight savings time to advance and set back the time of the clock.

12

Inheritance—Object.DaylightTime

```
public class System.Globalization.DaylightTime
  ' Constructors
  DaylightTime(start As DateTime, end As DateTime,
    delta As TimeSpan)
  ' Properties
  Delta As System.TimeSpan (read only)
  End As System.DateTime (read only)
  Start As System.DateTime (read only)
```

GregorianCalendar Class

Provides a representation of the Gregorian calendar. This class only recognizes the current era abbreviated as "AD" that represents Anno Domini (A.D., "in the year of the Lord") also known as Common Era (C.E.). The Gregorian calendar has 12 months with 28–31 days each.

Inheritance—Object.Calendar. GregorianCalendar

```
public class System.Globalization.GregorianCalendar
  ' Constructors
  GregorianCalendar(type As GregorianCalendarTypes)
  GregorianCalendar()
  ' Properties
  CalendarType As
    System.Globalization.GregorianCalendarTypes
  ' All properties below are available for all
  ' calendars that reference this one
  Eras As System.Int32() (read only)
  TwoDigitYearMax As System.Int32
  ' Methods
  AddWeeks(time As DateTime, weeks As Int32) As DateTime
  '   Other methods match calendars for
  AddMonths(time As DateTime, months As Int32) As DateTime
  AddYears(time As DateTime, years As Int32) As DateTime
  GetDayOfMonth(time As DateTime) As Int32
  GetDayOfWeek(time As DateTime) As DayOfWeek
  GetDayOfYear(time As DateTime) As Int32
  GetDaysInMonth(year As Int32, month As Int32,
    era As Int32) As Int32
  GetDaysInYear(year As Int32, era As Int32) As Int32
  GetEra(time As DateTime) As Int32
  GetMonth(time As DateTime) As Int32
  GetMonthsInYear(year As Int32, era As Int32) As Int32
  GetYear(time As DateTime) As Int32
  IsLeapDay(year As Int32, month As Int32, day As Int32,
    era As Int32) As Boolean
  IsLeapMonth(year As Int32, month As Int32,
    era As Int32) As Boolean
  IsLeapYear(year As Int32, era As Int32) As Boolean
  ToDateTime(year As Int32, month As Int32, day As Int32,
    hour As Int32, minute As Int32, second As Int32,
    millisecond As Int32, era As Int32) As DateTime
  ToFourDigitYear(year As Int32) As Int32
```

HebrewCalendar Class

Provides a representation of the Hebrew calendar. This class only recognizes the current era abbreviated as "AM" that represents Anno Mundi (A.M., "the year of the world"). The Hebrew calendar has 12 months in a common year and 13 months in a leap year.

Inheritance—Object.Calendar.HebrewCalendar

```
public class System.Globalization.HebrewCalendar
  ' Constructors
  HebrewCalendar()
  ' See GregorianCalendar class for
  ' methods and properties
```

HijriCalendar Class

Provides a representation of the Hijri calendar. This class only recognizes the current era abbreviated as "AM" that represents Anno Hegirae (A.M., "the year of the migration"). The Hijri calendar has 12 months with 29–30 days each.

Inheritance—Object.Calendar.HijriCalendar

```
public class System.Globalization.HijriCalendar
  ' Constructors
  HijriCalendar()
  ' See GregorianCalendar class for
  ' methods and properties
```


JapaneseCalendar Class

Provides a representation of the Japanese secondary calendar. Although the years and eras are different, this calendar works just like the Gregorian calendar.

Inheritance—Object.Calendar.JapaneseCalendar

```
public class System.Globalization.JapaneseCalendar
  ' Constructors
  JapaneseCalendar()
  ' See the GregorianCalendar class for
  ' methods and properties
```

JulianCalendar Class

Provides a representation of the Julian calendar, a predecessor to the Gregorian calendar. The Julian calendar only represents the current era and has 12 months with 28–31 days each.

Inheritance—Object.Calendar.JulianCalendar

```
public class System.Globalization.JulianCalendar
  ' Constructors
  JulianCalendar()
  ' See the GregorianCalendar class for
  ' methods and properties
```

KoreanCalendar Class

Provides a representation of the Korean calendar. Although the years and eras are different, this calendar works just like the Gregorian calendar.

Inheritance—Object.Calendar.KoreanCalendar

```
public class System.Globalization.KoreanCalendar
  ' Constructors
  KoreanCalendar()
  ' See the GregorianCalendar class for
  ' methods and properties
```

NumberFormatInfo Class

Provides a way of formatting numeric values for currency signs, decimal separators, and other symbols according to cultural standards. These case-insensitive modifiers can be used to specify the type of formatting: c (currency), d (decimal), e (scientific), f (fixed-point), g (general), n (number), r (roundtrip), and x (hexadecimal). Note that round-trip formatting (r) assures that numbers converted to strings will be formatted so that a conversion back to a number will result in exactly the same original value.

Inheritance—Object.NumberFormatInfo

```
public class System.Globalization.NumberFormatInfo
  ' Constructors
  NumberFormatInfo()
  ' Properties
  CurrencyDecimalDigits As System.Int32
  CurrencyDecimalSeparator As System.String
  CurrencyGroupSeparator As System.String
  CurrencyGroupSizes As System.Int32()
  CurrencyNegativePattern As System.Int32
  CurrencyPositivePattern As System.Int32
  CurrencySymbol As System.String
  CurrentInfo As
    System.Globalization.NumberFormatInfo (read only)
  InvariantInfo As
    System.Globalization.NumberFormatInfo (read only)
  IsReadOnly As System.Boolean (read only)
  NaNSymbol As System.String
  NegativeInfinitySymbol As System.String
  NegativeSign As System.String
  NumberDecimalDigits As System.Int32
  NumberDecimalSeparator As System.String
  NumberGroupSeparator As System.String
  NumberGroupSizes As System.Int32()
  NumberNegativePattern As System.Int32
  PercentDecimalDigits As System.Int32
  PercentDecimalSeparator As System.String
  PercentGroupSeparator As System.String
```

```
  PercentGroupSizes As System.Int32()
  PercentNegativePattern As System.Int32
  PercentPositivePattern As System.Int32
  PercentSymbol As System.String
  PerMilleSymbol As System.String
  PositiveInfinitySymbol As System.String
  PositiveSign As System.String
  ' Methods
  Clone() As Object
  GetFormat(formatType As Type) As Object
  GetInstance(formatProvider As IFormatProvider)
    As NumberFormatInfo
  ReadOnly(nfi As NumberFormatInfo) As NumberFormatInfo
```

RegionInfo Class

Holds region-specific information such as currency type names and measurement systems.

Inheritance—Object.RegionInfo

```
public class System.Globalization.RegionInfo
  ' Constructors
  RegionInfo(culture As Int32)
  RegionInfo(name As String)
  ' Properties
  CurrencySymbol As System.String (read only)
  CurrentRegion As
    System.Globalization.RegionInfo (read only)
  DisplayName As System.String (read only)
  EnglishName As System.String (read only)
  IsMetric As System.Boolean (read only)
  ISOCurrencySymbol As System.String (read only)
  Name As System.String (read only)
  ThreeLetterISORegionName As System.String (read only)
  ThreeLetterWindowsRegionName As System.String (read only)
  TwoLetterISORegionName As System.String (read only)
  ' Methods
  Equals(value As Object) As Boolean
  GetHashCode() As Int32
  ToString() As String
```

SortKey Class

Holds a repository of sort weights for a particular string. Strings can be evaluated for sorting in a variety of ways (alphabetic, case-sensitive, and diacritic) and this class holds the key for the sort weights of the characters in the related string.

Inheritance—Object.SortKey

```
public class System.Globalization.SortKey
  ' Properties
  KeyData As System.Byte() (read only)
  OriginalString As System.String (read only)
  ' Methods
  Compare(sortkey1 As SortKey, sortkey2 As SortKey)
    As Int32
  Equals(value As Object) As Boolean
  GetHashCode() As Int32
  ToString() As String
```

StringInfo Class

Provides a parsing routine to split a string into text elements and iterate through them. A text element is one or more characters that are displayed as a single character and might encompass a single character, a surrogate pair, or a combination character sequence.

Inheritance—Object.StringInfo

```
public class System.Globalization.StringInfo
  ' Constructors
  StringInfo()
  ' Methods
  GetNextTextElement(str As String, index As Int32)
    As String
  GetNextTextElement(str As String) As String
  GetTextElementEnumerator(str As String, index As Int32)
    As TextElementEnumerator
```

```
  GetTextElementEnumerator(str As String)
    As TextElementEnumerator
  ParseCombiningCharacters(str As String) As Int32()
```

TaiwanCalendar Class

Provides a representation of the Taiwanese calendar. Although the years and eras are different, this calendar works just like the Gregorian calendar.

Inheritance—Object.Calendar.TaiwanCalendar

```
public class System.Globalization.TaiwanCalendar
   ' Constructors
   TaiwanCalendar()
   ' See the GregorianCalendar class for
   ' methods and properties
```

TextElementEnumerator Class

Provides access to text elements within a string. A text element is one or more Unicode characters that are displayed as a single character and might encompass a single character, a surrogate pair, or a combination character sequence.

Inheritance—Object.TextElementEnumerator

```
public class System.Globalization.TextElementEnumerator
  ' Properties
  Current As System.Object (read only)
  ElementIndex As System.Int32 (read only)
  ' Methods
  GetTextElement() As String
  MoveNext() As Boolean
  Reset()
```

TextInfo Class

Holds definition information that indicates the scripts and orthographic rules used to present a language as text.

Inheritance—Object.TextInfo

```
public class System.Globalization.TextInfo
  ' Properties
  ANSICodePage As System.Int32 (read only)
  EBCDICCodePage As System.Int32 (read only)
  ListSeparator As System.String (read only)
  MacCodePage As System.Int32 (read only)
  OEMCodePage As System.Int32 (read only)
  ' Methods
  Equals(obj As Object) As Boolean
  GetHashCode() As Int32
  ToLower(str As String) As String
  ToLower(c As Char) As Char
  ToString() As String
  ToTitleCase(str As String) As String
  ToUpper(str As String) As String
  ToUpper(c As Char) As Char
```

ThaiBuddhistCalendar Class

Provides a representation of the Thai Buddhist calendar. Although the years and eras are different, this calendar works just like the Gregorian calendar.

Inheritance—Object.Calendar. ThaiBuddhistCalendar

```
public class System.Globalization.ThaiBuddhistCalendar
  ' Constructors
  ThaiBuddhistCalendar()
  ' See the GregorianCalendar class for
  ' methods and properties
```

Chapter 13
Security

With the release of Windows 2000 and its successor Windows XP, security has become a very important aspect of system configuration. Security reaches from a single desktop computer through the local area network all the way to the Internet. The Windows operating system now includes capabilities that allow protection granularity to extend down to individual assemblies and files.

The advance of the Internet makes security of paramount importance to even a medium size company. Connections to the Internet that are "always up" expose any security vulnerability to the world. On both the programming and system level, the .NET Framework comes with extensive capabilities to handle security and cryptography.

.NET Security

The programming access to the security interfaces included in the .NET Framework provides functionality to

- Secure encoded and decoded data
- Manage security configurations through the SecurityManager class
- Compute hash values
- Generate statistically secure random numbers
- Provide message authentication
- Manage a variety of cryptographic algorithms
- Authenticate and generate digital signatures for identity authorization and data integrity verification
- Encrypt XML-based objects

The underlying foundation for all of the security features available through the Common Language Runtime (CLR) are provided by classes found in the System.Security namespace. Some of the classes, such as the secure XML implementations, are not made to be used directly by developers, but are used for internal transmission between areas of the .NET framework.

The security systems available through the Windows-based operating systems include an extendable structure where each encryption/decryption system is represented as a Crypto Service Provider (CSP). Each CSP provides a code wrapper of an implementation of a specific algorithm. Classes that have a name ending with the suffix CryptoServiceProvider are CSPs.

Due to the sophistication, complexity, and specific nature of the security classes, full implementation details could not be included in a reference book of this size. Therefore, each security class contains a descriptive entry and the namespace location. For complete definition information, consult the Visual Studio documentation.

Generating Hash Codes

Hash algorithms are used extensively in cryptography for everything from indexing for fast searching to generating validity checksum codes. These algorithms map variable-length binary strings to fixed-length strings that are known as hash values or hash codes. A hash value may be computed using a number of different algorithms. Within the .NET Framework, specifiying an encoding algorithm is generally as simple as instantiating the necessary CSP and using the ComputeHash() method to retrieve the hash information.

The following example uses the MD5 and SHA1 algorithms to generate hash values. After the sample text string is computed as a hash code, the code is printed to the Console window. Add this header to the beginning of a new VB Windows application project:

```
Imports System.Security
Imports System.Security.Cryptography
Imports System.Text
```

Place a button on the default form and name it **cmdComputeHash**. Now insert the following code in the Click event of a button:

```
Sub cmdComputeHash_Click()
  Dim dataStr As String = "This will be encoded."
  Dim myEncoder As New ASCIIEncoding()
```

```
  ' Turn the string into a series of bytes
  ' for encoding
  Dim data() As Byte = myEncoder.GetBytes(dataStr)
  Dim cspMD5 As New MD5CryptoServiceProvider()
  Dim cspSHA1 As New SHA1CryptoServiceProvider()
  Dim result As Byte()
  Dim outputStr As String

  ' Compute hash with MD5 algorithm
  result = cspMD5.ComputeHash(data)
  outputStr = myEncoder.GetString(result)
  Console.WriteLine("MD5:" & outputStr)

  ' Compute hash with SHA1 algorithm
  result = cspSHA1.ComputeHash(data)
  outputStr = myEncoder.GetString(result)
  Console.WriteLine("SHA:" & outputStr)
End Sub
```

After you've executed the application and clicked the button, examine the output window to see the ASCII representation of the hash codes generated by the different algorithms.

AllMembershipCondition Class

Provides a membership condition that matches all code, so it traditionally provides the policy level of the root code group. This class is not inheritable. Found as System.Security.Policy. **AllMembershipCondition**.

ApplicationDirectory Class

Provides the application directory for policy evaluation. This class is not inheritable. Found as System.Security.Policy. **ApplicationDirectory**.

ApplicationDirectoryMembership Condition Class

Indicates if an assembly is a member of a code group by examining the Directory property of an ApplicationDirectory instance. If the code is not located in the path (or subpath) indicated by the Directory property, it will fail the code group membership test. This class is not inheritable. *See also* the HashMembershipCondition, PublisherMembershipCondition, SiteMembershipCondition, StrongNameMembershipCondition, UrlMembershipCondition, WebPageMembershipCondition, and ZoneMembershipCondition classes. Found as System.Security. Policy.**ApplicationDirectoryMembershipCondition**.

AsymmetricAlgorithm Class

Provides the abstract foundation class for all asymmetric (public key) algorithm classes. Found as System.Security.Cryptography. **AsymmetricAlgorithm**.

AsymmetricKeyExchangeDeformatter Class

Provides the abstract foundation class for all asymmetric (public key) exchange deformatter classes. Key exchange is the process of encrypting and sending secret information (such as a private key for symmetric data encryption) with an asymmetric algorithm. This symmetric information is then used as a basis for secure communication, since symmetric encryption and decryption are much faster and less processor intensive than asymmetric operations. Deformatting is the process of decrypting the key exchange data. Found as System.Security.Cryptography. **AsymmetricKeyExchangeDeformatter**.

AsymmetricKeyExchangeFormatter Class

Provides the abstract foundation class for all asymmetric (public key) exchange formatter classes. Key exchange is the process of encrypting and sending secret information (such as a private key for symmetrical data encryption) with an asymmetric algorithm. This information is then used as a basis for secure communication. Formatting is the process of encrypting the key exchange data. Found as System.Security. Cryptography.**AsymmetricKeyExchangeFormatter**.

AsymmetricSignatureDeformatter Class

Provides the abstract foundation class for all asymmetric (public key) signature deformatter classes. Signature deformatters verify digital signatures created by AsymmetricSignatureFormatter-based objects. Found as System.Security.Cryptography. **AsymmetricSignatureDeformatter**.

AsymmetricSignatureFormatter Class

Provides the abstract foundation class for all asymmetric (public key) exchange formatter classes. Signature formatters create digital signatures that are verified by AsymmetricSignatureDeformatter-based objects. Found as System.Security.Cryptography. **AsymmetricSignatureFormatter**.

CodeAccessPermission Class

Provides an access stack that is used to verify that all callers of the specified code have the proper permissions. If this object contains a null or Nothing reference, the code block is treated as if no access rights have been granted. If a class inherits from this class, it must override the Copy, Intersect, IsSubsetOf, ToXml, FromXml, and Union methods. Additionally, the constructor may take a PermissionState argument. Found as System.Security.**CodeAccessPermission**.

CodeGroup Class

Provides the abstract foundation class for all code group classes. Code groups are used to define policy-level access specification to blocks of code. Code groups are organized into a hierarchical topology that extends security behavior to multiple levels. Found as System.Security.Policy.**CodeGroup**.

CryptoAPITransform Class

Provides cryptographic transformation capabilities for use on a CryptoStream object. Found as System.Security.Cryptography.**CryptoAPITransform**.

CryptoConfig Class

Holds the cryptographic configuration information. The following list shows the simple name of the cryptographic scheme and the algorithm implementation of that scheme in parentheses: SHA (SHA1CryptoServiceProvider), SHA1 (SHA1CryptoServiceProvider), System.Security.Cryptography.SHA1 (SHA1CryptoServiceProvider), System.Security.Cryptography. HashAlgorithm (SHA1CryptoServiceProvider), MD5 (MD5CryptoServiceProvider), System.Security.Cryptography.MD5 (MD5CryptoServiceProvider), SHA256 (SHA256Managed), SHA-256 (SHA256Managed), System.Security.Cryptography.SHA256 (SHA256Managed), SHA384 (SHA384Managed), SHA-384 (SHA384Managed), System.Security.Cryptography.SHA384 (SHA384Managed), SHA512 (SHA512Managed), SHA-512 (SHA512Managed), System.Security.Cryptography.SHA512 (SHA512Managed), RSA (RSACryptoServiceProvider), System.Security.Cryptography.RSA (RSACryptoServiceProvider), System.Security.Cryptography.AsymmetricAlgorithm (RSACryptoServiceProvider), DSA (DSACryptoServiceProvider), System.Security.Cryptography.DSA (DSACryptoServiceProvider), DES (DESCryptoServiceProvider), System.Security.Cryptography.DES (DESCryptoServiceProvider), 3DES (TripleDESCryptoServiceProvider), TripleDES (TripleDESCryptoServiceProvider), Triple DES (TripleDESCryptoServiceProvider), System.Security. Cryptography.TripleDES (TripleDESCryptoServiceProvider), System.Security.Cryptography.SymmetricAlgorithm (TripleDESCryptoServiceProvider), RC2 (RC2CryptoServiceProvider), System.Security.Cryptography.RC2 (RC2CryptoServiceProvider), Rijndael (RijndaelManaged), and System.Security.Cryptography. Rijndael (RijndaelManaged). Found as System.Security. Cryptography.**CryptoConfig**.

CryptoStream Class

Provides a stream linking data streams to cryptographic transformations. The CryptoStream is the core object in the cryptographic stream in the Common Language Runtime (CLR). Any CryptoStream objects can be chained to any objects that are children of the Stream file object. The output of the Stream object is fed directly into the cryptographic implementation, so no unencrypted storage is necessary previous to encoding. Found as System.Security.Cryptography.**CryptoStream**.

CspParameters Class

Holds the parameter set that is passed to a Cryptographic Service Provider (CSP). Most classes that have a name ending with the suffix CryptoServiceProvider are CSPs. This class is not inheritable. Found as System.Security.Cryptography.**CspParameters**.

DeriveBytes Class

Provides the abstract foundation class for all classes that derive byte information from an integer. The PasswordDeriveBytes class is a child of this class. Found as System.Security.Cryptography. **DeriveBytes**.

DES Class

Provides the foundation class for the Data Encryption Standard (DES) algorithm for all classes that use DES. The DESCryptoServiceProvider class is a child of this class. Found as System.Security.Cryptography.**DES**.

DESCryptoServiceProvider Class

Provides the code wrapper for the CSP implementation for the Data Encryption Standard (DES) algorithm. This class is not inheritable. Found as System.Security.Cryptography. **DESCryptoServiceProvider**.

DSA Class

Provides the abstract foundation class for all Digital Signature Algorithm (DSA) classes. Digital signatures are used to authenticate an identity or to verify the integrity of data. Found as System.Security.Cryptography.**DSA**.

DSACryptoServiceProvider Class

Provides the code wrapper for the CSP implementation of the Digital Signature Algorithm (DSA). This class is not inheritable. Found as System.Security.Cryptography.**DSACryptoServiceProvider**.

DSASignatureDeformatter Class

Provides verification of a Digital Signature Algorithm (DSA) PKCS#1 v1.5 signature. *See also* the DSASignatureFormatter class. Found as System.Security.Cryptography.**DSASignatureDeformatter**.

DSASignatureFormatter Class

Creates a Digital Signature Algorithm (DSA) PKCS#1 v1.5 signature. *See also* the DSASignatureDeformatter class. Found as System.Security.Cryptography.**DSASignatureFormatter**.

EnvironmentPermission Class

Holds the permissions settings that allow users to access and modify system and user environment variables. Environmental variables are listed as one or more case-insensitive items separated by semicolons in a list. This class is not inheritable. Found as System.Security.Permissions.**EnvironmentPermission**.

Evidence Class

Holds a set of evidence (such as digital signatures or location of origin) for security permissions granted to access code. Evidence consists of a number of inputs that determine membership conditions for a code group. This class is not inheritable. Found as System.Security.Policy.**Evidence**.

FileCodeGroup Class

Holds permissions to modify file code assemblies. This class is a child of the CodeGroup class and is not inheritable. Found as System.Security.Policy.**FileCodeGroup**.

FileDialogPermission Class

Provides the initialization of the FileDialogPermissions class with either unrestricted or entirely restricted permissions. This class is not inheritable. Found as System.Security.Permissions.**FileDialogPermission**.

FileIOPermission Class

Holds permissions settings that allow or deny access to files and folders. The permissions may restrict three different and independent types of file or folder interaction: read, write, and append. This class is not inheritable. Found as System.Security. Permissions.**FileIOPermission**.

FirstMatchCodeGroup Class

Provides a method of selecting a code group similar to the functionality of a switch (C#, C++) or Select Case (VB) statement. This class is a child of the CodeGroup class and is not inheritable. Found as System.Security.Policy.**FirstMatchCodeGroup**.

FromBase64Transform Class

Provides a method of converting the content found in a CryptoStream from the Base64 transfer encoding format. *See also* the ToBase64Transform class. Found as System. Security.Cryptography.**FromBase64Transform**.

GenericIdentity Class

Provides a generic implementation of an identity object (represented by the IIdentity class) that indicates the user who is executing a set of code. *See also* the WindowsIdentity class. Found as System.Security.Principal.**GenericIdentity**.

GenericPrincipal Class

Provides a generic implementation of a principal object (represented by the IPrincipal class) that indicates the role membership of the specified user. Found as System.Security. Principal.**GenericPrincipal**.

Hash Class

Holds evidence (from the SHA1 and MD5 hash algorithms) for the hash value of an assembly that verifies an assembly's identity instead of using a digital signature. This class is not inheritable. Found as System.Security.Policy.**Hash**.

HashAlgorithm Class

Provides the abstract foundation class for all cryptographic hash algorithm classes. Hash algorithms map variable-length binary strings to fixed-length strings that are known as hash values. Cryptographic hash values, often used for digital signatures and data integrity, are values that are statistically unique, and it is computationally infeasible that two matching values will be generated. Found as System.Security.Cryptography. **HashAlgorithm**.

HashMembershipCondition Class

Provides a method of determining whether an assembly belongs to a specified code group based on its hash value. This class is not inheritable. *See also* the ApplicationDirectoryMembershipCondition, PublisherMembershipCondition, SiteMembershipCondition, StrongNameMembershipCondition, UrlMembershipCondition, WebPageMembershipCondition, and ZoneMembershipCondition classes. Found as System.Security.Policy.**HashMembershipCondition**.

HMACSHA1 Class

Provides the functionality of the Hash-based Message Authentication Code (HMAC) for determining whether a message sent on an insecure channel has been modified based on a secret key possessed by both the sender and receiver. The HMAC algorithm uses the SHA1 hash function to perform the verification. Found as System.Security.Cryptography.**HMACSHA1**.

IsolatedStorageFilePermission Class

Holds the file access permissions used by the Common Language Runtime (CLR) for a private virtual file system. This class is not inheritable. Found as System.Security.Permissions.**IsolatedStorageFilePermission**.

IsolatedStoragePermission Class

Provides the abstract foundation class for access permissions used by the Common Language Runtime (CLR) for generic isolated storage. Found as System.Security.Permissions.**IsolatedStoragePermission**.

KeyedHashAlgorithm Class

Provides the abstract foundation class for all keyed hash algorithm classes. Hash algorithms map variable-length binary strings to fixed-length strings that are known as hash values. Keyed hash values are one-way, key-dependent values used for message authentication. HMACSHA1 is a keyed hash algorithm. Found as System.Security.Cryptography.**KeyedHashAlgorithm**.

KeySizes Class

Provides a method of determining the set of valid key sizes available for symmetric cryptographic algorithms. This class, based on three parameters (MinSize, MaxSize, and SkipSize) will return a set of allowed sizes. For example, setting the MinSize, MaxSize, and SkipSize properties to 16, 40, and 8, respectively, will return a set of four possible key size values (16, 24, 32, and 40). Found as System.Security.Cryptography.**KeySizes**.

MACTripleDES Class

Provides a Message Authentication Code (MAC) on data received from a CryptoStream object based on the TripleDES encryption algorithm. Found as System.Security.Cryptography.**MACTripleDES**.

MaskGenerationMethod Class

Provides the abstract foundation class for all mask generator algorithm classes. This class is used to create masks for key exchange algorithms. Found as System.Security.Cryptography.**MaskGenerationMethod**.

MD5 Class

Provides the abstract foundation class for all MD5 hash algorithm classes. Hash algorithms map variable-length binary strings to fixed-length strings that are known as hash values. Found as System.Security.Cryptography.**MD5**.

MD5CryptoServiceProvider Class

Provides the code wrapper for the CSP implementation of the MD5 hash. This class is not inheritable. Found as System.Security. Cryptography.**MD5CryptoServiceProvider**.

NamedPermissionSet Class

Holds a named permission set that includes the set name, the set description, and the permission chain for authorization to resources. This class is not inheritable. Found as System.Security. **NamedPermissionSet**.

NetCodeGroup Class

Holds permissions to Web sites and sockets of the site where the specified assembly was downloaded. This class is a child of the CodeGroup class and is not inheritable. Found as System.Security. Policy.**NetCodeGroup**.

PasswordDeriveBytes Class

Provides a method of generating a hash key from a password. Found as System.Security.Cryptography.**PasswordDeriveBytes**.

PermissionRequestEvidence Class

Holds the evidence settings required to request access to code. Found as System.Security.Policy.**PermissionRequestEvidence**.

PermissionSet Class

Holds a collection of permissions and the methods to use and modify those permissions. Operations may be performed on an individual permission, or several kinds of permissions may be modified as a group. Found as System.Security.**PermissionSet**.

PKCS1MaskGenerationMethod Class

Provides a method to create masks for key exchange algorithms based on the PKCS #1 standard. This class is a child of the MaskGenerationMethod class. Found as System.Security. Cryptography.**PKCS1MaskGenerationMethod**.

PolicyLevel Class

Provides a representation of the Common Language Runtime (CLR) security policy level. Use the PolicyHierarchy() method on the SecurityManager object to enumerate the current policy levels available. This class is not inheritable. Found as System.Security. Policy.**PolicyLevel**.

PolicyStatement Class

Holds the permission set for granting and setting special attributes for a code group. This class is not inheritable. Found as System. Security.Policy.**PolicyStatement**.

PrincipalPermission Class

Provides a method of verifying that the identity of the active principal matches that of a specified user name and role. This class is not inheritable. Found as System.Security.Permissions. **PrincipalPermission**.

Publisher Class

Holds the Authenticode X.509 v.3 digital signature for a code assembly as evidence for security policy confirmation. The CLR implements Authenticode X.509 v.3 certificates, which are certificates signed with a private key, uniquely and positively identifying the holder of the certificate. This class is not inheritable. Found as System.Security.Policy.**Publisher.**

PublisherIdentityPermission Class

Holds the representation of the identity of a publisher. This class is not inheritable. Found as System.Security.Permissions. **PublisherIdentityPermission**.

PublisherMembershipCondition Class

Provides a method of determining whether the code group holds an assembly by testing its software publisher certificate. This class is not inheritable. See also the ApplicationDirectoryMembershipCondition, HashMembershipCondition, SiteMembershipCondition, StrongNameMembershipCondition, UrlMembershipCondition, WebPageMembershipCondition, and ZoneMembershipCondition classes. Found as System.Security.Policy. **PublisherMembershipCondition**.

RandomNumberGenerator Class

Provides the abstract foundation class for all cryptographic random number generator classes. Found as System.Security. Cryptography.**RandomNumberGenerator**.

RC2 Class

Provides the abstract foundation class for all implementations of cryptographic RC2 classes. Found as System.Security. Cryptography.**RC2**.

RC2CryptoServiceProvider Class

Provides the code wrapper for the CSP implementation of the RC2 algorithm. This class is not inheritable. Found as System.Security.Cryptography.**RC2CryptoServiceProvider**.

ReflectionPermission Class

Holds the permission settings for access to the class metadata available from the System.Reflection APIs. Without the proper permissions, only the Public members of loaded assemblies are available through metadata. This class is not inheritable. Found as System.Security.Permissions.**ReflectionPermission**.

RegistryPermission Class

Holds the permission settings that limit access to variables located in the system registry. This class is not inheritable. Found as System.Security.Permissions.**RegistryPermission**.

ResourcePermissionBase Class

Provides the abstract foundation class for all resource permission classes, including EventLogPermission, PerformanceCounterPermission, DirectoryServicesPermission, and ServiceControllerPermission. Found as System.Security. Permissions.**ResourcePermissionBase**.

ResourcePermissionBaseEntry Class

Holds a resource permission base entry. Found as System. Security.Permissions.**ResourcePermissionBaseEntry**.

Rijndael Class

Provides the abstract foundation class for all Rijndael symmetric encryption algorithm classes. Found as System.Security. Cryptography.**Rijndael**.

RijndaelManaged Class

Provides the code wrapper for a managed implementation of the Rijndael symmetric encryption algorithm. This class is not inheritable. Found as System.Security.Cryptography.**RijndaelManaged**.

RNGCryptoServiceProvider Class

Provides the wrapper for the CSP implementation of the cryptographic Random Number Generator (RNG). Found as System.Security.Cryptography.**RNGCryptoServiceProvider**.

RSA Class

Provides the abstract foundation class for all RSA algorithm classes. Found as System.Security.Cryptography.**RSA**.

RSACryptoServiceProvider Class

Provides the code wrapper for the CSP implementation of the RSA asymmetric encryption and decryption algorithm. This class is not inheritable. Found as System.Security. Cryptography.**RSACryptoServiceProvider**.

RSAOAEPKeyExchangeDeformatter Class

Provides a method of using RSA to decode key exchange data that has been encrypted using Optimal Asymmetric Encryption Padding (OAEP). Found as System.Security.Cryptography. **RSAOAEPKeyExchangeDeformatter**.

RSAOAEPKeyExchangeFormatter Class

Provides a method of using RSA to encode key exchange data that can be decrypted using Optimal Asymmetric Encryption Padding (OAEP). Found as System.Security.Cryptography. **RSAOAEPKeyExchangeFormatter**.

RSAPKCS1KeyExchangeDeformatter Class

Provides a method of using RSA to decode key exchange data that has been encrypted using PKCS #1. Found as System.Security. Cryptography.**RSAPKCS1KeyExchangeDeformatter**.

RSAPKCS1KeyExchangeFormatter Class

Provides a method of using RSA to encode key exchange data that can be decrypted using PKCS #1. Found as System.Security. Cryptography.**RSAPKCS1KeyExchangeFormatter**.

RSAPKCS1SignatureDeformatter Class

Provides a method of using RSA to verify an RSA PKCS #1 version 1.5 signature. Found as System.Security.Cryptography. **RSAPKCS1SignatureDeformatter**.

RSAPKCS1SignatureFormatter Class

Provides a method of using RSA to create an RSA PKCS #1 version 1.5 signature. Found as System.Security.Cryptography. **RSAPKCS1SignatureFormatter**.

SecurityElement Class

Provides an XML object model implementation of security object encoding. This class provides a primitive implementation of a simple XML object model. This class is not inheritable. Found as System.Security.**SecurityElement**.

SecurityManager Class

Provides the central abstract class that includes methods for interacting with the security policy system. For this class an instance is not created, but methods are executed directly from the abstract class. This class is not inheritable. Found as System.Security.**SecurityManager**.

SecurityPermission Class

Holds a collection of flags that are used by the security portion of the .NET Framework. Flags included in the SecurityPermissionFlag enumeration are AllFlags, Assertion, ControlAppDomain, ControlDomainPolicy, ControlEvidence, ControlPolicy, ControlPrincipal, ControlThread, Execution, Infrastructure, NoFlags, RemotingConfiguration, SerializationFormatter, SkipVerification, and UnmanagedCode. This class is not inheritable. Found as System.Security.Permissions. **SecurityPermission.**

SHA1 Class

Provides a method of processing the SHA1 hash to obtain the input data. The hash size used by the SHA1 algorithm is 160 bits. Found as System.Security.Cryptography.**SHA1**.

SHA1CryptoServiceProvider Class

Provides the code wrapper for the CSP implementation for computing the SHA1 hash for input data. This class is not inheritable. Found as System.Security.Cryptography.**SHA1CryptoServiceProvider**.

SHA1Managed Class

Provides a method of processing the SHA1 hash to obtain the input data purely using the managed library (so it does not wrap CAPI). The hash size used by the SHA1 algorithm is 160 bits. Found as System.Security.Cryptography.**SHA1Managed**.

SHA256 Class

Provides an abstract class for processing the SHA256 hash to obtain the input data. The SHA256Managed class is an implementation of this class. The hash size used by the SHA256 algorithm is 256 bits. This class is not inheritable. Found as System.Security.Cryptography.**SHA256**.

SHA256Managed Class

Provides a method of processing the SHA256 hash to obtain the input data purely using the managed library (so it does not wrap CAPI). The hash size used by the SHA256 algorithm is 256 bits. Found as System.Security.Cryptography.**SHA256Managed**.

SHA384 Class

Provides an abstract class for processing the SHA384 hash to obtain the input data. The SHA384Managed class is an implementation of this class. The hash size used by the SHA384 algorithm is 384 bits. This class is not inheritable. Found as System.Security.Cryptography.**SHA384**.

SHA384Managed Class

Provides a method of processing the SHA384 hash to obtain the input data purely using the managed library (so it does not wrap CAPI). The hash size used by the SHA384 algorithm is 384 bits. Found as System.Security.Cryptography.**SHA384Managed**.

SHA512 Class

Provides an abstract class for processing the SHA512 hash to obtain the input data. The SHA512Managed class is an implementation of this class. The hash size used by the SHA512 algorithm is 512 bits. This class is not inheritable. Found as System.Security.Cryptography.**SHA512**.

SHA512Managed Class

Provides a method of processing the SHA512 hash to obtain the input data purely using the managed library (so it does not wrap CAPI). The hash size used by the SHA512 algorithm is 512 bits. Found as System.Security.Cryptography.**SHA512Managed**.

SignatureDescription Class

Provides deformatter, digest, formatter, and key algorithms. Found as System.Security.Cryptography.**SignatureDescription**.

Site Class

Holds the Web site identity for a code assembly as evidence for security policy confirmation. This class is used by the SiteIdentityPermission class to verify that the calling code originates from the specified Web site. This class is not inheritable. Found as System.Security.Policy.**Site**.

SiteIdentityPermission Class

Holds the identity permission for the Web site where the specified code originated. This class is not inheritable. Found as System. Security.Permissions.**SiteIdentityPermission**.

SiteMembershipCondition Class

Provides a method of determining whether the code group holds an assembly by testing the site where it originated. *See also* the ApplicationDirectoryMembershipCondition, HashMembershipCondition, PublisherMembershipCondition, StrongNameMembershipCondition, UrlMembershipCondition, WebPageMembershipCondition, and ZoneMembershipCondition classes. Found as System.Security.Policy.**SiteMembershipCondition**.

SkipVerificationMembershipCondition Class

Holds an indicator whether verification of membership can be skipped based on the evidence for an assembly. Found as System.Security.Policy.**SkipVerificationMembershipCondition**.

StrongName Class

Holds the strong name for a code assembly as evidence for security policy confirmation. A strong name is made up of a public key, a given name, and version parts. This class is not inheritable. Found as System.Security.Policy.**StrongName**.

StrongNameIdentityPermission Class

Holds the identity permission for the strong name based on a cryptographic public key (called a blob) and a simple name. Found as System.Security.Permissions.**StrongNameIdentityPermission**.

StrongNameMembershipCondition Class

Provides a method of determining whether the code group holds an assembly by testing its strong name. This class is not inheritable. *See also* the ApplicationDirectoryMembershipCondition, HashMembershipCondition, PublisherMembershipCondition, SiteMembershipCondition, UrlMembershipCondition, WebPageMembershipCondition, and ZoneMembershipCondition classes. Found as System.Security.Policy. **StrongNameMembershipCondition**.

StrongNamePublicKeyBlob Class

Holds the public key information (a blob) for a strong name. This class is not inheritable. Found as System. Security.Permissions.**StrongNamePublicKeyBlob**.

SymmetricAlgorithm Class

Provides the abstract foundation class for all symmetric algorithm classes. Symmetric algorithms use a single secret key for encrypting and decrypting, in contrast to asymmetric algorithms that use separate keys (public and private) for these two processes. Symmetric algorithms tend to require far less processing power and execute faster than asymmetric algorithms. Children of this class include DES, RC2, Rijndael, and TripleDES classes. Found as System.Security.Cryptography.**SymmetricAlgorithm**.

ToBase64Transform Class

Provides a method of converting the content found in a CryptoStream to the Base64 transfer encoding format. *See also* the FromBase64Transform class. Found as System.Security.Cryptography.**ToBase64Transform**.

TripleDES Class

Provides the foundation class for the Triple Data Encryption Standard (DES) algorithm for all classes that use TripleDES. The TripleDESCryptoServiceProvider class is a child of this class. Found as System.Security.Cryptography.**TripleDES**.

TripleDESCryptoServiceProvider Class

Provides the code wrapper for the CSP implementation of the Triple DES algorithm. This class is not inheritable. Found as System.Security.Cryptography.**TripleDESCryptoServiceProvider**.

UIPermission Class

Holds the access control permissions to user interface features (such as window drawing and user input events) and the clipboard. For user interface features, the following settings are available: unrestricted use, use limited to safe top-level windows, only safe subwindows may be used, or no window drawing/user input access allowed. For clipboard access, the following settings are available: unrestricted, limited to paste from the same application, or fully restricted. This class is not inheritable. Found as System.Security.Permissions.**UIPermission**.

UnionCodeGroup Class

Holds a code group that is a union of the security policy statements of the parent group and all of its children. This class represents the most common type of code group. This class is not inheritable. Found as System.Security.Policy.**UnionCodeGroup**.

Url Class

Holds the URL for a code assembly as evidence for security policy confirmation. This class is not inheritable. URLs must either match exactly or may end with a wildcard character (such as http://www.microsoft.com/*). Found as System.Security.Policy.**Url**.

UrlIdentityPermission Class

Holds the identity permission of the URL where the specified code originated. URLs must either match exactly or may end with a wildcard character (such as http://www.microsoft.com/*). Found as System.Security.Permissions.**UrlIdentityPermission**.

UrlMembershipCondition Class

Provides a method of determining whether the code group holds an assembly by testing its URL. URLs must either match exactly or may end with a wildcard character (such as http://www.microsoft.com/*). *See also* the ApplicationDirectoryMembershipCondition, HashMembershipCondition, PublisherMembershipCondition, SiteMembershipCondition, StrongNameMembershipCondition, WebPageMembershipCondition, and ZoneMembershipCondition classes. This class is not inheritable. Found as System.Security. Policy.**UrlMembershipCondition**.

WebPage Class

Holds the Web page for a code assembly as evidence for security policy confirmation. This class is not inheritable. Found as System. Security.Policy.**WebPage**.

WebPageMembershipCondition Class

Provides a method of determining whether the code group holds an assembly by testing its Web page. This class is not inheritable. *See also* the ApplicationDirectoryMembershipCondition, HashMembershipCondition, PublisherMembershipCondition, SiteMembershipCondition, StrongNameMembershipCondition, UrlMembershipCondition, and ZoneMembershipCondition classes. Found as System.Security.Policy.**WebPageMembershipCondition**.

WindowsIdentity Class

Provides a Windows user implementation of an identity object (represented by the IIdentity class) that identifies which user is executing a set of code. Calling the GetCurrent() method will return an instance of this class that represents the current user. *See also* the GenericIdentity class. Found as System.Security. Principal.**WindowsIdentity**.

WindowsImpersonationContext Class

Holds the identity of a Windows user temporarily to allow a reversion to that identity after the user completes the impersonation of another user (such as during a Web server transaction). Note that impersonation can only take place on Windows NT–based systems, including NT 4, Windows 2000, and Windows XP. Found as System.Security.Principal. **WindowsImpersonationContext**.

WindowsPrincipal Class

Provides the functionality to allow code to confirm the membership of a specified Windows user in a particular Windows group. Found as System.Security.Principal.**WindowsPrincipal**.

X509Certificate Class

Provides the Common Language Runtime (CLR) implementation of an Authenticode X.509 v.3 certificate. This class can create an instance of the certificate from either a certification or a signed file. Found as System.Security.Cryptography.X509Certificates. **X509Certificate**.

X509CertificateCollection Class

Holds a collection of X509Certificate objects. Found as System. Security.Cryptography.X509Certificates.**X509CertificateCollection**.

Zone Class

Holds the security zone of origin for a code assembly as evidence for security policy confirmation. This class is used to verify that calling code originates from a particular zone. Found as System. Security.Policy.**Zone**.

ZoneIdentityPermission Class

Holds the permission settings for the code's zone of origin. Zones are typically configured in the Microsoft Internet Explorer and include the following types: local machine zone, local intranet zone, Internet zone, trusted sites zone, and restricted sites zone. This class is not inheritable. Found as System.Security.Permissions. **ZoneIdentityPermission**.

ZoneMembershipCondition Class

Provides a method of determining whether the specified code group holds a desired assembly by testing the zone of origin. Zones are typically configured in the Microsoft Internet Explorer and include the following types: local machine zone, local intranet zone, Internet zone, trusted sites zone, and restricted sites zone. This class is not inheritable. *See also* the ApplicationDirectoryMembershipCondition, HashMembershipCondition, PublisherMembershipCondition, SiteMembershipCondition, StrongNameMembershipCondition, UrlMembershipCondition, and WebPageMembershipCondition classes. Found as System.Security.Policy. **ZoneMembershipCondition**.

INDEX

NOTE: Page numbers in *italics* refer to illustrations or charts.

A

B

C

D

I

J

K

L

M

N

O

Z

INTERNATIONAL CONTACT INFORMATION

AUSTRALIA
McGraw-Hill Book Company Australia Pty. Ltd.
TEL +61-2-9417-9899
FAX +61-2-9417-5687
http://www.mcgraw-hill.com.au
books-it_sydney@mcgraw-hill.com

CANADA
McGraw-Hill Ryerson Ltd.
TEL +905-430-5000
FAX +905-430-5020
http://www.mcgrawhill.ca

GREECE, MIDDLE EAST, NORTHERN AFRICA
McGraw-Hill Hellas
TEL +30-1-656-0990-3-4
FAX +30-1-654-5525

MEXICO (Also serving Latin America)
McGraw-Hill Interamericana Editores S.A. de C.V.
TEL +525-117-1583
FAX +525-117-1589
http://www.mcgraw-hill.com.mx
fernando_castellanos@mcgraw-hill.com

SINGAPORE (Serving Asia)
McGraw-Hill Book Company
TEL +65-863-1580
FAX +65-862-3354
http://www.mcgraw-hill.com.sg
mghasia@mcgraw-hill.com

SOUTH AFRICA
McGraw-Hill South Africa
TEL +27-11-622-7512
FAX +27-11-622-9045
robyn_swanepoel@mcgraw-hill.con

UNITED KINGDOM & EUROPI (Excluding Southern Europe)
McGraw-Hill Education Europe
TEL +44-1-628-502500
FAX +44-1-628-770224
http://www.mcgraw-hill.co.uk
computing_neurope@mcgraw-hill.c

ALL OTHER INQUIRIES Conta
Osborne/McGraw-Hill
TEL +1-510-549-6600
FAX +1-510-883-7600
http://www.osborne.com
omg_international@mcgraw-hill.co